W9-BPP-201

Wilton Baking and Decorating for Special Occasions

Publications International, Ltd.

© 2014 Publications International, Ltd.

Recipes, text and photographs © 2014 Wilton Industries, Inc. All rights reserved.

This publication may not be reproduced or quoted in whole or in part by any means whatsoever without written permission from:

Louis Weber, CEO
Publications International, Ltd.
7373 North Cicero Avenue
Lincolnwood, IL 60712

Permission is never granted for commercial purposes.

Wilton, the Wilton logo, All-Occasion Checkerboard Cake Pan Set, Amazing has never been so easy!, Bake Easy!, Baker's Best, Cake Release, Cake Sparkles and design, Candy Melts, Chocolate Pro, Colorburst, ColorCups, Color Flow Mix, Color Mist, the Cookie Icing design, Cookie Master Plus, Cookie Pro Ultra II, Creepy Sprinkles Lab, Cupcakes-N-More, Cut-Outs, Decorator Preferred, Dessert Decorator Pro, Dimensions, the Edible Accents design, Featherweight, FoodWriter, Fun Pix, Gum-Tex, Icing Writer, Pearl Dust and design, Performance Pans, the Pops! design, Recipe Right Non-Stick, Ruffle Boards, Scoop-It, Show-N-Serve, Sugar Sheets! & design, The Wilton Method of Cake Decorating, The Wilton Rose, The Wilton Method, Tilt-N-Turn Ultra, Trim-N-Turn Plus, Trim-N-Turn Ultra, Tuk-N-Ruffle, We Make It Easy... You Make It Amazing and Wilton Method Classes and associated trademarks are owned by and used under license from Wilton Industries, Inc.

Pictured on the front cover (left to right, top to bottom): Party Cap Mini Cakes *(page 34)*, Tot Cookie Pops *(page 54)*, Dazzling Dots Cake *(page 24)*, Swirl Topped Petit Fours *(page 102)*, Sundaes on a Stick Cake Pops *(page 98)* and Fall Favorite Cupcakes *(page 135)*.

Pictured on the back cover: Cupcake Bouquet *(page 19)*.

ISBN: 978-1-4508-7786-2

Library of Congress Control Number: 2013943700

Manufactured in China.

8 7 6 5 4 3 2 1

Microwave Cooking: Microwave ovens vary in wattage. Use the cooking times as guidelines and check for doneness before adding more time.

CONTENTS

55

81

104

162

Historical Wilton photograph courtesy of Norman Wilton.

The Wilton Story

WE MAKE IT EASY ... YOU MAKE IT AMAZING!™

• •

Since 1929, Wilton has made cake decorating accessible and easy for everyone. We believe that decorating cakes and sweet treats isn't magic and that everyone can enjoy doing it. Through our decorating courses, ideas, instructions and tools, Wilton has empowered people to create cakes and sweet treats that make their celebrations unforgettable.

Like most iconic American brands, Wilton was conceived by a visionary founder. Dewey McKinley Wilton dedicated his life and career to teaching cake decorating to anyone who wanted to learn. He developed and taught The Wilton Method of Cake Decorating™, which combined the best of European fine artistry with the traditional American desire for elegance and simplicity.

Today The Wilton Method® is a worldwide phenomenon, taught through a network of professional instructors who truly bring the "social" to social education. Outside the classroom, Wilton publishes the most beautiful creative content about cakes and sweet treats in the world—content that inspires consumers wherever they are. Wilton also designs and produces the tools and edible embellishments you need to make an amazing cake or sweet treat. The result is a decorating experience that virtually guarantees your success.

Now you can experience that success with this publication. Let Wilton help you bake and decorate amazing treats for a birthday bash catered to adults and kids alike, as well as for other special occasions. We've got fun ideas for cakes, cake pops and cupcakes, along with time-tested recipes, decorating tips and techniques. Whatever the theme, our ideas will make every party more exciting for your friends and family. Let us show you how...Amazing has never been so easy!™

Birthday Bonanza

MAKE YOUR NEXT BIRTHDAY PARTY A BLOWOUT BASH WITH A SPECTACULAR CAKE, CUPCAKE OR POPS DISPLAY

ABUNDANT ROSES CAKE

A simple white cake can instantly become a vision of beauty with the addition of piped roses and rosebuds.

RECIPES:

Royal Icing (p. 181)

Yellow, White or Chocolate Cake (p. 176-177)

Buttercream Icing (p. 181)

INGREDIENTS:

Meringue Powder

Icing Colors: Pink, Kelly Green

TOOLS:

12 in. Disposable Decorating Bags

Decorating Tips: 12, 104, 3, 352

Pre-Cut Icing Flower Squares

Flower Nail No. 7

Parchment Paper

10 in. x 14 in. Cake Board

8 in. x 2 in. Square Pan

Cooling Grid

13 in. Angled Spatula

TECHNIQUES:

Tip Techniques (p. 204)

SERVES: 20.

INSTRUCTIONS:

STEP 1 One day in advance, make roses and rosebuds. Prepare royal icing following recipe directions. Tint pink. Use tips 12 and 104 to pipe 24 pink roses (p. 215) and 24 pink rosebuds (p. 210). Let dry on parchment paper-covered board 24 hours.

STEP 2 Bake and cool 2-layer cake. Place cake on serving plate. Prepare buttercream icing following recipe directions. Tint small portion green and majority light pink. Ice cake smooth with light pink icing.

STEP 3 Use tip 3 to attach rosebuds and tip 12 to attach roses on cake. Use tip 3 to pipe calyxes (p. 210) on rosebuds. Use tip 352 to pipe leaves (p. 208) around roses at base.

CANDY SWIRLS BIRTHDAY CAKE

Personal touches and sweet candy swirls make this birthday cake irresistible.

RECIPES:

Yellow, White or Chocolate Cake (p. 176-177)

Chocolate Buttercream Icing (p. 181)

INGREDIENTS:

Candy Melts Candy: White, Light Cocoa

Candy Color Sets: Primary (yellow and orange used), **Garden** (pink and green used)

Flowerful Medley 6-Cell Sprinkles

TOOLS:

10-Pack Candy Mold Set

Dessert Accents Candy Mold

15 in. Parchment Triangles

8 in. x 2 in. Square Pan

Cooling Grid

13 in. Angled Spatula

12 in. Disposable Decorating Bags

Decorating Tips: 2, 6, 10

Hot Colors Twist Candles

TECHNIQUES:

Candy/Pop Making Techniques (p. 230)

Tip Techniques (p. 204)

SERVES: 20.

INSTRUCTIONS:

STEP 1 In advance, make candy trims. Melt Candy Melts candy according to package directions. Tint portions of melted white candy yellow, orange, pink and green using candy colors from sets.

Mold two-tone letters in mold set using layering method. Fill cavities ¼ in. deep with melted pink candy. Chill until firm 3 to 5 minutes. Fill remainder of mold with melted light cocoa candy. Chill until firm 10 to 15 minutes.

Mold four swirls in each color using dessert accents mold. Chill until firm.

STEP 2 Bake and cool 2-layer cake. Prepare chocolate buttercream icing following recipe directions. Ice cake smooth with chocolate icing. Place on serving plate.

Use tip 2 to attach candy swirls and confetti sprinkles to cake sides with dots (p. 206) of icing. Use tip 6 to pipe bead (p. 205) top border and use tip 10 to pipe bead bottom border. Position letters.

Use tip 10 to pipe dots for candle holders and insert candles.

CANDY-COATED SURPRISE CUPCAKES

What a sweet surprise for anyone! Dip cupcakes in melted Candy Melts candy to give them their baking cups.

RECIPES:

Yellow or Chocolate Cupcakes (p. 178)

Buttercream Icing (p. 181)

INGREDIENTS:

Cake Release Pan Coating

White Candy Melts Candy (3 pks.)

Candy Color Sets: Garden (green, violet and pink used), **Primary** (yellow and blue used)

Sour cherry candies

TOOLS:

12-Cup Standard Muffin Pan

Pastry Brush

Cooling Grid

Cookie Sheet

15 in. Parchment Triangles

Scissors

12 in. Disposable Decorating Bag

Decorating Tip: 1M

TECHNIQUES:

Candy/Pop Making Techniques (p. 230)

Tip Techniques (p. 204)

INSTRUCTIONS:

STEP 1 Brush pan cavities with Cake Release pan coating. Bake and cool cupcakes without baking cups.

STEP 2 Melt Candy Melts candy according to package directions. Divide 2 pks. melted candy into thirds. Tint portions violet, yellow and light pink using candy colors from sets.

STEP 3 Place cupcakes upside down on cooling grid over cookie sheet. Cover with melted candy (p. 232). Chill until firm 10 to 15 minutes. Repeat if needed to coat completely.

STEP 4 Divide remaining white melted candy into fifths. Tint portions dark pink, green, dark violet, orange and blue using candy colors from sets. Use melted candy and cut parchment bags to pipe stripes, swirls and dots on sides of cupcakes.

STEP 5 Prepare buttercream icing following recipe directions. Use tip 1M to pipe swirl (p. 204) on cupcake tops. Position cherry candy.

BIRTHDAY CANDLEPOWER CAKE

This cake is a work of art. Spark interest by adding tiers of vibrant fondant candles detailed with shapes, flames and waxy drips.

RECIPES:

Yellow, White or Chocolate Cake (p. 176-177)

Buttercream Icing (p. 181)

Thinned Fondant Adhesive (p. 189)

INGREDIENTS:

White Ready-To-Use Rolled Fondant (220 oz.)

Icing Colors: Rose*, Orange, Leaf Green, Lemon Yellow, Violet*, Sky Blue

Yellow Colored Sugar

Cornstarch

Piping Gel

TOOLS:

20 in. Fondant Roller

Roll-N-Cut Mat

Cut-Outs Fondant Cutters: Leaf, Round

Brush Set

Plastic ruler

Toothpicks

10 in. x 14 in. Cake Boards

Stepsaving Rose Bouquet Flower Cutter Set

Knife

Fondant Shaping Foam

10-Pc. Gum Paste/Fondant Tool Set

Plastic Dowel Rods (5 pks. for candles; 40-6 in. lengths)

14 in. Silver Cake Bases (2)

Transparent cellophane tape

Cake Dividing Chart

Knife

Round Pans: 6 in. x 2 in., 8 in. x 2 in., 10 in. x 2 in.

Cooling Grid

13 in. Angled Spatula

Fondant Smoother

Cake Circles: 6 in., 8 in., 10 in.

Bamboo Dowel Rods

Scissors

TECHNIQUES:

Fondant and Gum Paste Decorating Techniques (p. 220)

Tiered Construction (p. 227)

SERVES: 60.

*Combine Violet with Rose for violet shown.

INSTRUCTIONS:

STEP 1 Two days in advance, make flames, candles and base. Tint fondant 5 oz. each rose, orange, green, yellow, violet and blue for candles; 36 oz. rose, 48 oz. orange and 72 oz. green to cover cakes; and 24 oz. yellow for base board. Roll out ⅛ in. thick unless otherwise specified. Reserve any excess fondant.

STEP 2 Cut 40 yellow flames using smallest leaf Cut-Out. Brush with damp brush and sprinkle on yellow sugar. Insert toothpick at bottom, leaving 2 in. exposed to insert into candle. Let dry 24 hours on cornstarch-dusted board.

STEP 3 Make four dot and four striped candles in each color (rose, orange, violet, blue and green). Roll out fondant ¹⁄₁₆ in. thick. For dots, cut six to eight circles for each candle using smallest round Cut-Out. For stripes, cut strips, 12 in. x ½ in. Attach trims to 6 in. dowel rods using piping gel.

Roll 40 white fondant logs, 1½ in. long x ⅝ in. dia. Brush inside top 1 in. of dowel rod with piping gel. Push in one fondant log until even with top.

For wax drips, roll out white fondant ⅛ in. thick. Use small rose cutter from set to cut 40 flowers. Set on thin foam and use small ball tool from set to slightly elongate petals. Attach over top of dowel rod using piping gel and shape with fingers. Insert flame. Let dry 24 hours.

STEP 4 Prepare base. Tape two cake bases together and brush with piping gel. Cover with rolled fondant. Use cake dividing chart to divide base into 12ths. Roll out remaining yellow fondant. Cut strips, 5 in. x ½ in. Twist and attach between marks using thinned fondant adhesive. Roll ½ in. dia. balls and attach to cover ends. Let dry 24 hours.

STEP 5 Bake and cool three 2 in. high layers for each size cake. Prepare buttercream icing following recipe directions. Prepare cake for fondant by icing in buttercream. Cover cake with fondant and smooth with fondant smoother. Prepare for stacked construction (p. 228). Attach candles to cake sides, 1½ in. apart, using thinned fondant adhesive. Push five candles into cake top.

PRETTY PASTEL CAKE POPS

Display these pretty pastel pops on a decorated stand that's perfect for any party. Both the pops and the stand will make your guests smile!

RECIPES:
Basic Cake Ball Pops (p. 180)

INGREDIENTS:
White Candy Melts Candy

Candy Color Sets: Primary (yellow and blue used), **Garden** (pink and green used)

White Sparkling Sugar

Flowerful Medley 6-Cell Sprinkles

TOOLS:
9 in. x 13 in. x 2 in. Sheet Pan

4 in. Lollipop Sticks

Chocolate Pro Melting Pot

15 in. Parchment Triangles

Pops Display Stand

TECHNIQUES:
Candy/Pop Making Techniques (p. 230)

INSTRUCTIONS:

STEP 1 Prepare small cake balls and insert sticks following recipe directions. Chill until firm.

STEP 2 Melt Candy Melts candy according to package directions. Tint melted candy yellow, green, pink and blue using candy colors from sets. Dip cake pops in melted candy. Immediately roll in sugar to coat bottom half. Chill until firm 10 to 15 minutes.

STEP 3 Use melted candy and a cut parchment bag to attach confetti sprinkles to pops display stand. Place pops on stand.

PRINCESS'S CROWN MINI CAKES

Crown your precious princess or make Mom queen for the day with these individual bejeweled cakes.

RECIPES:
Lemon Pound Cake (p. 177)

INGREDIENTS:
White Candy Melts Candy

Garden Candy Color Set (pink used)

Jumbo Confetti Sprinkles

Flowerful Medley 6-Cell Sprinkles

Red Sparkle Gel

TOOLS:
Parchment Paper

9 in. x 13 in. x 2 in. Sheet Pan

Cooling Grid

Daisy Comfort-Grip Cutter

Circle Metal Cutter

Knife

9 in. Angled Spatula

Cookie Sheet

15 in. Parchment Triangles

Plastic ruler

TECHNIQUES:
Candy/Pop Making Techniques (p. 230)

INSTRUCTIONS:

STEP 1 Bake and cool 1 in. cake in sheet pan. Remove from pan. Cut daisy shapes with cutter. Using edge of circle cutter, cut daisy 2½ in. from top point for bottom curve of crown. Trim side points to create straight edge.

STEP 2 Melt Candy Melts candy according to package directions. Tint melted candy pink using candy color from set. Cover bottoms of treats with melted candy. Chill until firm 15 to 20 minutes. Cover treats with melted candy (p. 232). Chill until firm 15 to 20 minutes. Use melted white candy and a cut parchment bag to pipe band at bottom of crown and pipe diamond shapes, ½ in. high x ⅜ in. wide, at points. Chill until firm 5 minutes.

STEP 3 Attach confetti sprinkles with dots of melted candy. Let set. Cover diamonds with sparkle gel.

A NEW SPIN ON AGING CAKE

Complete the statement, "You are older than…" with comic relief by putting A New Spin on Aging. This colorful round cake adds a jolt of fun with a board game-style spinner to answer that age-old question.

RECIPES:

Yellow, White or Chocolate Cake (p. 176-177)

Buttercream Icing (p. 181)

Thinned Fondant Adhesive (p. 189)

INGREDIENTS:

Icing Colors: Royal Blue, Kelly Green, Rose, Golden Yellow, Black

Ready-To-Use Rolled Fondant: White (24 oz.), **Chocolate** (48 oz.)

TOOLS:

12 in. Cake Circle

Fanci-Foil Wrap

Towering Tiers Cake Stand (14 in. plate; 4.25 in. short center post; four base feet; center post foot; cake corer used)

12 in. x 2 in. Round Pan

Cooling Grid

13 in. Angled Spatula

20 in. Fondant Roller

Roll-N-Cut Mat

Fondant Smoother

Fondant Trimmer

Knife

12 in. Disposable Decorating Bags

Decorating Tip: 2

Brush Set

Plastic Dowel Rod

Cardboard

TECHNIQUES:

Tip Techniques (p. 204)

Using Rolled Fondant (p. 217)

PATTERNS:

Game Wedge, Spinner (p. 236)

SERVES: 28.

INSTRUCTIONS:

STEP 1 Prepare cake board. Prepare for towering tiers construction following instructions in kit.

STEP 2 Bake and cool 2-layer cake. Prepare buttercream icing following recipe directions. Core and prepare cake for fondant by icing in buttercream.

STEP 3 Cover cake with chocolate fondant; smooth with fondant smoother. Position cake on stand with short center post.

STEP 4 Set aside 3 oz. of white fondant. Divide remainder of white fondant into fourths. Tint blue, green, rose and yellow. Using wedge pattern, roll out and cut out two wedges in each color. Position wedges on cake. Trim cake center with knife.

STEP 5 Use pattern to cut spinner from cardboard and wrap with foil. Cut opening in middle to fit snuggly over dowel rod.

STEP 6 Use tip 2 to print (p. 209) messages on spinner and wedges.

STEP 7 Use fondant trimmer to cut strips of white fondant, ¼ in. wide. Position and attach with damp brush at seams between wedges.

STEP 8 Cut two strips, ¼ in. wide, of matching fondant for each wedge. Attach strips with damp brush to cake sides as double drop strings.

STEP 9 Roll balls, ½ in., of white fondant; flatten slightly. Attach at ends of drapes with damp brush. Cut dowel rod to 5¼ in. Place in center of short center post. Position spinner on dowel rod.

STEP 10 Cover dowel rod opening with a 1½ in. dia. ball of yellow fondant.

STEP 11 Roll 1 in. dia. balls of chocolate fondant and attach to base of cake with thinned fondant adhesive.

MEDIEVAL FORTRESS CASTLE CAKE

Opt for realism with this castle cake by etching stone patterns into gray fondant walls accented with colorful turrets, windowsills and pennants.

RECIPES:

Yellow, White or Chocolate Cake (p. 176-177)

Buttercream Icing (p. 181)

Thinned Fondant Adhesive (p. 189)

INGREDIENTS:

Ready-To-Use Rolled Fondant: White (120 oz.), **Natural Colors Multi Pack, Primary Colors Multi Pack**

Icing Colors: Black, Kelly Green, Royal Blue

Piping Gel

White Candy Melts Candy

Cornstarch

Imitation Clear Vanilla Extract

TOOLS:

Romantic Castle Cake Set

20 in. Fondant Roller

Roll-N-Cut Mat

Detail Embosser

Plastic Dowel Rods

Brush Set

Cut-Outs Fondant Cutters: Square, Oval

Toothpicks

Paring knife

Thin wooden skewers

10 in. x 14 in. Cake Boards

4 in. Lollipop Sticks

Square Pans: 6 in. x 2 in., 10 in. x 2 in.

Cooling Grid

11 in. Straight Spatula

Fondant Smoother

16 in. Round Silver Cake Base

Construction paper

Plastic ruler

Transparent cellophane tape

TECHNIQUES:

Using Rolled Fondant (p. 217)

Tiered Construction (p. 227)

SERVES: 42.

INSTRUCTIONS:

STEP 1 Tint 96 oz. white fondant light gray using black color. Remove 8 oz. and tint dark gray. Tint remaining white fondant blue. Use door piece as pattern to cut out ½ in. thick brown fondant for drawbridge. Score wood lines with straight wheel of detail embosser.

STEP 2 Melt Candy Melts candy according to package directions. For castle towers, attach dowel rods, cut 1 in. shorter than height of tier, to bottoms of four small and one medium turret towers using melted candy. Brush all towers lightly with piping gel. Roll out light gray fondant ⅛ in. thick. Cover towers with light gray fondant and smooth with fingers dipped in cornstarch.

STEP 3 For castle bricks, imprint towers with small square Cut-Out. Roll out blue fondant ⅛ in. thick. Mark four small, one medium and four large turret peak patterns from included kit with toothpick. Cut out with knife. Brush turret peaks lightly with piping gel. Attach fondant pieces, wrapping around peaks. Roll out black fondant ⅛ in. thick. Mark small and large/medium window patterns from kit for corresponding towers. Cut out with knife. Attach to towers with damp brush.

STEP 4 For window ledges, roll out yellow fondant ⅛ in. thick. Cut oval using medium Cut-Out. Attach with damp brush, trimming to fit.

For stonework around castle tower windows, shape balls of dark gray fondant in various sizes. Flatten and attach.

STEP 5 For bunting beneath windows, roll out red fondant ⅟₁₆ in. thick. Use knife to cut a strip, 1½ in. x 2 in. Gather strip and form folds in fondant by placing one skewer under bottom edge of strip and one on top, next to the first skewer. Repeat with more skewers to form three folds. Remove skewers and gather fondant at each end. Pinch ends of fondant and taper. Trim as needed. Brush back of strip with damp brush and attach below window.

STEP 6 For battlement squares on cake top borders, roll out light gray fondant ⅛ in. thick. Cut squares using smallest Cut-Out. Let dry on cornstarch-dusted board overnight.

For flag bases, roll a ⅜ in. ball of blue fondant. Flatten slightly and insert a lollipop stick cut to 2 in., supporting with thinned fondant adhesive if needed. Let dry on cornstarch-dusted board overnight.

For drawbridge ropes, paint two 4 in. lollipop sticks with mixture of black icing color and vanilla extract. Let dry 10 to 15 minutes.

STEP 7 Bake and cool 3-layer 10 in. cake (bake three 10 in. x 2 in. layers; trim one layer to 1 in. high to make a 5 in. high cake) and 2-layer 6 in. cake. Prepare buttercream icing following recipe directions. Prepare cake for fondant by icing in buttercream. Cover cakes with light gray fondant. Smooth with fondant smoother. Prepare cakes for stacked construction (p. 228).

STEP 8 For bricks, imprint sides with smallest square Cut-Out. Roll out black fondant ⅛ in. thick. Mark door and large window patterns with toothpick on cake sides. Attach windows with damp brush. Cut and attach window ledges and bunting as for towers; shape and attach stonework around windows as above. Attach battlement squares with thinned fondant adhesive around top borders.

STEP 9 Position cake on silver cake base. Attach large towers to sides of 10 in. cake with icing.

STEP 10 Insert medium tower at center of 6 in. cake and four small towers in 10 in. cake. Cut 2¼ in. x 1 in. high flags from construction paper. Attach to sticks with tape, then attach bases to turret peaks with thinned fondant adhesive. Ice cake base fluffy in icing. Position drawbridge on cake base. Attach ropes diagonally on each side of drawbridge.

BALLOONS & GIFTS BIRTHDAY CAKE

This cake captures everyone's attention! After covering a 2-layer 8 in. cake in white fondant, decorate it with fondant balloons and gifts.

RECIPES:

Yellow, White or Chocolate Cake (p. 176-177)

Buttercream Icing (p. 181)

INGREDIENTS:

Ready-To-Use Rolled Fondant: White (36 oz.), **Primary Colors Multi Pack**

TOOLS:

10 in. x 14 in. Cake Board

Fanci-Foil Wrap

8 in. x 2 in. Square Pan

Cooling Grid

13 in. Angled Spatula

20 in. Fondant Roller

Roll-N-Cut Mat

Fondant Trimmer

Fondant Smoother

Cut-Outs Fondant Cutters: Round, Square

Brush Set

Plastic ruler

TECHNIQUES:

Using Rolled Fondant (p. 217)

SERVES: 20.

INSTRUCTIONS:

STEP 1 Trim cake board to square. Wrap cake board with foil. Bake and cool 2-layer cake. Prepare buttercream icing following recipe directions. Prepare cake for fondant by icing in buttercream. Cover cake with white fondant. Smooth with fondant smoother. Place cake on prepared board.

STEP 2 Make balloons and gifts. Roll out primary colors fondant ⅛ in. thick. Use medium and large round and square Cut-Outs to cut balloons and gifts. Attach all decorations with damp brush.

STEP 3 For balloon strings, roll thin ropes of fondant. For gift ribbons, cut strips ⅛ in. wide. For dots on gifts, roll ¹⁄₁₆ in. balls, flatten and attach. For bows, flatten two balls, ¼ in. For confetti, cut strips, ⅛ in. wide, in pieces. For bottom border, roll ½ in. balls in various colors. Use damp brush to attach all decorations.

CUPCAKE BOUQUET

What a sweet surprise to give someone special on his or her birthday: a bouquet of cupcakes. And, you can even eat the baking cups!

RECIPES:

Yellow or Chocolate Cupcakes (p. 178)

Buttercream Icing (p. 181)

INGREDIENTS:

White Candy Melts Candy

Candy Color Sets: Garden (pink and green used),
   Primary (yellow, blue and orange used)

Cake Release Pan Coating

Colored Sugars: Yellow, Pink, Green, Blue, Orange

TOOLS:

White Mini Baking Cups

Decorator Brush Set

Mini Muffin Pan

Cooling Grid

8 in. Cookie Treat Sticks

12 in. Disposable Decorating Bags

Decorating Tip: 21

8 in. x 2 in. round craft block

½ in. wide satin ribbon (30 in.)

2 in. wide satin ribbon (30 in.)

Straight pins

Plastic ruler

White curling ribbon

TECHNIQUES:

Candy/Pop Making Techniques (p. 230)

Tip Techniques (p. 204)

INSTRUCTIONS:

STEP 1 In advance, make candy cups (p. 231). Melt Candy Melts candy according to package directions. Tint melted candy yellow, pink, green, blue and orange using candy colors from sets. Place baking cups in pan and make candy shells in cups. Chill until firm 5 to 8 minutes. Peel off paper.

STEP 2 Brush mini muffin pan cavities with Cake Release pan coating. Bake and cool cupcakes without cups. Make small hole through bottom of candy cup and insert cookie stick, positioning halfway to top edge. Attach stick with melted candy. Let set. Slide mini cupcake inside candy cup onto stick.

STEP 3 Prepare buttercream icing following recipe directions. Use tip 21 to pipe swirl (p. 204) top. Sprinkle with colored sugar. Wrap 2 in. and ½ in. wide ribbons around craft block, securing with pins. Insert sticks into craft block. Cut curling ribbon into 18 in. lengths. Curl and position around sticks.

CURLY BOW CAKE

Place this impressive parcel center stage at birthday parties and springtime buffets.

RECIPES:

Yellow, White or Chocolate Cake (p. 176-177)

Buttercream Icing (p. 181)

Thinned Fondant Adhesive (p. 189)

INGREDIENTS:

Gum-Tex

Ready-To-Use Rolled Fondant: White (24 oz.), **Pastel Colors Multi Pack** (2 pks.)

Cornstarch

TOOLS:

Roll-N-Cut Mat

20 in. Fondant Roller

Ribbon Cutter

Plastic ruler

Paper napkins

Bamboo Dowel Rods

8 in. x 2 in. Round Pan

Cooling Grid

8 in. Cake Circles

13 in. Angled Spatula

Fondant Trimmer

Fondant Smoother

Cake Dividing Chart

Brush Set

Paring knife

TECHNIQUES:

Using Rolled Fondant (p. 217)

Fondant and Gum Paste Decorating Techniques (p. 220)

SERVES: 20.

INSTRUCTIONS:

STEP 1 One day in advance, make bow. Knead ½ teaspoon of Gum-Tex to each color of fondant. Make two bow loops (p. 220) each in pastel pink, blue, green and yellow and one center loop in green.

Roll out fondant ⅛ in. thick and cut the following loop strips using zigzag cutting wheels and ½ in. spacers from cutter. (You can use three wheels and two spacers to cut two strips at once.)

Cut one green center loop, 4½ in. long. Cut two loops each in pink, blue, green and yellow, 6½ in. long.

Shape center and loops, supporting with crumbled paper napkins. Let dry on cornstarch-dusted board 24 hours. Reserve remaining fondant.

STEP 2 Make curlicues. Roll out colored fondant ¹⁄₁₆ in. thick on mat lightly dusted with cornstarch. Cut into thin strips, ⅜ in. wide in various lengths from 8 in. to 12 in.

Loosely wrap strips several times around a dowel rod to form curls. Let set 5 to 10 minutes. Slide curl off dowel rod and let dry 24 hours.

STEP 3 Bake and cool 2-layer cake. Prepare buttercream icing following recipe directions. Prepare cake for fondant by icing in buttercream. Cover cake with white fondant. Smooth with fondant smoother.

STEP 4 Use cake dividing chart to divide cake in eighths. Roll out reserved pink, blue, green and yellow fondant ⅛ in. thick and cut two ribbon strips in each color, 8 in. long, using same wheels as for loops.

Attach at each cake division with damp brush and trim excess. Trim off corners of bow loop ends to form an outward V shape.

Attach ends where ribbon strips meet with thinned fondant adhesive. Attach center loop and curlicues with thinned fondant adhesive.

STEP 5 Roll out balls, ¼ in., of white fondant. Attach to bow loops and ribbon strips, ½ in. apart, with damp brush.

THE PRINCESS'S CASTLE CAKE

This bold castle will make her day. It's the ultimate princess palace with 12 sparkling peaked towers, sprays of fondant flowers and windows laced with lattice.

RECIPES:

Royal Icing (p. 181)

Yellow, White or Chocolate Cake (p. 176-177)

Buttercream Icing (p. 181)

INGREDIENTS:

White Ready-To-Use Rolled Fondant (12 oz.)

Icing Colors: Rose*, Violet*, Kelly Green

Cornstarch

Meringue Powder

White Cake Sparkles (2 pks.)

White Candy Melts Candy

TOOLS:

Gum Paste Flower Cutter Set

20 in. Fondant Roller

Roll-N-Cut Mat

10-Pc. Gum Paste/Fondant Tool Set

Fondant Shaping Foam

12 in. Disposable Decorating Bags

Decorating Tips: 2, 3, 5, 349, 12

Romantic Castle Cake Set

Plastic Dowel Rods

Round Pans: 6 in. x 2 in., 10 in. x 2 in.

Cooling Grid

Cake Circles: 6 in., 10 in.

13 in. Angled Spatula

14 in. Silver Cake Base

Plastic ruler

TECHNIQUES:

Using Rolled Fondant (p. 217)

Fondant and Gum Paste Decorating Techniques (p. 220)

Tip Techniques (p. 204)

Tiered Construction (p. 227)

SERVES: 40.

*Combine Violet with Rose for violet shown.

INSTRUCTIONS:

STEP 1 One day in advance, make flowers using small blossom cutter from flower cutter set. Tint 8 oz. fondant rose. Roll out ⅟₁₆ in. thick. Cut 285 flowers. Make extras to allow for breakage.

Place cut flowers on thick foam and cup centers using rounded end of thick modeling stick dipped in cornstarch. Prepare royal icing following recipe directions. Tint portion violet. Use tip 2 to pipe dot (p. 206) centers. Let dry 24 hours.

STEP 2 Add trims to Romantic Castle Cake Set pieces in violet royal icing. Ice tower peaks; sprinkle with Cake Sparkles. Use tip 3 to pipe arch around windows on towers and main roof. Sprinkle with Cake Sparkles. Use tip 5 to outline (p. 208) door and windows for cake sides. Sprinkle with Cake Sparkles. Ice sides of main roof and use tip 5 to overpipe scalloped edge. Sprinkle with Cake Sparkles. Let dry 24 hours.

STEP 3 Prepare towers to insert in cake. Make one large, four medium and two small towers more stable to be inserted into cakes. Attach plastic dowel rods, cut 1 in. shorter than height of cake, to bottom of towers. Stand tower upside down. Melt Candy Melts candy according to package directions. Attach cut dowel rod to base with melted candy. Chill until firm 10 to 15 minutes.

STEP 4 Bake and cool 2-layer cakes. Prepare buttercream icing following recipe directions. Tint small portion green. Ice cakes smooth with buttercream. Prepare for stacked construction (p. 228). Position 6 in. cake ½ in. from center toward back of 10 in. cake to allow for main roof in front. Working from top to bottom, assemble and decorate using buttercream icing.

STEP 5 Decorate three towers (small, medium and large) for 6 in. cake top. Attach tower peaks and flowers under windows. Use tip 3 to pipe dots on battlements and use tip 2 to pipe double drop strings (p. 207) above windows. Use tip 349 to pipe leaves (p. 208).

STEP 6 Insert first three towers into cake top. Use tip 5 to pipe bead border (p. 205) around tower bases and bottom of 6 in. cake. Attach flowers for top border. Use tip 349 to pipe leaves. Insert four plastic windows around sides of 6 in. cake. Attach flowers under windows. Use tip 349 to pipe leaves. Position main roof on 10 in. cake.

Prepare three medium towers and one small tower as described above. Insert in 10 in. cake. Use tip 5 to pipe bead border around bases and bottom border of 10 in. cake. Attach flowers for top border. Use tip 349 to add leaves. Insert door at front and two plastic windows on sides of 10 in. cake.

Attach flowers under windows and around door. Use tip 349 to pipe leaves. Prepare three large and two small towers as described above for sides of cake. Attach to cake board, touching cake sides. Use tip 12 to pipe random green zigzag (p. 215) around base. Position flowers and use tip 349 to pipe leaves.

DAZZLING DOTS CAKE

This cake is gifted with eye-popping color and a fun attitude, thanks to the bow and dazzling dotted sprinkle accents. A great way to top off any birthday celebration!

RECIPES:

Gum Glue Adhesive (p. 189)

Yellow, White or Chocolate Cake (p. 176-177)

Buttercream Icing (p. 181)

INGREDIENTS:

White Ready-To-Use Rolled Fondant (42 oz.)

Ready-To-Use Gum Paste (6 oz.)

Cornstarch

Golden Yellow Icing Color

White Candy Melts Candy

Jumbo Confetti Sprinkles

Flowerful Medley 6-Cell Sprinkles

TOOLS:

Roll-N-Cut Mat

Fondant Rollers: 9 in., 20 in.

Ribbon Cutter

Plastic ruler

Round Cut-Outs Fondant Cutters

Paper napkins

8 in. x 2 in. Square Pan

Cooling Grid

10 in. x 14 in. Cake Board

13 in. Angled Spatula

Fondant Smoother

Brush Set

12 in. Disposable Decorating Bags

Decorating Tip: 2

Knife

TECHNIQUES:

Fondant and Gum Paste Decorating Techniques (p. 220)

Using Rolled Fondant (p. 217)

SERVES: 20.

INSTRUCTIONS:

STEP 1 One day in advance, make bow. Mix 6 oz. fondant and 6 oz. gum paste. Roll out ⅛ in. thick and cut 12 to 14 strips, each 1¼ in. wide x 6 in. long, using ribbon cutter with one 1 in. spacer and one ¼ in. spacer. Fold strips over to form loops. Attach ends with gum glue adhesive. Stand loop sides on cornstarch-dusted cake board. Using large round Cut-Out, cut out a circle for bow base. Let dry 24 hours. Reserve remaining fondant/gum paste blend.

STEP 2 Assemble bow. Melt Candy Melts candy according to package directions. Position six or seven loops in a circle on bow base, using melted candy and a cut disposable bag. Attach remaining loops, filling in center area of bow. Support with crumbled paper napkins if needed. Remove after 1 hour.

STEP 3 Bake and cool 2-layer cake. Prepare buttercream icing following recipe directions. Prepare cake for fondant by icing in buttercream. Tint 36 oz. white fondant light golden yellow. Cover cake with fondant. Smooth with fondant smoother.

For ribbons, roll out fondant/gum paste blend ¹⁄₁₆ in. thick. Cut four strips, each 8 in. x 1¼ in., using ribbon cutter with one 1 in. spacer and one ¼ in. spacer. Attach to cake with damp brush. Attach bow to cake top with melted candy and a cut disposable bag. Attach large and small confetti to cake top and sides with tip 2 dots of icing.

TWINKLING STAR CUPCAKES

Give treats a starring role at your next birthday party. Star cookies sparkle with royal icing and sugar coatings, placed proudly in a cloud of matching buttercream on cupcakes.

RECIPES:

Roll-Out Cookies (p. 183)

Color Flow Icing (p. 182)

Yellow Cupcakes (p. 178)

Buttercream Icing (p. 181)

INGREDIENTS:

Color Flow Mix

Icing Colors: Lemon Yellow, Violet, Rose, Sky Blue

Sparkling Sugars: Yellow, Violet, Pink, Blue

Color Mist Food Color Sprays: Yellow, Violet, Pink, Blue

TOOLS:

12 in. Rolling Pin

4-Pc. Stars Nesting Metal Cutter Set

Cookie Sheet

Cooling Grid

12 in. Disposable Decorating Bags

Decorating Tip: 2

15 in. Parchment Triangles

White Standard Baking Cups

Standard Muffin Pan

9 in. Angled Spatula

13-Ct. Cupcakes-N-More Dessert Stand

INSTRUCTIONS:

STEP 1 In advance, make cookies. Prepare and roll out dough following recipe directions. Cut cookies using smallest star cutter from set. Bake and cool cookies.

STEP 2 Prepare Color Flow icing following recipe directions. Tint portions yellow, violet, rose and blue. Outline cookies with tip 2 and tinted full-strength icing. Flow in with thinned tinted icing in cut parchment bag. Let set 10 minutes, then sprinkle with matching sparkling sugar. Let dry 24 hours.

STEP 3 Bake and cool cupcakes. Prepare buttercream icing following recipe directions. Ice cupcakes smooth with icing. Spray with various food color sprays and sprinkle with matching sparkling sugar. Insert cookie and support with icing if needed. Position cupcakes on stand.

COLORFUL CELEBRATION CAKE

Become a cake sculptor! Decorate these tiered cakes with brightly hued fondant ropes and swags with fluffy white faux filling.

RECIPES:

Thinned Fondant Adhesive (p. 189)

Yellow, White or Chocolate Cake (p. 176-177)

Buttercream Icing (p. 181)

INGREDIENTS:

White Ready-To-Use Rolled Fondant (144 oz.)

Icing Colors: Rose*, Royal Blue, Leaf Green*, Lemon Yellow*, Violet*

Cornstarch

Black shoestring licorice

Piping Gel

TOOLS:

Fondant Rollers: 9 in., 20 in.

Roll-N-Cut Mat

Star Cut-Outs Fondant Cutters

10 in. x 14 in. Cake Boards

Brush Set

Plastic Dowel Rods (2 pks.)

Knife

Plastic ruler

12 in. Round Silver Cake Base

8 in. x 2 in. Round Pan

8 in. Cake Circles

Fondant Smoother

Circle Metal Cutter

TECHNIQUES:

Using Rolled Fondant (p. 217)

Tiered Construction (p. 227)

SERVES: 60.

*Combine Leaf Green with Lemon Yellow for green shown.
 Combine Violet with Rose for violet shown.

INSTRUCTIONS:

STEP 1 One day in advance, make fondant star flames and candles. Tint fondant 32 oz. rose, 22 oz. blue, 26 oz. green, 24 oz. yellow and 6 oz. violet. Also tint 2 oz. portions in a darker shade of each color. For flames, roll out dark yellow fondant ⅛ in. thick. Cut five stars with medium star Cut-Out. Let dry on cornstarch-dusted board 24 hours.

For wicks, attach 1¼ in. long pieces of licorice to backs of stars with thinned fondant adhesive. Let dry 1 hour.

For candles, cut four dowel rods to 5 in. long and one to 6 in. long. Roll out all light colors except yellow ⅛ in. thick. Cut strips, 2½ in. x 5 in. or 6 in. long (length of dowel rod). Wrap strips around dowel rods (use green for 6 in. candle). Trim off excess and smooth with fingers dipped in cornstarch.

For spiral trim, roll out dark fondant ⅛ in. thick. Cut strips, ¼ in. x 8 in. Attach strips around dowel rods with damp brush. Insert a matching-color fondant ball at top of each dowel rod. Insert wicks.

STEP 2 Prepare cake base for fondant by brushing with piping gel. Roll out 14 oz. light blue fondant ⅛ in. thick. Cover cake base with fondant. Smooth with fondant smoother.

STEP 3 Bake and cool three 2-layer cakes. Prepare buttercream icing following recipe directions. Prepare cakes for fondant by icing in buttercream. Cover cakes with 24 oz. yellow, rose and green fondant. Smooth with fondant smoother. Place on prepared board. Prepare for stacked construction (p. 228).

STEP 4 For icing between cakes, roll a ¾ in. dia. white fondant rope. Indent with fingers to create irregular shapes. Attach ropes with damp brush.

STEP 5 For swags, roll out light rose, blue and violet fondant ⅛ in. thick. Cut crescent shapes using circle cutter. First cut circles, then move up cutter 1 in. and cut again to make a 3 in. long crescent. Attach to cake with damp brush, halfway down side.

STEP 6 Roll ⅜ in. balls of light violet, green and blue. Attach at swag points with damp brush. Insert candles in cake top.

TEDDY BEAR TRAIN CUPCAKES

Everyone stops for this train! The square cupcake cars are decorated with dazzling candies, including a cargo of colorful Sugar Gems and cute teddy bear icing decorations.

RECIPES:

Yellow or Chocolate Cupcakes (p. 178)

Buttercream Icing (p. 181)

INGREDIENTS:

Flowerful Medley Sprinkles

Large and small spice drops

Jumbo Nonpareils Sprinkles

Sugar Gems: Blue, Red, Green, Pink

Pinwheel candies

Bear with Gum Drop Icing Decorations

TOOLS:

Bar Pan

White Square Baking Cups

10 in. x 16 in. Cooling Grid

Cupcake Spatula

Knife

Decorating Tips: 5, 1, 2A

9 in. Fondant Roller

TECHNIQUES:

Tip Techniques (p. 204)

INSTRUCTIONS:

STEP 1 Bake and cool seven square cupcakes in bar pan. Reserve two for train cab.

Prepare buttercream icing following recipe directions. Ice five remaining cupcakes smooth with icing.

STEP 2 Use knife to trim tops of reserved cab cupcakes level. Sandwich together with thin layer of icing. Use tip 5 and icing to pipe zigzags (p. 215) over seam on sides of cupcakes. Attach confetti to icing. For side window, use 9 in. rolling pin with purple guide rings to roll out spice drop, ⅛ in. thick. Use knife to cut a rectangle, ½ in. x ¾ in. Use tip 5 and icing to pipe dots (p. 206) to attach window to top cab cupcake. Use tip 1 and icing to pipe dots to attach jumbo nonpareils around window.

STEP 3 On engine cupcake, position large spice drop, narrow end down, for smokestack. Use tip 2A to pipe swirl (p. 204) smoke. For headlight, use knife to cut small red spice drop in half. Use tip 5 and icing to pipe dots to attach headlight to front of engine.

STEP 4 On remaining train car cupcakes, sprinkle each top with a different Sugar Gems color.

STEP 5 Assemble train at party. Position engine, cab and four cars. For wheels, use tip 5 dots to attach pinwheel candies to sides. Use tip 5 dots to attach jumbo confetti to center of each wheel. Use tip 5 and icing to pipe dots to attach bear icing decoration to cab and cars.

CRISPY RICE CAKE SLICE

Fool their eyes by serving double-layer cake slices shaped from crisped rice cereal treats. Melted-candy icing and rainbow jimmies further the piece-of-cake illusion.

RECIPES:

Crisped Rice Cereal Treat (2 batches) (p. 180)

INGREDIENTS:

Brown Icing Color

Bake Easy! Non-Stick Pan Spray

Candy Melts Candy: White, Light Cocoa

Garden Candy Color Set (pink used)

Rainbow Jimmies Sprinkles

Candy-coated chocolates

TOOLS:

6 in. x 2 in. Round Pan

Parchment Paper

8 in. Cake Circles

Transparent cellophane tape

Serrated knife

15 in. Parchment Triangles

9 in. Angled Spatula

Smiley Flames Chunky Candles

INSTRUCTIONS:

STEP 1 Prepare two recipes of cereal treats. Tint approximately 2 cups of mixture brown.

STEP 2 Press brown mixture into pan, ½ in. deep. Unmold onto parchment paper-covered board sprayed with non-stick pan spray. Press plain mixture into pan, 2 in. deep, for one layer. Immediately unmold. Repeat for second layer.

STEP 3 Press together two plain layers with brown layer in between. Let set. With serrated knife, cut into six wedges.

STEP 4 Melt Candy Melts candy according to package directions. Tint melted white candy pink using candy color from set.

STEP 5 Use melted candy and a cut parchment bag to pipe "icing" on wedges, working from side to top. Smooth with spatula. Immediately sprinkle wedges with jimmies.

STEP 6 Position candy-coated chocolates for top border, attaching with melted candy.

STEP 7 Insert candle. Repeat with other wedges using melted light cocoa candy for icing.

DAZZLING DESSERT DUO CAKE

Cupcakes top this birthday cake making it every little girl's wish! Personalize the cake to make it extra special.

RECIPES:

Yellow, White or Chocolate Cake (p. 176-177)

Yellow or Chocolate Cupcakes (p. 178)

Buttercream Icing (p. 181)

INGREDIENTS:

White Ready-To-Use Rolled Fondant (66 oz.)

Icing Colors: Violet, Rose, Lemon Yellow, Orange, Royal Blue, Leaf Green

Piping Gel

Flowerful Medley 6-Cell Sprinkles

Colored Sugars: Pink, Yellow, Blue, Orange, Green

TOOLS:

20 in. Fondant Roller

Roll-N-Cut Mat

12 in. Silver Cake Base

Brush Set

Fondant Smoother

10 in. x 2 in. Round Pan

Pastel Silicone Baking Cups

Cookie Sheet

Cooling Grid

12 in. Disposable Decorating Bags

Decorating Tip: 1M

13 in. Angled Spatula

Plastic ruler

101 Cookie Cutter Set

Star Cut-Outs Fondant Cutters

Stars Chunky Candles (2 pks.)

TECHNIQUES:

Using Rolled Fondant (p. 217)

Tip Techniques (p. 204)

SERVES: 28.

INSTRUCTIONS:

STEP 1 In advance, prepare cake base. Tint 16 oz. fondant violet. Roll out ⅛ in. thick. Prepare cake base for fondant by brushing with piping gel. Cover with fondant. Smooth with fondant smoother.

STEP 2 Bake and cool 2-layer cake. Bake and cool seven cupcakes in silicone cups supported by cookie sheet. Prepare buttercream icing following recipe directions. Prepare cake for fondant by icing in buttercream.

STEP 3 Use tip 1M to pipe swirl (p. 204) on cupcakes. Top with confetti sprinkles.

STEP 4 Tint fondant 36 oz. rose, 12 oz. yellow and divide 2 oz. for orange, blue and green. Roll out rose fondant ⅛ in. thick. Cover cake and smooth with fondant smoother. Position cake on prepared base. Roll ¾ in. yellow balls; attach for bottom border with piping gel.

STEP 5 Roll out remaining tinted fondant ⅛ in. thick. Cut letters using alphabet cutters from set and stars using medium star Cut-Out. Brush with piping gel and sprinkle with matching sugars. Attach to cake with damp brush. Position cupcakes and insert candles.

ONE-derful Cakes

CELEBRATE BABY'S FIRST BIRTHDAY WITH A CAKE TO REMEMBER

• •

PARTY CAP MINI CAKES

It wouldn't be a party without festive hats! Make individual cap cakes for every guest using our Mini Wonder Mold pan and delightfully delicious pull-out icing fringe and pompom trims.

RECIPES:

Lemon Pound Cake (p. 177)

Buttercream Icing (p. 181)

INGREDIENTS:

Icing Colors: Leaf Green, Violet*, Rose*, Orange, Sky Blue

TOOLS:

Mini Wonder Mold

Cooling Grid

Paring knife

12 in. Disposable Decorating Bags

Decorating Tips: 16, 18, 5

TECHNIQUES:

Tip Techniques (p. 204)

*Combine Violet with Rose for violet shown.

INSTRUCTIONS:

STEP 1 Bake and cool cakes. Use knife to trim ¼ in. off sides for straighter hat shape. Prepare buttercream icing following recipe directions. Tint portions green, violet, orange and blue. Use icing to build up point of hat.

STEP 2 Use wide end of tip 16 to mark dots. Fill in dots, then background, with tip 16 stars (p. 212).

STEP 3 Use tip 18 to pipe pull-out star (p. 212) fringe and pompom. Use tip 5 to pipe number (p. 209).

BABY STARTING OUT ON TOP! CAKE

A first birthday can be marvelously messy with this treat cake. A candy plaque No. 1 declares this milestone as it perches atop a 2-tiered cake covered with fondant letters and trim.

RECIPES:

Thinned Fondant Adhesive (p. 189)

Yellow, White or Chocolate Cake (p. 176-177)

Buttercream Icing (p. 181)

INGREDIENTS:

Gum-Tex

White Ready-To-Use White Rolled Fondant (24 oz.)

Icing Colors: Sky Blue*, Violet*, Rose*, Lemon Yellow*, Leaf Green*

White Candy Melts Candy (2 pks.)

Cornstarch

TOOLS:

9 in. Fondant Roller

Roll-N-Cut Mat

101 Cookie Cutter Set

Round Cut-Outs Fondant Cutters

Parchment Paper

10 in. x 14 in. Cake Boards

Brush Set

6 in. Lollipop Sticks

Knife

#1 Pan

10-Pack Candy Mold Set

Round Pans: 10 in. x 3 in., 14 in. x 3 in.

Decorator Preferred Heating Core

Cooling Grid

13 in. Angled Spatula

16 in. Round Silver Cake Base

10 in. Cake Circles

Ribbon Cutter

Detail Embosser

Plastic Dowel Rods

12 in. Disposable Decorating Bags

Decorating Tip: 5

TECHNIQUES:

Using Rolled Fondant (p. 217)

Fondant and Gum Paste Decorating Techniques (p. 220)

Candy/Pop Making Techniques (p. 230)

Tiered Construction (p. 227)

Tip Techniques (p. 204)

SERVES: 48.

*Combine Violet with Rose for violet shown. Combine Leaf Green with Lemon Yellow for green shown.

INSTRUCTIONS:

STEP 1 Two days in advance, make fondant "Happy Birthday." Knead ¾ teaspoon Gum-Tex into 8 oz. fondant; tint blue. Roll out ⅛ in. thick. Cut out letters using alphabet cutters from 101 Cookie Cutter Set. Let dry on parchment paper-covered board 24 hours.

Roll out remaining blue fondant ¼ in. thick. Cut 13 circles using smallest Cut-Out. Attach a circle to the back of each letter using damp brush. Cut lollipop sticks to 3 in. long. Dip end in thinned fondant adhesive and push into circle at right angle to letter. Shape fondant circle around stick for support. Let dry 24 hours.

STEP 2 Make candy plaque. Melt Candy Melts candy according to package directions. Use #1 pan and fill just the recessed number area with melted candy. Chill until firm. Unmold and bring to room temperature. Roll out remaining blue fondant ⅛ in. thick. Use smallest Cut-Out to cut circles. Attach around edge of plaque with melted candy. Tint 4 oz. fondant violet. Press into alphabet mold dusted with cornstarch to make name letters. Unmold. Use knife to trim and smooth edges. Reserve leftover fondant. Attach name letters to candy plaque with melted candy. Store out of direct sunlight to prevent fading.

STEP 3 Bake and cool 1-layer 14 in. cake and 2-layer 10 in. cake. Prepare buttercream icing following recipe directions. Tint yellow and rose. Ice cakes smooth with icing. Place on cake base. Prepare for stacked construction (p. 228).

STEP 4 Make circles. Tint 3 oz. portions of fondant green, yellow and rose. Use remaining violet. Roll out colors ⅛ in. thick. Use medium Cut-Out to cut six circles in each color. Attach to sides of 10 in. cake. Use extra icing if needed.

STEP 5 Make strips. Use ribbon cutter to make nine to 10 strips each in yellow, green and violet for side of 14 in. cake. Cut yellow using two wavy cutting wheels with ¼ in. spacer. Cut green using two zigzag cutting wheels with ¼ in. spacer. Cut violet using two straight cutting wheels with ½ in. spacer. Imprint with bead border from detail embosser. Attach to cake sides, about 1 in. apart. Use extra icing if needed.

STEP 6 Add accents. Use tip 5 to pipe ball bottom border (p. 204) on both cakes. Use melted candy to attach two plastic dowel rods to back of candy plaque, leaving 6 in. exposed at bottom; let set. Insert letters on sides of 10 in. cake, set about 1 in. away from cake side.

STEP 7 At party, insert candy plaque.

CUPCAKE STACK

A towering stack of cupcakes—from mini to giant—will take any celebration to new heights.

RECIPES:

Lemon Pound Cake (p. 177)

Yellow, White or Chocolate Cake (p. 176-177)

Buttercream Icing (p. 181)

INGREDIENTS:

Icing Colors: Orange, Rose*, Leaf Green*, Lemon Yellow*, Violet*

White Ready-To-Use Rolled Fondant (10 oz.)

Cornstarch

TOOLS:

Dimensions Large Cupcake Pan

Jumbo Muffin Pan

Standard Muffin Pan

Mini Muffin Pan

Knife

11 in. Straight Spatula

9 in. Fondant Roller

Roll-N-Cut Mat

Ribbon Cutter

Plastic ruler

Brush Set

12 in. Disposable Decorating Bags

Decorating Tips: 12, 2

Bamboo Dowel Rod

Assorted Celebration Candles

TECHNIQUES:

Using Rolled Fondant (p. 217)

SERVES: 15.

*Combine Violet with Rose for violet shown. Combine Leaf Green with Lemon Yellow for green shown.

INSTRUCTIONS:

STEP 1 Bake and cool large cupcake and one of each size muffin. Trim off crowns. Bake and cool two additional swirl tops for tiers two and three using Dimensions pan. Use only ½ cup cake batter for tier 2, and ⅓ cup for tier 3. Trim off pointed tops. Trim sides to match diameters of jumbo and standard muffins. Prepare buttercream icing following recipe directions. Tint portions orange, rose, green and yellow; reserve some white. Ice bottoms smooth with tinted icing.

STEP 2 Tint 2 oz. fondant in each color. Roll out ¹⁄₁₆ in. thick. For bottom tier, cut 17 wavy strips, each 3½ in. long, using ribbon cutter fitted with two wavy wheels and ¼ in. spacer. Attach with damp brush about 1 in. apart. Cut 17 plain strips, each 3½ in. long, using cutter fitted with two straight wheels and ¼ in. spacer. Attach over wavy strips.

STEP 3 For second tier, cut 12 circles using wide end of tip 12. Attach. Use tip 2 and icing to pipe swirls.

STEP 4 For third tier, cut 12 zigzag strips, each 1½ in. long, using cutter fitted with two zigzag wheels and no spacer. Attach about ½ in. apart.

STEP 5 For top tier, cut 10 dots using small end of tip 12. Attach. Ice tops fluffy for bottom three tiers. Assemble bottom tiers. Insert dowel rod into stacked cakes. Ice mini muffin top and position on tower. Position candle.

IT'S FUN BEING NO. 1! CAKE

First birthdays are fun for clowning around! Playfully perched atop a colorful candy No. 1, these clowns seem to say, "Go ahead... dig in!"

RECIPES:

Royal Icing (p. 181)

Yellow, White or Chocolate Cake (p. 176-177)

Buttercream Icing (p. 181)

INGREDIENTS:

White Candy Melts Candy (4 pks.)

Primary Candy Color Set (orange used)

Jumbo Confetti Sprinkles

Icing Colors: Sky Blue, Violet*, Rose*, Leaf Green, Red-Red, Black, Orange, Lemon Yellow

Cornstarch

TOOLS:

Candy Melting Plate

4 in. Lollipop Sticks

#1 Pan

15 in. Parchment Triangles

12 in. Disposable Decorating Bags

Decorating Tips: 12, 6, 3, 2, 8, 13, 101

Parchment Paper

13 in. x 19 in. Cake Boards

Soft towel

Dowel Rods: Plastic and Bamboo

Oval Pan Set

Cooling Grid

Fanci-Foil Wrap

Toothpicks

Plastic ruler

9 in. Straight Spatula

13 in. Angled Spatula

TECHNIQUES:

Candy/Pop Making Techniques (p. 230)

Tiered Construction (p. 227)

Tip Techniques (p. 204)

SERVES: 37.

*Combine Violet with Rose for violet shown.

INSTRUCTIONS:

STEP 1 Several days in advance, make clown heads. Melt Candy Melts candy according to package directions. Tint portion orange using candy color from set. Mold heads in candy melting plate. Chill until firm 10 to 15 minutes. Attach lollipop sticks to backs with melted candy. Chill until completely firm 3 to 5 minutes.

STEP 2 Also, mold candy plaque (p. 231) in #1 pan using 3 pks. melted white candy. Chill until completely firm about 30 minutes. Remove from pan. Attach confetti sprinkles to border using dots of melted candy.

STEP 3 Pipe royal icing clowns. Place prepared candy plaque face up on parchment paper-covered board. Position candy clown heads by attaching sticks to back of plaque with melted candy, leaving space for piped bodies; let set.

Prepare royal icing following recipe directions. Tint portions blue, violet, green, rose, yellow, red and black. Use tip 12 to pipe bodies over sticks and to pipe arms and legs. Use tip 6 to pipe hands and cone-shaped hats. Use tip 3 to pipe swirl hair and dot (p. 206) noses. Use tip 2 to outline (p. 208) mouth, dot eyes and cheeks, and pipe pull-out dot trims on hats. Use tip 8 to pipe shoes, tip 13 to pipe rosette (p. 210) buttons and tip 101 to pipe ruffles (p. 211). Let dry for 48 hours.

Once dried, set plaque face down on board cushioned with soft towel. Use melted candy to attach two plastic dowel rods to candy plaque, 1 in. from narrow side edges with 2 in. exposed at the bottom. Reinforce back of clowns with tip 6 and royal icing. Let set several hours.

STEP 4 Make cakes. Wrap cake board with foil (p. 192). Bake and cool I-layer cakes using two largest ovals from set. Prepare buttercream icing following recipe directions. Tint portions yellow, rose, orange, green and blue; reserve majority white. Ice cakes smooth with white icing. Place on prepared board. Prepare for stacked construction (p. 228).

STEP 5 Decorate cake. Beginning in back, mark cake edge for garlands 3 in. apart on top cake, 3¾ in. apart on bottom cake. Use tip 3 to pipe double drop strings

(p. 207), ¾ in. and 1 in. deep, between marks. Use tip 12 to pipe balls (p. 204) for balloons. Pat smooth with finger dipped in cornstarch. Use tip 8 to pipe bead bottom borders (p. 205). Use tip 6 to print (p. 209) name.

Lightly mark where plaque dowel rods will go into cake. Sharpen two bamboo dowel rods and push through both cakes at marks. Position plaque by sliding plastic dowel rods over bamboo rods and through top cake.

FIRST BIRTHDAY FEAST CANDY AND CUPCAKES

A candy teddy bear heads up the cheers for the first birthday girl or boy! The easy swirled mini cupcakes that surround him will be a smashing success with any one-year old.

RECIPES:

Yellow, White or Chocolate Cake (p. 176–177)

Buttercream Icing (p. 181)

INGREDIENTS:

Candy Melts Candy: Light Cocoa, White (1 pk. each)

Large marshmallows

Garden Candy Color Set (black, pink used)

Rainbow Jimmies Sprinkles

Cinnamon Drops Sprinkles

TOOLS:

Dessert Dome Candy Mold

Warming tray

15 in. Parchment Triangles

Parchment paper

10 in. x 14 in. Cake Boards

Scissors

Decorating Tips: 2, 12

Transparent cellophane tape

Pink Party Mini Baking Cups

Decorator Brush Set

Letters/Numbers Fondant & Gum Paste Mold

Mini Muffin Pan

10 in. x 16 in. Cooling Grid

4-Pc. Circles Nesting Metal Cutter Set

13.25 in. x 9.25 in. x 0.5 in. Non-Stick Cookie Sheet

10 in. Cake Circles

Fanci-Foil Wrap

TECHNIQUES:

Candy/Pop Making Techniques (p. 230)

Tip Techniques (p. 204)

INSTRUCTIONS:

STEP 1 One day in advance, make candy bear. Melt light cocoa and white Candy Melts candy, separately, according to package directions. Mix 8 oz. melted light cocoa candy with 4 oz. melted white candy for lighter brown shown. Follow dessert dome mold instructions to make four half shells (p. 231) in large cavity. Chill until firm; unmold. Run edges over warming tray, then attach halves, positioning seams vertically, to make balls for head and body.

For ears, use melted light cocoa candy in cut parchment bag to pipe two circles, ¾ in. dia., on parchment paper-covered board; chill until firm.

For arms and legs, use scissors to cut two marshmallows in half. Dip in melted light cocoa candy; let set on waxed paper.

To assemble bear, flatten both ends of body ball by running lightly over warming tray; stand on parchment paper. Flatten bottom of head ball; attach to body, flat side down. Use melted candy in a cut parchment bag to attach ears, arms and legs. Tint portion of white candy black using candy color from set; place in cut parchment bag with tip 2 taped to the outside. Pipe dot eyes, pipe in nose and outline facial features.

STEP 2 Also in advance, make candy shell cupcake for top of head. Tint 4 oz. melted white candy pink to match baking cups. Pour melted pink candy into fondant mold to make number. Chill until firm; unmold.

Use mini baking cup in mini muffin pan and melted pink candy to make candy shell cupcake bottom, ⅛ in. thick. For bear base, place largest circle cutter from set on cookie sheet. Fill ¼ in. deep with melted pink candy. Chill until firm.

STEP 3 Bake and cool desired number of mini cupcakes following recipe directions.

Prepare buttercream icing following recipe directions. Use tip 12 and buttercream icing to pipe swirl (p. 204) on cupcake tops and fill candy cupcake shell. Sprinkle with jimmies. Position cinnamon drops sprinkles on cupcakes. Insert candy number in candy cupcake.

Use melted light cocoa candy in cut parchment bag to attach candy bear to base and candy cupcake to head. Position bear on foil-wrapped cake circle. Surround with mini cupcakes.

FIRST BIRTHDAY TEDDY BEAR CAKE

A tiered cake is a wonderful thing to behold, but when topped with a cute teddy bear holding a No. 1 cookie, it's absolutely awesome!

RECIPES:

Roll-Out Cookies (p. 183)

Buttercream Icing (p. 181)

Yellow, White or Chocolate Cake (p. 176–177)

Lemon Pound Cake (p. 177)

Chocolate Buttercream Icing (p. 181)

INGREDIENTS:

Cornstarch

Icing Colors: Rose, Lemon Yellow, Royal Blue, Black, Kelly Green, Violet

Sugar ice cream cone

White Ready-To-Use Rolled Fondant (11 oz.)

TOOLS:

12 in. Rolling Pin

Parchment Paper

Scissors

Knife

Cookie Sheet

Cooling Grid

11 in. Straight Spatula

Angled Spatulas: 9 in., 13 in.

12 in. Disposable Decorating Bags

Decorating Tips: 5, 4, 233, 8, 1A, 12, 125, 16

Cake Circles: 6 in., 10 in., 16 in.

18 in. dia. plywood or foam core circle (½ in. thick)

Fanci-Foil Wrap

Transparent cellophane tape

Round Pans: 10 in. x 2 in., 16 in. x 2 in.

3-D Bear Pan Set

Plastic ruler

9 in. Fondant Roller

Roll-N-Cut Mat

Brush Set

11¾ in. Lollipop Sticks

Dowel Rods

TECHNIQUES:

Tip Techniques (p. 204)

Tiered Construction (p. 227)

Using Rolled Fondant (p. 217)

PATTERNS:

Number 1 (p. 242)

SERVES: 117.

INSTRUCTIONS:

STEP 1 Prepare and roll out cookie dough following recipe directions. Trace pattern on parchment paper, cut out shape and then lay on dough and cut shape with knife. Bake and cool cookie. Prepare buttercream icing following recipe directions. Tint portions yellow and blue; reserve some white. Ice cookie smooth with icing. Use tip 5 to outline (p. 208) cookie and print (p. 209) name.

STEP 2 Wrap 18 in. circle with foil. Bake and cool 2-layer 10 in. and 16 in. round cakes. Bake and cool pound cake in 3-D bear pan according to pan directions. Ice 2-layer round cakes smooth with white and yellow icing. Prepare for stacked construction (p. 228) on prepared base board. Trim right arm off bear cake; position bear on stacked cakes.

STEP 3 Prepare chocolate buttercream icing following recipe directions. Tint a small portion black and lighten a portion of chocolate icing with a little white icing. Ice smooth footpads and inside ears with light brown icing.

STEP 4 Use tip 4 and black icing to pipe nose and eyes. Pat smooth with finger dipped in cornstarch. Use tip 4 to pipe in mouth and add outline smile. Use tip 233 and chocolate icing to cover bear with pull-out fur (p. 207).

STEP 5 For hat, trim ice cream cone to 3½ in. high. Ice smooth with yellow icing.

STEP 6 Use tip 8 to print message on cake.

STEP 7 For polka dots, tint 2 oz. portions of fondant green, violet, rose and blue. Roll out colors ⅛ in. thick and cut various size circles using both ends of tip 1A and large ends of tips 12 and 125. Attach circles to cakes and cone with damp brush.

STEP 8 Use tip 8 to pipe ball (p. 204) top borders on 10 in. and 16 in. cakes and bottom border on 10 in. cake. Use tip 12 to pipe ball bottom border on 16 in. cake.

STEP 9 Attach hat. Insert lollipop stick in bear's head, leaving 3 in. exposed. Position cone hat. Use tip 16 to pipe pull-out star (p. 212) fringe.

STEP 10 Position cookie. Insert two lollipop sticks in cake for cookie support. Position cookie, attaching to sticks with icing.

STEP 11 Shape a fondant log arm, 1 in. dia. x 3 in. long. Attach to bear with a damp brush. Shape paw around cookie. Cover arm with tip 233 pull-out fur.

CUTE CATERPILLAR CAKE

A mischievous caterpillar surprises you with a row of Mini Ball Cakes covered in icing stars.

RECIPES:

Yellow, White or Chocolate Cake (p. 176-177)

Buttercream Icing (p. 181)

INGREDIENTS:

Icing Colors: Lemon Yellow, Rose*, Leaf Green, Orange, Violet*, Sky Blue

Black twist licorice

Large spice drops

Candy-coated chocolates

Jelly beans

TOOLS:

Mini Ball Pan

Cooling Grid

12 in. Disposable Decorating Bags

Decorating Tip: 16

13 in. x 19 in. Cake Board

Fanci-Foil Wrap

Scissors

Transparent cellophane tape

Knife

Plastic ruler

TECHNIQUES:

Tip Techniques (p. 204)

SERVES: 6.

*Combine Violet with Rose for violet shown.

INSTRUCTIONS:

STEP 1 Bake and cool two cake halves for each ball. Prepare buttercream icing following recipe directions. Tint portions yellow, rose, green, orange, violet and blue. Attach halves with icing. Use tip 16 and tinted icing to cover in stars (p. 212).

STEP 2 Cover cake board with foil (p. 192). Position mini ball cakes on board in curved arrangement.

STEP 3 Attach candy facial features and 2¼ in. long twist for mouth with icing. For antennae, cut spice drops in half and position on end of 2½ in. licorice twist. Insert in top of head.

Shower Mom With Love

TREAT MOM AND MOM-TO-BE WITH SUPER SPECIAL SWEETS FOR MOTHER'S DAY AND BABY SHOWERS

BABY STEPS COOKIES

The pitter-patter of little feet always sounds sweet. Step up the cuteness factor of any baby shower with simple-to-make baby feet cookies.

RECIPES:

Roll-Out Cookies (p. 183)

Color Flow Icing (p. 182)

INGREDIENTS:

Color Flow Mix

Icing Colors: Rose, Royal Blue

TOOLS:

12 in. Rolling Pin

101 Cookie Cutter Set

Scissors

Cookie Sheet

Cooling Grid

15 in. Parchment Triangles

Decorating Tip: 2

INSTRUCTIONS:

STEP 1 Prepare and roll out dough following recipe directions. For each pair, cut two feet using foot cutter from set, reversing one. Bake and cool cookies.

STEP 2 Prepare Color Flow icing following recipe directions. Tint portions rose and blue. Use tip 2 and tinted icing to outline base of foot and toes (about ¼ in. from edge). Flow in using thinned icing and a cut parchment bag. Let dry 24 hours.

EVERYTHING'S COMING UP CUPCAKES

April showers may bring these flowers. As a sweet treat for Mother's Day, Easter or a bridal shower, simple and elegant cupcake flowers bloom and grow.

RECIPES:

Yellow or Chocolate Cupcakes (p. 178)

Buttercream Icing (p. 181)

INGREDIENTS:

Icing Colors: Golden Yellow, Violet*, Rose*

White Sugar Pearls

Yellow Sparkling Sugar

TOOLS:

Standard Petal Baking Cups

Standard Muffin Pan

Cooling Grid

12 in. Disposable Decorating Bags

Decorating Tip: 1M

TECHNIQUES:

Tip Techniques (p. 204)

*Combine Violet with Rose for violet shown.

INSTRUCTIONS:

STEP 1 Bake and cool cupcakes in assorted baking cups.

STEP 2 Prepare buttercream icing following recipe directions. Tint portions yellow and violet; reserve some white. Use tip 1M to cover tops of cupcakes with swirl (p. 204). Position Sugar Pearls or sprinkle with sparkling sugar.

DUCK CUPCAKES

Rubber duckies make bath time—and party time—lots of fun. Bubble cookies froth from underneath the tower of candy rubber duckies floating on cupcake "tubs." They'll squeak some extra fun into a baby shower.

RECIPES:

Roll-Out Cookies (p. 183)

Royal Icing (p. 181)

Yellow or Chocolate Cupcakes (p. 178)

Buttercream Icing (p. 181)

INGREDIENTS:

Meringue Powder

Icing Colors: Sky Blue, Leaf Green, Orange, Rose, Violet

Sapphire Blue Pearl Dust

Candy Melts Candy: Yellow, White, Light Cocoa

Large and mini marshmallows

Primary Candy Color Set (orange used)

White Ready-To-Use Rolled Fondant (5 oz.)

TOOLS:

12 in. Rolling Pin

101 Cookie Cutter Set

Cookie Sheet

Cooling Grid

12 in. Disposable Decorating Bags

Decorating Tips: 3, 1, 2

Decorator Brush Set

Rubber Ducky Candy Mold

15 in. Parchment Triangles

9 in. Fondant Roller

Roll-N-Cut Mat

Plastic ruler

Knife

Regular Muffin Pan

Rubber Ducky Baking Cups

9 in. Angled Spatula

23-Ct. Standard Cupcakes-N-More Dessert Stand

TECHNIQUES:

Candy/Pop Making Techniques (p. 230)

Using Rolled Fondant (p. 217)

Tip Techniques (p. 204)

INSTRUCTIONS:

STEP 1 In advance, make cookies. Prepare and roll out dough following recipe directions. Cut 13 medium and 13 small cookies using small and medium round cutters from set. Bake and cool cookies. Prepare royal icing following recipe directions. Tint small portion blue; reserve majority white. Outline with tip 3 and full-strength blue icing. Let dry 1 to 2 hours. Flow in with thinned white icing. Let dry 24 hours. Lightly brush on sapphire blue Pearl Dust highlights. Melt Candy Melts candy according to package directions. Use melted candy to attach large marshmallow to back of medium cookies and mini marshmallow to small cookies. Position marshmallows near bottom edge so cookie will stand. Let set 5 to 10 minutes.

STEP 2 Also, make 23 candy ducks. Tint portion of melted white candy orange using candy color from set. Use piping method (p. 230) to fill in white of eye and orange beak first. Chill until firm. Fill with melted yellow candy. Chill until firm. Use melted light cocoa candy and a cut parchment bag to pipe dot pupil. Let set.

STEP 3 Tint fondant 1 oz. each green, orange, rose, blue and violet. Roll out ⅛ in. thick. Cut triangles for hats, ⅝ in. wide x ¾ in. high. Attach to ducks with melted candy.

STEP 4 Bake and cool 23 cupcakes. Prepare buttercream icing following recipe directions. Tint blue. Ice tops fluffy with icing. Position ducks. Use tip 1 to pipe zigzag (p. 215) brim and pull-out pompom on hats. Use tip 2 to pipe bubbles in assorted sizes. Position cupcakes on stand and cookies around base.

BABY CARRIAGE BROWNIES

First comes love, then comes marriage, then comes this delicious baby carriage made from candy-coated brownies.

RECIPES:

Cake Brownies or Fudgy Brownies (p. 179)

Buttercream Icing (p. 181)

INGREDIENTS:

Light Cocoa Candy Melts Candy

Icing Colors: Juniper Green*, Leaf Green*, Sky Blue

TOOLS:

15 in. Parchment Triangles

Classic Mint Discs Candy Mold

Dessert Accents Candy Mold

9 in. x 13 in. x 2 in. Sheet Pan

Cooling Grid

4-Pc. Baby Colored Metal Cutter Set

10 in. x 14 in. Cake Boards

Parchment Paper

12 in. Disposable Decorating Bags

Decorating Tip: 2

TECHNIQUES:

Candy/Pop Making Techniques (p. 230)

Tip Techniques (p. 204)

*Combine Juniper Green with Leaf Green for green shown.

INSTRUCTIONS:

STEP 1 In advance, make wheels and handles. Melt Candy Melts candy according to package directions. Mold two candy wheels for each treat in mint discs mold and handle in double scroll cavity of dessert accents mold (use larger scroll). Chill until firm 10 to 15 minutes. Overpipe scrolls on back side. Chill until firm 5 to 10 minutes.

STEP 2 Bake and cool brownies in sheet pan. Cut out carriage shapes using cutter. Coat back of carriages in melted candy. Let set on parchment paper-covered cake board. Chill until firm 10 to 15 minutes. Cover carriages with melted candy. Let set. Chill until firm 10 to 15 minutes. Trim off excess candy if needed.

STEP 3 Attach wheels and handle with melted candy. Let set 10 to 15 minutes. Prepare buttercream icing following recipe directions. Tint portions green and blue; reserve some white. Use tip 2 to pipe dots (p. 206) for wheel axles and on carriage hood in scroll design.

TOT COOKIE POPS

Adorable cookie pops will have everyone going ga-ga! Simple and sweet, they've got the cutest little baby faces.

RECIPES:

Roll-Out Cookies (p. 183)

Color Flow Icing (p. 182)

INGREDIENTS:

Color Flow Mix

Icing Colors: Pink, Brown*, Red-Red*, Black

White Candy Melts Candy

Cornstarch

TOOLS:

12 in. Rolling Pin

4-Pc. Blossoms Nesting Metal Cutter Set

Round Cut-Outs Fondant Cutters

Cookie Sheet

Cooling Grid

Parchment Paper

10 in. x 14 in. Cake Boards

15 in. Parchment Triangles

Decorating Tips: 3, 2

8 in. Cookie Treats Sticks

¼ in. wide ribbon (10 in. for each bow)

*Combine Brown with Red-Red for brown (skin tone shown).

INSTRUCTIONS:

STEP 1 In advance, make cookies. Prepare and roll out dough following recipe directions. For each treat, cut one bonnet using second largest blossom cutter from set and one face using large round Cut-Out. Bake and cool cookies.

STEP 2 Place round cookies on cooling grid. Prepare Color Flow icing following recipe directions. Tint portions pink and brown; reserve some white. Cover with thinned

icing (p. 233). Let dry on parchment paper-covered boards overnight.

STEP 3 Attach head to bonnet cookie using full-strength icing. Outline bonnet with tip 3 and full-strength icing. Flow in with thinned icing in cut parchment bag. Let dry 24 hours.

STEP 4 Melt Candy Melts candy according to package directions. Attach cookies to cookie sticks with melted candy. Let set 3 to 5 minutes. For faces, pipe hair curl, outline (p. 208) smile and dot (p. 206) eyes with tip 2 and full-strength icing. Pipe dot nose. Pipe tip 3 dot cheeks and flatten slightly with finger dipped in cornstarch. Let dry. Tie ribbon around stick.

CUTE AND CONTENTED BABY CUPCAKES

Wish the family congrats with Cute and Contented Baby Cupcakes. Candy pacifiers help to make this treat as sweet as the new bundle of joy.

RECIPES:

Yellow or Chocolate Cupcakes (p. 178)

Buttercream Icing (p. 181)

INGREDIENTS:

Copper Icing Color (light skin tone shown)

Candy Melts Candy: Light Cocoa, Yellow

Yellow hollow-center candy

TOOLS:

Standard Muffin Pan

White Standard Baking Cups

Cooling Grid

9 in. Angled Spatula

15 in. Parchment Triangles

Decorating Tip: 2

Parchment Paper

10 in. x 14 in. Cake Boards

TECHNIQUES:

Tip Techniques (p. 204)

INSTRUCTIONS:

STEP 1 Bake and cool cupcakes. Prepare buttercream icing following recipe directions. Tint copper. Ice cupcakes smooth with icing.

STEP 2 Melt Candy Melts candy according to package directions. For pacifier base, pipe ovals, 1¼ in. x 1⅛ in., with melted yellow candy on parchment paper-covered cake board. Chill until firm 5 to 10 minutes. Attach yellow candy to center of base with melted candy. Chill until set 3 to 5 minutes.

STEP 3 For hair, pipe melted light cocoa candy curls on parchment paper. Chill until set 5 to 10 minutes. Insert into top of cupcake.

STEP 4 Use melted candy and a cut parchment bag to outline eyes and mouth. Use tip 2 and icing to pipe dot (p. 206) nose.

STEP 5 Position pacifier on cupcake.

MOM-TO-BE BABY SHOWER CAKE

The spotlight should be on the mom-to-be! A baby shower will be right on point with this sweet fondant-covered, polka-dotted cake. Get to the heart of the matter with a wonderful way to say congratulations!

RECIPES:

Yellow, White or Chocolate Cake (p. 176-177)

Buttercream Icing (p. 181)

INGREDIENTS:

White Ready-To-Use Rolled Fondant (60 oz.)

Icing Colors: Rose, Leaf Green

Solid vegetable shortening

TOOLS:

12 in. x 3 in. Round Pan

Cooling Grid

13 in. Angled Spatula

20 in. Fondant Roller

20 in. Fondant Roller Guide Rings

Roll-N-Cut Mat

Fondant Smoother

Knife

Toothpicks

Brush Set

101 Cookie Cutter Set

Decorating Tip: 12

Plastic ruler

TECHNIQUES:

Using Rolled Fondant (p. 217)

PATTERNS:

Half Scalloped Circle (p. 244)

SERVES: 20.

INSTRUCTIONS:

STEP 1 Bake and cool 1-layer cake. Prepare buttercream icing following recipe directions. Prepare cake for fondant by icing in buttercream. Tint fondant 36 oz. rose, 6 oz. green and 4 oz. light rose. Roll out ⅛ in. thick unless otherwise specified. Cover cake with rose fondant. Smooth with fondant smoother. Place cake on serving platter.

STEP 2 Use white fondant and pattern to cut full scalloped circle. Attach to cake top using damp brush.

STEP 3 Use cutters from set and fondant to cut green letters and large rose heart. Attach to circle using damp brush. Roll out light rose fondant. Cut large dots using wide end of tip 12. Cut small dots using narrow end of tip 12. Attach to cake sides and heart using damp brush.

STEP 4 Soften remaining green fondant by adding 1½ teaspoons shortening. Roll logs, ⅛ in. dia., for scalloped circle trims. Cut and shape "to be" and ⅜ in. long stitching lines. Attach using damp brush.

STEP 5 For bottom border, roll logs, ¼ in. dia., totaling 38 in. Attach for bottom border with damp brush.

QUEEN MOM CAKE POPS

Crown Mom "Queen for the Day" with these cute cake pops.

RECIPES:

Basic Cake Ball Pops (p. 180)

Thinned Fondant Adhesive (p. 189)

INGREDIENTS:

White Ready-To-Use Rolled Fondant (6 oz. makes 24 pops)

Icing Colors: Rose, Lemon Yellow*, Golden Yellow*

Candy Melts Candy: White, Light Cocoa

Candy Color Sets: Garden (pink and black used), **Primary** (red and orange used)

Sugar Pearls: Pink, Yellow

TOOLS:

9 in. Fondant Roller

Roll-N-Cut Mat

Knife

Brush Set

Cotton balls

9 in. x 13 in. x 2 in. Sheet Pan

8 in. Lollipop Sticks

Chocolate Pro Melting Pot

15 in. Parchment Triangles

Pops Decorating Stand

TECHNIQUES:

Using Rolled Fondant (p. 217)

Candy/Pop Making Techniques (p. 230)

PATTERNS:

Crown (p. 243)

*Combine Golden Yellow with Lemon Yellow for yellow shown.

INSTRUCTIONS:

STEP 1 One day in advance, make crowns. For each crown, tint ¼ oz. fondant rose or yellow. Roll out ¹⁄₁₆ in. thick. Cut crown shapes using pattern. Curve and attach ends with damp brush. Curl points down slightly. Support with cotton balls, if needed. Let dry overnight.

STEP 2 Prepare medium cake ball pops and insert sticks following recipe directions. Chill until firm 10 to 15 minutes.

STEP 3 Melt Candy Melts candy according to package directions. For dark skin tone, combine melted light cocoa candy with melted white candy. For light skin tone, combine melted white candy with a small amount of orange candy color from set. Dip each pop in melted candy. Chill until set 10 to 15 minutes.

STEP 4 Tint melted white candy black and red using candy colors from sets. Use cut parchment bag to pipe facial features and hair onto pops. Attach crowns with melted candy. Let dry in decorating stand 10 to 15 minutes. Use thinned fondant adhesive to attach Sugar Pearls to points of crown and around base of crown.

WHOOPIE PIES FOR MOM!

Get the celebration started for Mom with delicious whoopie pies created especially for her.

RECIPES:

Chocolate Whoopie Pies (p. 186)

Whoopie Pie Filling (p. 187)

INGREDIENTS:

Sugar Pearls: Pink, Yellow

White Ready-To-Use Rolled Fondant (3½ oz. for four treats)

Icing Colors: Violet*, Rose*, Lemon Yellow*, Golden Yellow*, Leaf Green

White Pearl Dust

TOOLS:

12-Cavity Whoopie Pie Pan

Cooling Grid

9 in. Straight Spatula

9 in. Fondant Roller

Roll-N-Cut Mat

Knife

Plastic ruler

Detail Embosser

Stepsaving Rose Bouquets Flower Cutter Set

Decorating Tip: 3

Brush Set

Alphabet/Numbers Cut-Outs Fondant Cutters

TECHNIQUES:

Using Rolled Fondant (p. 217)

*Combine Violet with Rose for violet shown. Combine Lemon Yellow with Golden Yellow for yellow shown.

INSTRUCTIONS:

STEP 1 Bake and cool whoopie pies.

STEP 2 Prepare whoopie pie filling following recipe directions. Using spatula, spread filling on pies and sandwich two together. Roll edges in colored Sugar Pearls.

STEP 3 Tint fondant 1 oz. rose, 1 oz. yellow, ½ oz. violet and ½ oz. green. Reserve ½ oz. white.

STEP 4 For flowers, roll rose and yellow fondant ⅛ in. thick. Cut a strip, 2½ in. x 5 in. Imprint using straight wheel from detail embosser. Cut two flowers using large rose cutter.

Roll white fondant ⅛ in. thick. Use wide end of tip 3 to cut centers for flowers. Attach with damp brush. Brush flowers with white Pearl Dust. Use tip 3 and dot of whoopie pie filling to attach flowers to whoopie pies.

STEP 5 For lettering, roll green and violet fondant ⅛ in. thick. Use alphabet Cut-Outs to cut name. Use tip 3 and dot of whoopie pie filling to attach names to whoopie pies.

Inspired Springtime Sweets

CELEBRATE EASTER, BAPTISMS AND OTHER RELIGIOUS CELEBRATIONS WITH FUN COOKIES AND INTRICATELY DECORATED CROSS CAKES

• •

ECLECTIC EGG COOKIES

Polka dots, stripes, swirls in every color of the Easter egg rainbow! Imagine a basket of creative cookie eggs gracing your Easter feast. Get cracking!

RECIPES:

Roll-Out Cookies (p. 183)

Color Flow Icing (p. 182)

INGREDIENTS:

Color Flow Mix

Icing Colors: Violet, Lemon Yellow, Orange, Rose, Sky Blue, Leaf Green

White Pearl Dust

Imitation Clear Vanilla Extract

TOOLS:

12 in. Rolling Pin

4-Pc. Grippy Easter Cutter Set

Cookie Sheet

Cooling Grid

12 in. Disposable Decorating Bags

Decorating Tips: 2, 44

Plastic ruler

Parchment Paper

10 in. x 14 in. Cake Boards

15 in. Parchment Triangles

Brush Set

TECHNIQUES:

Puddle Dots (p. 233)

Pearl Dust and Color Dust Color Effects (p. 226)

INSTRUCTIONS:

STEP 1 One day in advance, make cookies. Prepare and roll out dough following recipe directions. Cut using egg cutter. Bake and cool cookies.

STEP 2 Prepare Color Flow icing following recipe directions. Tint portions violet, yellow, orange, rose, blue and green; reserve some white. Use tip 2 and full-strength icing to outline cookies. Flow in with thinned icing in cut parchment bag. Let dry on parchment paper-covered boards 24 hours.

STEP 3 Make puddle dots (p. 233). Use tip 2 and thinned icing to pipe ¼ in. dots (p. 206) on parchment paper covered board (about 14 per cookie). Let dry 24 hours.

STEP 4 Decorate cookies with full-strength icing. Use tip 44 to pipe stripes and tip 2 to pipe spirals. Attach puddle dots with icing. Let dry 4 to 5 hours.

STEP 5 Paint cookies with Pearl Dust/vanilla mixture (p. 226). Let dry 15 minutes.

BONNIE EASTER BASKET CAKE POPS

An Easter basket you can devour in one bite! Use White Candy Melts candy and Colorful Egg Sprinkles to create your bite-sized basket cake pops.

RECIPES:

Basic Cake Ball Pops (p. 180)

INGREDIENTS:

White Candy Melts Candy

Candy Color Sets: Primary (blue used), **Garden** (green used)

White Ready-To-Use Rolled Fondant (6 oz.)

Colorful Egg Sprinkles Mix

TOOLS:

9 in. x 13 in. x 2 in. Sheet Pan

8 in. Lollipop Sticks

Pops Decorating Stand

9 in. Fondant Roller

Roll-N-Cut Mat

Round Cut-Outs Fondant Cutters

Toothpicks

Plastic ruler

Knife

Deluxe Brush Set

15 in. Parchment Triangles

TECHNIQUES:

Candy/Pop Making Techniques (p. 230)

Using Rolled Fondant (p. 217)

Tip Techniques (p. 204)

INSTRUCTIONS:

STEP 1 Prepare medium cake balls and insert sticks following recipe directions. Chill until firm 10 to 15 minutes.

STEP 2 Melt Candy Melts candy according to package directions. Tint portions blue and green using candy colors from sets. Dip cake balls into melted blue candy. Place in decorating stand. Chill until firm 15 to 20 minutes.

STEP 3 Roll white fondant 1/16 in. thick. Cut with largest round Cut-Out. Slide up sticks and attach to cake pops with damp brush. Use toothpick to mark basketweave.

STEP 4 For each pop, roll remaining fondant into two logs, 2¼ in. long x ⅛ in. wide. Twist together and attach to top of pops with damp brush.

STEP 5 Attach eggs from sprinkles mix to pop using melted candy and a cut parchment bag.

STEP 6 Use melted green candy and a cut parchment bag to pipe pull-out grass around fondant basket.

AS YOUR JOURNEY BEGINS CAKE

Let this cake proclaim your pride in taking the next step on a religious journey. Perfect for a Bar or Bat Mitzvah, this Star of David cake features beautiful details like royal icing scrollwork and initials.

RECIPES:

Yellow, White or Chocolate Cake (p. 176-177)

Royal Icing (p. 181)

Buttercream Icing (p. 181)

INGREDIENTS:

Gum-Tex

White Ready-To-Use Rolled Fondant (108 oz.)

Royal Blue Icing Color

Cornstarch

Sugar cubes

TOOLS:

20 in. Fondant Roller

10-Pc. Gum Paste/Fondant Tool Set

10 in. x 14 in. Cake Boards

Hexagon Pan Set

Plastic ruler

12 in. Disposable Decorating Bags

Decorating Tips: 14, 5, 3, 2

16 in. Cake Circles

Parchment Paper

30 in. x 30 in. foam core or plywood board (¼ in. thick)

Fanci-Foil Wrap

Toothpicks

Cooling Grid

Fondant Smoother

TECHNIQUES:

Using Rolled Fondant (p. 217)

Tip Techniques (p. 204)

PATTERNS:

Triangles, Initials (p. 237-238)

SERVES: 24.

INSTRUCTIONS:

STEP 1 A week in advance, make triangles and open hexagon section. Knead 6 teaspoons Gum-Tex into 60 oz. fondant. Tint 3 oz. fondant blue. Roll out blue and white fondant ⅛ in. thick. Use patterns to cut six large white triangles, six medium white triangles and six small blue triangles. For open hexagon to frame initials, using bottom of 15 in. hexagon pan as pattern, position on fondant and cut 2 in. in from edges. Cut and remove center. Let all dry on cornstarch-dusted cake boards.

STEP 2 Several days in advance, decorate fondant pieces. Prepare royal icing following recipe directions. Use royal icing to add details to fondant pieces and make initials. Use patterns to mark scrolls on medium triangles and on hexagon. Use tip 14 to outline (p. 208) scrolls. Overpipe with tip 5, then overpipe again with tip 3. Add tip 3 dot (p. 206) accents to medium triangles. Use tip 3 to pipe beads (p. 205) ½ in. from edge on large triangles and on 15 in. hexagon. Let dry 48 hours.

STEP 3 Enlarge initial patterns to 3 in. tall. Tape letters to board and tape parchment paper over letters. Use tip 2 to outline letters. Let dry slightly. Fill in and pat smooth with finger dipped in cornstarch. Top with tip 2 beads and let dry 24 hours. Also, prepare foam core board. Cut a star shape with points 5 in. larger than hexagon pan; wrap with foil.

STEP 4 Bake and cool 1-layer hexagon cake in 15 in. x 2 in. pan. Prepare buttercream icing following recipe directions. Prepare cake for fondant by icing in buttercream. Tint remaining 48 oz. fondant blue. Cover cake with fondant. Smooth with fondant smoother. Position cake in center of prepared board. Position large triangles on each side of hexagon and secure with dots of icing. Attach three sugar cubes to large triangles with tip 3 dots of royal icing and attach medium triangles to sugar cubes with icing. Repeat with sugar cubes and blue triangles. Attach open hexagon to cake top with dots of icing. Position initials.

SWEET-N-PINK CROSS CAKE

This symbol of faith adds an extra blessing to celebrating a christening, first communion, confirmation or any spiritual occasion. Fondant ribbons, flowers and flourishes dress this cake up in Sunday best.

RECIPES:

Buttercream Icing (p. 181)

Yellow, White or Chocolate Cake (p. 176-177)

INGREDIENTS:

White Ready-To-Use Rolled Fondant (66 oz.)

Rose Icing Color

Gum-Tex

Cornstarch

TOOLS:

20 in. Fondant Roller

Roll-N-Cut Mat

Ribbon Cutter

Knife

Plastic ruler

Wave Flower Former Set

Brush Set

101 Cookie Cutter Set

Mini Ball Pan

Gum Paste Flower Cutter Set

Fondant Shaping Foam

10-Pc. Gum Paste/Fondant Tool Set

12 in. Disposable Decorating Bags

Decorating Tip: 2

Cross Pan

Cooling Grid

13 in. x 19 in. Cake Boards

Fanci-Foil Wrap

Scissors

Transparent cellophane tape

Fondant Smoother

TECHNIQUES:

Using Rolled Fondant (p. 217)

Fondant and Gum Paste Decorating Techniques (p. 220)

SERVES: 24.

INSTRUCTIONS:

STEP 1 At least one day in advance, make fondant curves, center circle and flowers. For fondant curves, tint 6 oz. fondant dark rose. Knead in 1 teaspoon Gum-Tex. Roll out ⅛ in. thick. Use wavy-edge wheels and 1 in. spacer with ribbon cutter to cut a long strip. Using knife and plastic ruler, cut into 10 strips, 2 in. long. Let dry on back of small flower former dusted with cornstarch 24 hours.

STEP 2 For center bands, roll out white fondant ⅛ in. thick. Use straight edge wheels with ribbon cutter to cut a long strip. Cut into 10 strips, each 2 in. long. Attach to top of curves with damp brush.

STEP 3 For center circle, knead ½ teaspoon Gum-Tex into 4 oz. white fondant. Roll out fondant ⅛ in. thick and cut a circle using largest cutter from set. Position circle on back of mini ball pan cavity dusted with cornstarch. Let dry 24 hours.

STEP 4 For flowers, tint 6 oz. fondant light rose. Roll out light rose and white fondant ¹⁄₁₆ in. thick. Use small blossom cutter from flower cutter set to cut 60 light rose and 160 white flowers. Reserve remaining light rose fondant. Position flowers on thick foam. Cup centers using end of thick modeling stick. Let dry on cornstarch-dusted board 24 hours.

STEP 5 Bake and cool cross cake. Place cake on a foil-wrapped, cut-to-fit cake board (p. 191-192). Prepare buttercream icing following recipe directions. Prepare cake for fondant by icing in buttercream. Cover cake with 36 oz.

white fondant. Smooth with fondant smoother. For border, roll out reserved light rose fondant ⅛ in. thick. Use cutter to cut into strips, 1½ in. wide. Attach around bottom border with damp brush. Trim excess at edges. Attach center circle to top of cake with icing. Use tip 2 and icing to print (p. 209) message.

STEP 6 Attach light rose flowers around base of circle with tip 2 dots of icing. Use tip 2 to pipe dots (p. 206) in center of flowers. Attach fondant curves to cake top with icing, trimming if necessary to fit evenly. Attach light rose flowers to bands with icing. Attach white flowers around bottom border.

CROSS COOKIES

Share blessings in a sweet way at baptisms, confirmations or first communion celebrations. These cookies will add beauty and a meaningful, personal touch to the special day.

RECIPES:

Roll-Out Cookies (p. 183)

Color Flow Icing (p. 182)

INGREDIENTS:

Color Flow Mix

Icing Colors: Rose, Blue

White Pearl Dust

Imitation Clear Vanilla Extract

White Ready-To-Use Rolled Fondant (½ oz. per daisy)

Cornstarch

White Sugar Pearls

TOOLS:

Cross Metal Cookie Cutter

Cookie Sheet

Cooling Grid

15 in. Parchment Triangles

Decorating Tips: 3, 5, 2

Cake Boards

Parchment Paper

Transparent cellophane tape

Plastic ruler

9 in. Fondant Roller

Roll-N-Cut Mat

Daisy Cut-Outs Fondant Cutters

Brush Set

TECHNIQUES:

Pearl Dust and Color Dust Color Effects (p. 226)

Puddle Dots (p. 233)

INSTRUCTIONS:

STEP 1 Two days in advance, make cookies. Prepare and roll out dough following recipe directions. Cut using cross cutter. Bake and cool cookies.

STEP 2 Prepare Color Flow icing following recipe directions. Tint small portions rose and blue; reserve majority white. Outline cookies with tip 3 and full-strength white icing or tip 5 and full-strength rose icing. Let outline dry 1 to 2 hours. Flow in with thinned icing. Let dry 24 hours.

STEP 3 For blue cross cookies, make monogrammed disks. Use thinned white icing to pipe 1⅛ in. dia. disk on parchment paper-covered board. Let dry 24 hours. Use tip 2 to pipe initials (p. 209) on disks with full-strength blue icing. Let dry 3 to 4 hours. Pipe blue cross on some of white outlined cookies. Outline with tip 3 and full-strength blue icing. Flow in with thinned icing. Let dry 24 hours. Paint initial and blue cross section with Pearl Dust/vanilla mixture (p. 226). Attach disks using full-strength icing.

STEP 4 For daisy cookies, roll out fondant ⅛ in. thick. Cut using medium daisy cutter from set. Roll ¼ in. dia. ball and attach to center using damp brush. Flatten ball and petals with finger dipped in cornstarch. Attach daisies using full-strength icing. Paint rose edges of cookie with Pearl Dust/vanilla mixture.

STEP 5 For all-white cookies, paint outer edges with Pearl Dust/vanilla mixture. Use tip 5 to pipe center cross with full-strength white icing. Flatten with finger dipped in cornstarch. Position Sugar Pearls. Attach with full-strength icing.

· ·

INSPIRED INSCRIPTION CAKE

Inspired Inscription Cake offers a spiritual design to serve at christening, communion or confirmation parties.

RECIPES:

Yellow, White or Chocolate Cake (p. 176-177)

Buttercream Icing (p. 181)

INGREDIENTS:

Piping Gel

White Ready-To-Use Rolled Fondant (18 oz.)

Royal Blue Icing Color

TOOLS:

13 in. x 19 in. Cake Boards

Plastic ruler

Fanci-Foil Wrap

Pastry Brush

20 in. Fondant Roller

Roll-N-Cut Mat

Fondant Smoother

Book Pan

Cooling Grid

3-Pc. Icing Comb Set

101 Cookie Cutter Set

12 in. Disposable Decorating Bags

Decorating Tips: 1, 2, 349, 7

Italic Make-Any-Message Press Set

TECHNIQUES:

Using Rolled Fondant (p. 217)

Tip Techniques (p. 204)

SERVES: 12.

INSTRUCTIONS:

STEP 1 At least one day in advance, cover cake base. Use pan as pattern to cut cake base from double-thick cake boards, making base 1 in. larger than pan on all sides. Wrap base with foil and lightly brush with piping gel. Tint 24 oz. fondant blue and roll out ⅛ in. thick. Cover board with fondant. Smooth with fondant smoother.

STEP 2 Bake and cool cake. Prepare buttercream icing following recipe directions. Tint portion blue; reserve some white. Ice cake top smooth in blue icing and sides ½ in. thick in white icing. Comb sides with tooth edge of icing comb to resemble book pages. Place on prepared board.

STEP 3 For page borders, roll out white fondant ⅛ in. thick; cut ½ in. wide strips. Position around page edges.

STEP 4 For center binding, cut 1 in. wide fondant strip. Position at center.

STEP 5 For message and chalice areas, cut two fondant rectangles, 8 in. x 4½ in. Position at center of each page. Cut chalice and host using trophy and smallest round cutter from set. Trim handles from trophy. Position on cake.

STEP 6 Outline chalice base with tip 1 and print letters on host. Add tip 2 scrolls and dots (p. 206) on chalice. Imprint message on right page using message press. Outline (p. 208) with tip 2.

STEP 7 For background of both pages, use tip 2 to pipe scrolls with tip 349 leaves (p. 208). Use tip 7 to pipe ball bottom border (p. 204).

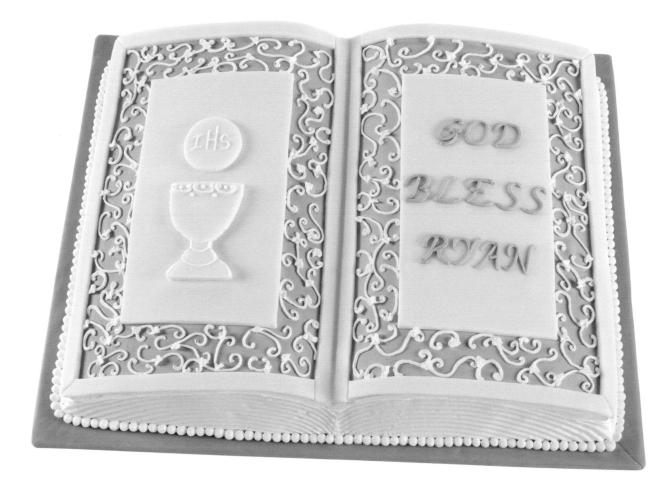

CANDY CURLS LAMB CAKE

The sweetest lamb cake you'll ever create for Easter celebrations is easy with the Stand-Up Lamb Pan Set and candy curls for white-as-snow fleece.

RECIPES:

Lemon Pound Cake (p. 177)

Buttercream Icing (p. 181)

INGREDIENTS:

White Candy Melts Candy

Solid vegetable shortening

Icing Colors: Brown*, Red-Red*, Rose

Cornstarch

TOOLS:

Mini Loaf Pans

Potato peeler (for tighter curls)

Cheese plane (for looser curls)

10 in. x 14 in. Cake Boards

Fanci-Foil Wrap

Stand-Up Lamb Pan Set

Cooling Grid

9 in. Angled Spatula

12 in. Disposable Decorating Bags

Decorating Tip: 3

*Combine Brown with Red-Red for brown shown.

SERVES: 12.

INSTRUCTIONS:

STEP 1 Make candy curls. Melt 12 oz. Candy Melts candy and add 1 tablespoon plus 1 teaspoon shortening. Pour melted mixture into mini loaf pans, 1 in. thick in one, ½ in. thick in another. Chill until firm 30 minutes. Unmold and bring to room temperature. Run potato peeler or cheese plane across narrow edge of candy to make various size curls. Wrap cake board with foil (p. 192).

STEP 2 Bake and cool lamb cake according to pan package directions. Place on prepared board. Prepare buttercream icing following recipe directions. Tint small amount brown and rose; reserve majority white. Ice face and ears smooth with icing. Use tip 3 and brown icing to pipe nose and add dot (p. 206) eyes and string (p. 207) mouth. Pat smooth with finger dipped in cornstarch. Use tip 3 and pink icing to pipe ears. Pat smooth with finger dipped in cornstarch.

STEP 3 Spatula ice remainder of cake and cover with candy curls.

Milestones & Memories

CELEBRATE TREMENDOUS ACHIEVEMENTS AT GRADUATION AND RETIREMENT PARTIES WITH THESE SPECIAL SWEETS

• •

CAPPING OFF SUCCESS GRADUATION CAKE

Create a graduation cake with a surprise inside—the school colors presented in a checkerboard pattern! Cap it off with a cookie hat. Who knows, the graduate might just give you "extra credit."

RECIPES:

Roll-Out Cookies (p. 183)

Color Flow Icing (p. 182)

Buttercream Icing (p. 181)

INGREDIENTS:

Color Flow Mix

3 boxes white cake mix (16.5 to 18.25 oz. each)

Icing Colors: Royal Blue, Lemon Yellow*, Golden Yellow*

TOOLS:

12 in. Rolling Pin

3-Pc. Graduation Cookie Cutter Set

Cookie Sheet

Cooling Grid

12 in. Disposable Decorating Bags

Decorating Tips: 3, 18, 6

15 in. Parchment Triangles

Toothpicks

Checkerboard Cake Pan Set

TECHNIQUES:

Tip Techniques (p. 204)

SERVES: 20.

*Combine Lemon Yellow with Golden Yellow for yellow shown.

INSTRUCTIONS:

STEP 1 In advance, make cookie. Prepare and roll out dough following recipe directions. Cut dough using graduation cap cutter from set. Bake and cool cookie. Prepare Color Flow icing following recipe directions. Tint portions blue and yellow. Outline with tip 3 and full-strength blue icing; flow in with thinned icing in cut parchment bag. Let dry 24 hours. Use tip 3 and full-strength yellow icing to pipe tassel. Let dry 1 to 2 hours.

STEP 2 Prepare three boxes of white cake mix, separately, following package instructions.

STEP 3 In one portion of batter, gently stir in royal blue icing color to desired shade (use clean toothpicks to transfer color from jar to batter). Repeat with lemon yellow and golden yellow icing colors to color second portion. Reserve one portion batter white.

STEP 4 Place batter dividing ring in the first prepared pan. Pour blue batter in outer section, yellow batter in middle section and white batter in center section. Fill sections halfway. Remove ring from pan by carefully lifting straight up on handles. Rinse and completely dry ring.

STEP 5 Place clean and dry ring in second pan. Pour white batter in outer section, blue batter in middle section and yellow batter in center section. Fill sections halfway. Remove ring from pan as before; rinse and completely dry.

STEP 6 Place clean and dry ring in third pan. Pour yellow batter in outer section, white batter in middle section and blue batter in center section. Fill sections halfway. Remove ring from pan as before. Bake and cool cakes following package directions.

DO NOT PUT DIVIDING RING IN OVEN.

STEP 7 Prepare buttercream icing following recipe directions. Tint portions blue and yellow; reserve some white. Assemble cake layers, spreading white icing between layers. Ice cake smooth with white icing. Use tip 18 and blue icing to pipe stars (p. 212) on cake sides. Use tip 6 and yellow icing to pipe top and bottom bead borders (p. 205). Position cookie on cake top, securing with icing.

CONGRATULATE THE GRAD CAKE

This book-shaped graduation cake looks good enough to read! With all the reading your graduate has done over the past years, this personalized graduation cake is a perfect way to say, "Job well done."

RECIPES:

Yellow, White or Chocolate Cake (p. 176-177)

Buttercream Icing (p. 181)

INGREDIENTS:

Piping Gel

Ready-To-Use Rolled Fondant: Red (48 oz.), **White** (36 oz.), **Black** (10 oz.)

Icing Colors: Christmas Red*, Red-Red*, Black

TOOLS:

13 in. x 19 in. Cake Boards (2)

Scissors

Transparent cellophane tape

Fanci-Foil Wrap

Brush Set

20 in. Fondant Roller

Roll-N-Cut Mat

Fondant Smoother

Book Pan

Cooling Grid

13 in. Angled Spatula

3-Pc. Icing Comb Set

12 in. Disposable Decorating Bags

Decorating Tips: 3, 2, 5

Star Cut-Outs Fondant Cutters

Knife

Cardstock

TECHNIQUES:

Using Rolled Fondant (p. 217)

Tip Techniques (p. 204)

PATTERNS:

Graduate (p. 235)

SERVES: 24.

*Combine Christmas Red with Red-Red for red shown.

INSTRUCTIONS:

STEP 1 Two days in advance, cut two cake boards to 13 in. x 17 in. and tape together. Wrap board with foil and brush with piping gel. Roll out red fondant ⅛ in. thick. Cover board with fondant and smooth with fondant smoother.

STEP 2 Bake and cool cake. Prepare buttercream icing following recipe directions. Tint small portions red and black; reserve majority white. Ice cake top lightly and sides thick with white icing. Use toothed edge of icing comb set to comb cake sides to resemble book pages.

STEP 3 Roll out white fondant ⅛ in. thick. Using top of book pan as guide, place fondant on pan and trim to size. Position on cake. Position cake on prepared board and secure with white icing.

STEP 4 Roll out black fondant ⅛ in. thick. Cut graduate silhouette using pattern. Reserve remaining fondant. Attach to cake with damp brush.

STEP 5 Use tip 3 and black icing to print (p. 209) message. Use tip 3 and red icing to highlight message. Outline (p. 208) scroll design with tip 2 and black icing. Use tip 2 and black icing to pipe starburst lines around message.

STEP 6 Roll out remaining black fondant ⅛ in. thick. Cut stars using small and medium Cut-Outs and attach to cake with damp brush.

STEP 7 Use tip 5 and white icing to pipe bead top and bottom borders (p. 205) and to print name.

SALUTE THE STUDENTS CAKE

Congratulate your graduate on reaching the next level with this 2-level cake featuring dignified diploma pillars and celebratory stars. This cake has all the pomp and circumstance to make graduation special!

RECIPES:

Yellow, White or Chocolate Cake (p. 176-177)

Buttercream Icing (p. 181)

Thinned Fondant Adhesive (p. 189)

INGREDIENTS:

Gum-Tex

Ready-To-Use Rolled Fondant: White (108 oz.), **Red** (16 oz.), **Black** (16 oz.)

Cornstarch

Pearl Dust: Gold, Yellow, Ruby Red, Sapphire, Leaf Green

Pure Lemon Extract

Icing Colors: Lemon Yellow*, Golden Yellow*

Piping Gel

TOOLS:

20 in. Fondant Roller

Roll-N-Cut Mat

Star Nesting Plastic Cutter Set

11¾ in. Lollipop Sticks

Curling ribbon

Scissors

10 in. x 14 in. Cake Boards

Parchment Paper

Alphabet/Numbers Cut-Outs Fondant Cutters

A-B-C and 1-2-3 Plastic Cutter Set

Brush Set

Fondant Smoother

Round Pans: 6 in. x 2 in., 10 in. x 2 in.

Cooling Grid

12 in. Round Silver Cake Base

8 in. Decorator Preferred Smooth Edge Plate

Bakers Best Disposable Pillars with Rings

Star Power Fondant Imprint Mat

Cake Circles: 6 in., 10 in.

Knife

Plastic ruler

TECHNIQUES:

Pearl Dust and Color Dust Color Effects (p. 226)

Using Rolled Fondant (p. 217)

Fondant and Gum Paste Decorating Techniques (p. 220)

Tiered Construction (p. 227)

SERVES: 40.

*Combine Lemon Yellow with Golden Yellow for yellow shown.

INSTRUCTIONS:

STEP 1 Two days in advance, prepare fondant stars. Knead ½ teaspoon Gum-Tex into 6 oz. white fondant. Roll out ⅛ in. thick. Cut four stars using third smallest cutter and one star using largest cutter from set. Let dry on cornstarch-dusted board 24 hours. Mix gold Pearl Dust with lemon extract. Paint over small stars and around edge of large star. Let dry 24 hours. Attach lollipop sticks and curling ribbon to backs using thinned fondant adhesive. Let set 1 to 2 hours.

STEP 2 Knead ½ teaspoon Gum-Tex into 6 oz. red fondant. Roll out ⅛ in. thick. Cut numbers using small plastic cutters and cut message using alphabet Cut-Outs. Attach to stars using damp brush. Let dry 24 hours. Also, make four simple bows (p. 220). Reserve remaining red fondant.

STEP 3 Prepare cake bases for fondant by wrapping with foil and brushing with piping gel. Roll out black fondant ⅛ in. thick. Cover 12 in. cake base with black fondant. Cover 8 in. plate with reserved red fondant. Reserve remaining fondant.

STEP 4 Bake and cool 2-layer cakes. Prepare buttercream icing following recipe directions. Tint 54 oz. white fondant pale yellow. Reserve remaining white fondant. Prepare cakes for fondant by icing in buttercream. Cover cakes with pale yellow fondant and smooth with fondant smoother. Prepare for push-in pillar construction (p. 228). Roll out remaining 48 oz. white fondant ⅛ in. thick. Cut a strip, 19 in. x 4 in.; place diagonally across imprint mat and roll over once to transfer design. Trim to match height of 6 in. cake.

Brush sides of 6 in. cake with water and attach fondant strip, smoothing gently with hands. Repeat using 24 in. x 4 in. and 8 in. x 4 in. strips to cover sides of 10 in. cake; reserve remaining fondant. Paint design with Pearl Dust/lemon extract mixture (p. 226), using assorted colors for stars, gold for streamers and backgrounds behind larger stars.

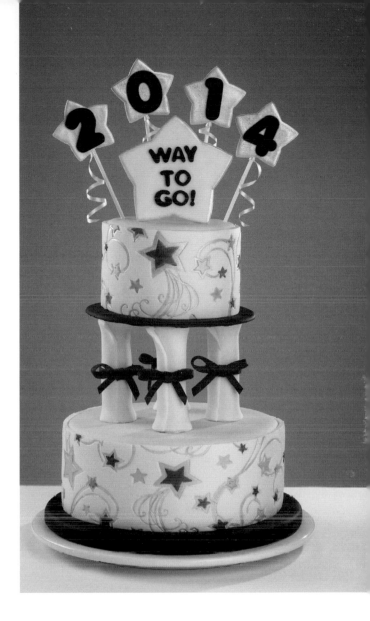

Position pillars in 10 in. cake. Roll out reserved white fondant ¼ in. thick. Cut four strips, each 3 in. x 3½ in. Brush straight section of pillars with piping gel. Wrap strips around pillars to create wider pillar. Roll out white fondant ⅛ in. thick. Cut four squares, each 5 in. Wrap around whole pillar to create diploma. Roll out red fondant ⅛ in. thick. Cut four strips, 4 in. x ¼ in. Attach around diplomas using damp brush. Attach bows with fondant adhesive.

STEP 5 At party, position 6 in. cake. Insert stars.

DIPLOMA MINI CAKES

Everyone shares in the sweet success when you serve these delightful diplomas. The breezy bow adds the colorful touch that ties it all together.

RECIPES:

Your favorite jelly roll cake recipe

Buttercream Icing (p. 181)

INGREDIENTS:

Sugar Sheets! Edible Decorating Paper: White (1 sheet; makes 2 treats), **Red** (1 sheet; makes 18 ribbons)

Piping Gel

TOOLS:

10.5 in. x 15.5 in. x 1 in. Jelly Roll Pan

Cooling Grid

Parchment Paper

Knife

Plastic ruler

9 in. Angled Spatula

Pastry Wheel

Brush Set

INSTRUCTIONS:

STEP 1 Bake and prepare jelly roll following your recipe directions, rolling tightly lengthwise. Cut into 1½ in. dia. x 3½ in. long cakes. Prepare buttercream icing following recipe directions. Ice smooth with icing.

STEP 2 Turn white edible decorating paper horizontally. Use pastry wheel to cut sections, each 4 in. x 7½ in. Brush back of sections with piping gel and wrap around cakes.

STEP 3 For bow loops, use knife and red edible decorating paper to cut two strips, each ⅜ in. x 3 in. Secure ends with piping gel and stand on side edge to dry.

STEP 4 For diploma band, cut a red strip, ⅜ in. x 5 in. Wrap around cake and secure ends with piping gel.

STEP 5 For streamers, cut two red strips, each ⅜ in. x 2 in. Cut V-shaped ends on each strip. Attach to band with piping gel.

STEP 6 Attach loops together with piping gel.

STEP 7 For knot, cut a red strip, ⅜ in. x 1½ in. long. Wrap around loops and secure with piping gel. Attach to cake with piping gel.

BLACK GRADUATION CAP COOKIES

A black graduation cap is the symbol of higher education. Great for high school, college and advanced degree celebrations. Hats off to the graduate!

RECIPES:
Roll-Out Cookies (p. 183)
Color Flow Icing (p. 182)

INGREDIENTS:
Color Flow Mix
Icing Colors: Black, Lemon Yellow*, Golden Yellow*

TOOLS:
12 in. Rolling Pin
Mortarboard Cookie Cutter
Cookie Sheet
Cooling Grid
15 in. Parchment Triangles
Decorating Tip: 3

*Combine Lemon Yellow with Golden Yellow for yellow shown.

INSTRUCTIONS:

STEP 1 Prepare and roll out dough following recipe directions. Cut dough using cutter. Bake and cool cookies.

STEP 2 Prepare Color Flow icing following recipe directions. Tint portions black and yellow; reserve a small amount white. Outline cap with tip 3 and full-strength white icing. Let outline dry 1 to 2 hours before filling in. Flow in cap with thinned black icing in cut parchment bag. Let dry 48 hours. Use tip 3 and full-strength yellow icing to pipe tassel, dot button on top of cap and dot knot on tassel. Let dry 1 to 2 hours.

DREAM SCHEDULE CAKE

It's time to take it easy. Celebrate the milestone of retirement with a 2-tier cake that says, "You're off the clock now."

RECIPES:

Yellow, White or Chocolate Cake (p. 176-177)

Buttercream Icing (p. 181)

INGREDIENTS:

Icing Colors: Leaf Green, Black, Lemon Yellow, Violet, Royal Blue, Christmas Red, Orange

TOOLS:

Round Pans: 10 in. x 2 in., 16 in. x 2 in.

Cooling Grids

Cake Dividing Chart

12 in. Disposable Decorating Bags

Decorating Tips: 2, 17, 4, 101, 6, 3

TECHNIQUES:

Tip Techniques (p. 204)

Tiered Construction (p. 227)

SERVES: 52.

INSTRUCTIONS:

STEP 1 Bake and cool 1-layer cakes. Prepare buttercream icing following recipe directions. Tint portions green, black, yellow, violet, blue, red and orange; reserve some white. Ice cake tops smooth with white icing and sides with green and yellow icing.

STEP 2 Use cake dividing chart to divide 10 in. cake in 12ths. At division marks, use tip 2 and black icing to pipe numbers, tasks and clock hands. Stack cakes (p. 227).

STEP 3 Use tip 17 and green and violet icing to pipe shell (p. 211) top and bottom borders.

STEP 4 On 16 in. cake, use tip 4 and tinted icing to pipe dot (p. 206) confetti on cake sides and use tip 101 to pipe ribbon streamers onto bottom border.

STEP 5 Use tip 6 to print (p. 209) message on 16 in. cake. Overpipe using tip 3.

TOP GRADUATE COOKIES

Congratulate the graduate with these big, bold cookies!

RECIPES:

Roll-Out Cookies (p. 183)

Color Flow Icing (p. 182)

INGREDIENTS:

Color Flow Mix

Icing Colors: Copper (for light skin tone shown), **Brown*, Black, Golden Yellow, Royal Blue, Red-Red***

White Ready-To-Use Rolled Fondant (3 oz. for each figure)

Cornstarch

Toothpick

TOOLS:

12 in. Rolling Pin

101 Cookie Cutter Set

Cookie Sheet

Cooling Grid

15 in. Parchment Triangles

Decorating Tips: 3, 2, 4, 1

9 in. Fondant Roller

Roll-N-Cut Mat

Knife

Plastic ruler

Brush Set

10 in. x 14 in. Cake Boards

TECHNIQUES:

Using Rolled Fondant (p. 217)

Tip Techniques (p. 204)

PATTERNS:

Mortarboard (p. 241)

*Combine Brown with Red-Red for brown shown.

INSTRUCTIONS:

STEP 1 One day in advance, make cookies. Prepare and roll out dough. Cut figures with large gingerbread girl cutter from set. Bake and cool cookies. Prepare Color Flow icing following recipe directions. Tint portions copper, brown, black and yellow; reserve some white. Outline head and hands with tip 3 and full-strength copper icing; flow in with thinned icing in cut parchment bag. Let dry 24 hours.

STEP 2 Also, make fondant caps. Reserve a ¾ in. dia. ball of white fondant for trims on each figure. Tint remaining fondant favorite school color. Roll out ⅛ in. thick. Use pattern to cut out mortarboard. Let dry 24 hours. Shape an oval, 1⅜ in. x ½ in. x ⁵⁄₁₆ in. high, for cap base. Attach mortarboard using damp brush. Let dry on cornstarch-dusted board 1 to 2 hours.

STEP 3 Roll out fondant ⅛ in. thick as needed. Use cookie cutter to cut gown; set over cookie. Trim at head, hands and feet to shape gown. Lightly brush gown with piping gel and attach.

Use knife tip to score center line. Cut semi-circles or triangles for collars, ¾ in. wide. Attach using damp brush. Cut thin strips for sleeve trims and small semi-circles for girl's shoes and attach. Roll remaining fondant into log, ¼ in. dia. x ¾ in. Flatten slightly to shape for diploma. Imprint scroll line on ends with toothpick.

STEP 4 Add details using full-strength icing. Use tip 2 to outline (p. 208) and fill in boy's tie and shoes. Use tip 2 to pipe dot (p. 206) eyes and outline mouth. Use tip 4 to pipe zigzag (p. 215) girl's hair. Use tip 2 to pipe boy's hair. Attach cap. Use tip 2 to outline tassel and pipe dot knot. Attach diploma. Use tip 1 to pipe bow on diploma. Let dry 1 to 2 hours.

DRIVING THROUGH THE WOODS CUPCAKES SCENE

This tower of cupcakes will make any man's retirement party a hole-in-one success.

RECIPES:

Royal Icing (p. 181)

Yellow or Chocolate Cupcakes (p. 178)

Buttercream Icing (p. 181)

INGREDIENTS:

Meringue Powder

Sugar ice cream cones (2 boxes or 19 cones)

Kelly Green Icing Color

TOOLS:

Plastic ruler

Scissors

12 in. Disposable Decorating Bags

Decorating Tips: 3, 14, 233

Construction paper

Black marker

Glue stick

4 in. Lollipop Sticks

Circle Metal Cutter

Pencil

Parchment Paper

White Standard Baking Cups

Standard Muffin Pan

9 in. Angled Spatula

38-Ct. Cupcakes-N-More Dessert Stand

Golf Topper Set

INGREDIENTS:

STEP 1 Two days in advance, make base for topper. Use circle cutter to draw pattern on parchment paper-covered board. Prepare royal icing following recipe directions. Tint green. Outline circle with tip 3 and green icing; flow in with thinned royal icing. Let dry 48 hours.

STEP 2 Also in advance, make royal icing trees. Trim ½ in. off six cones, 1 in. off six cones and 1½ in. off seven cones. Use tip 14 and green icing to pipe pull-out star (p. 212) leaves, working from bottom to top. Let dry 24 hours.

STEP 3 Make construction paper flags. Cut 18 triangles, each 1⅜ in. x 2 in. Add hole numbers 1 to 18 with marker. Glue flags to top of lollipop sticks.

STEP 4 Bake and cool 37 cupcakes. Prepare buttercream icing following recipe directions. Tint green. Ice cupcakes smooth with icing. Position trees on cupcakes. Use tip 233 and green icing to decorate remaining cupcakes with pull-out star (p. 212) grass. Insert flags. Attach topper to base with icing and let set.

STEP 5 At party, position cupcakes and attach topper to stand with full-strength royal icing.

Sizzling Summer Fun

LIGHT UP YOUR 4TH OF JULY WITH THESE RED, WHITE AND BLUE TREATS, AND BRING SIZZLE TO YOUR SUMMER WITH CREATIVE, WHIMSICAL SWEETS

• •

SAM LEADS THE PARADE CAKE POPS

Bring a bunch of Yankee Doodle Dandies to your patriotic party. Fashion adorable Uncle Sam sweets with candy hats set atop cake pops.

RECIPES:

Basic Cake Ball Pops (p. 180)

Buttercream Icing (p. 181)

INGREDIENTS:

White Candy Melts Candy

Primary Colors Candy Color Set (blue and orange used)

Icing Colors: Christmas Red*, Red-Red*, Black

TOOLS:

Cordial Cups Candy Mold

9 in. x 13 in. x 2 in. Sheet Pan

Parchment Paper

Round Cut-Outs Fondant Cutters

6 in. Cookie Treat Sticks

Chocolate Pro Melting Pot

Pops Decorating Stand

15 in. Parchment Triangles

Decorating Tips: 3, 46

TECHNIQUES:

Candy/Pop Making Techniques (p. 230)

Tip Techniques (p. 204)

*Combine Christmas Red with Red-Red for red shown.

INSTRUCTIONS:

STEP 1 In advance, make candy hats. Melt Candy Melts candy according to package directions. Tint portions blue and light orange using candy colors from set; reserve some white. For top, fill cordial cups mold about ¾ full with melted white candy. Tap to settle. Chill until firm 5 to 10 minutes. For brim, line pan with parchment paper. Set medium round Cut-Out on pan and fill ⅛ in. thick with melted blue candy. Tap to settle. Chill until firm. Attach to top using melted candy.

STEP 2 Prepare medium cake balls and insert sticks following recipe directions. Chill until firm. Dip pops in melted light orange candy. Place in decorating stand. Chill until set. Prepare buttercream icing following recipe directions. Tint small portions red and black; reserve some white. Use tip 3 to pipe hair with white icing. Attach hat using melted white candy and a cut parchment bag. Pipe nose using melted light orange candy and a cut parchment bag. Use tip 3 to pipe facial features with white and black icing. Use tip 46 to pipe red and white stripes.

AMERICAN AS APPLE PIE

Pump up the patriotism on July 4th with a star-spangled apple pie. Our version of the stars and stripes is filled with all-American good taste!

RECIPES:

Deep Dish Apple Pie (p. 187)

INGREDIENTS:

Pearl Dust: Ruby Red, Sapphire Blue

Pure Lemon Extract

White Decorating Gel-Tube

TOOLS:

Star Pan

Knife

Fanci-Foil Wrap

12 in. Rolling Pin

Brush Set

Plastic ruler

TECHNIQUES:

Pearl Dust and Color Dust Color Effects (p. 226)

SERVES: 12.

INSTRUCTIONS:

STEP 1 Bake and cool pie following recipe directions.

STEP 2 Paint pie with Pearl Dust/lemon extract mixture (p. 226), making a deep blue field across two star points and red stripes, 1 in. wide. For stars, pipe dots with decorating gel. Immediately pull out star points using tip of brush.

SPARKLING STARS CUPCAKES

Sparkling star cookies set in patriotic-themed baking cups are a great way to get the fireworks started. A perfect dessert for Memorial Day, July 4th and Labor Day celebrations.

RECIPES:

Roll-Out Cookies (p. 183)

Buttercream Icing (p. 181)

Yellow or Chocolate Cupcakes (p. 178)

INGREDIENTS:

Colored Sugars: Red, Blue

White Sparkling Sugar

White Candy Melts Candy

TOOLS:

12 in. Rolling Pin

Stars Nesting Metal Cutter Set

Cookie Sheet

Cooling Grid

9 in. Tapered Spatula

4 in. Lollipop Sticks

Patriotic-Themed Baking Cups

Standard Muffin Pan

12 in. Disposable Decorating Bags

Decorating Tip: 1M

TECHNIQUES:

Tip Techniques (p. 204)

INSTRUCTIONS:

STEP 1 Prepare and roll out dough following recipe directions. Cut two star cookies for each cupcake using smallest star cutter from set. Bake and cool cookies.

STEP 2 Prepare buttercream icing following recipe directions. Ice cookies smooth with icing. Sprinkle immediately with colored sugars. Let dry. Melt Candy Melts candy according to package directions. Attach lollipop sticks to backs with melted candy. Chill to set 5 to 10 minutes.

STEP 3 Bake and cool cupcakes.

STEP 4 Use tip 1M to pipe swirls (p. 204) on cupcake tops. Immediately sprinkle cupcakes with white sugar.

STEP 5 Insert cookies in cupcakes. Trim sticks as needed for staggered heights.

HINT: Carry out the patriotic theme with a cookie-topped cake. Bake a cake, ice and top with assorted-size cookies made with the Stars Nesting Metal Cutter Set, using the same decorating method as above.

POPPING FIREWORKS COOKIE POPS

These firework cookie pops are bursting with patriotic style.

RECIPES:

Vanilla Sugar Cookies on a Stick (p. 185)

INGREDIENTS:

White Candy Melts Candy

Red Colored Sugar

White Ready-To-Use Rolled Fondant
  (¼ oz. per treat)

Royal Blue Icing Color

TOOLS:

Star Cookie Treat Pan

6 in. Cookie Treat Sticks

Cooling Grid

Parchment Paper

Cookie Sheet

15 in. Parchment Triangles

9 in. Fondant Roller

Roll-N-Cut Mat

Star Cut-Outs Fondant Cutters

Brush Set

White curling ribbon (12 in. per treat)

TECHNIQUES:

Candy/Pop Making Techniques (p. 230)

INSTRUCTIONS:

STEP 1 Bake and cool cookies with sticks according to pan package directions. Set on cooling grid over parchment paper-covered cookie sheet. Melt Candy Melts candy according to package directions. Cover with melted white candy. Tap to settle and chill until firm on parchment paper-covered surface. Use melted candy and a cut parchment bag to pipe stripes. Immediately sprinkle on red sugar. Let set.

STEP 2 Tint fondant blue. Roll out ¹⁄₁₆ in. thick. Cut stars using medium Cut-Out. Attach using melted candy. Tie ribbon around stick.

A SLICE OF SUMMERTIME CAKE

Create a dessert sure to delight. Impress one and all with a watermelon-slice cake sporting chocolate-chip seeds and a fondant rind.

RECIPES:

White Cake (p. 177)

Buttercream Icing (p. 181)

INGREDIENTS:

Icing Colors: Red-Red, Leaf Green*, Kelly Green*

Mini chocolate chips

White Ready-To-Use Rolled Fondant (8 oz.)

Bold Tip Primary FoodWriter Edible Color Markers

TOOLS:

8 in. x 2 in. Round Pan

Cooling Grid

Small Cake Leveler

10 in. Cake Circle

16 In. Featherweight Decorating Bag

Decorating Tip: 789

20 in. Fondant Roller

Roll-N-Cut Mat

Pastry Wheel

TECHNIQUES:

Using Rolled Fondant (p. 217)

SERVES: 6.

*Combine Leaf Green with Kelly Green for green fondant shown.

INSTRUCTIONS:

STEP 1 Prepare cake batter and tint with ¼ teaspoon of Red-Red Icing Color. Blend in ½ cup mini chocolate chips. Bake and cool 1-layer cake.

STEP 2 Refrigerate cake until mini chocolate chips are hardened. Trim off top of cake with cake leveler. Prepare buttercream icing following recipe directions. Tint leaf green. Use tip 789 to ice cake side. For rind, tint 8 oz. fondant green. Roll out ⅛ in. thick. Using pastry wheel, cut a strip, 1½ in. wide, and attach to cake sides. Trim to fit. Draw lines on rind with green edible color marker.

SIZZLING SUMMER MINI CAKES

What a great way to extend the barbecue all the way through dessert.

RECIPES:

Lemon Pound Cake (p. 177), Yellow Cake or
   Chocolate Cake (p. 176)

Candy Clay (p. 189)

INGREDIENTS:

Candy Melts Candy: Red, White, Black

Candy Color Sets: Primary (red*, yellow, green* used),
   Garden (black* used)

TOOLS:

Mini Ball Pan

Cooling Grid

Cookie Sheet

9 in. Angled Spatula

6 in. Cookie Treat Sticks

Fanci-Foil Wrap

Glue stick

9 in. Fondant Roller

Parchment Paper

Paring knife

Plastic ruler

TECHNIQUES:

Candy/Pop Making Techniques (p. 230)

*Combine red with green candy colors for brown shown. Use
   a little black candy color to make gray shown.

INSTRUCTIONS:

STEP 1 Bake and cool mini ball cakes. Prepare candy clay using white candy. Let set according to recipe directions. Divide clay into five portions and tint large portion red, smaller portions gray, brown, black and yellow.

STEP 2 Place mini ball cakes flat side down on cooling grid over parchment paper-covered cookie sheet. Melt Candy Melts candy according to package directions. Cover with melted red candy. Chill to set 5 to 10 minutes. Turn cakes over. Use spatula to ice flat side with melted black candy. Chill to set.

STEP 3 Make legs and connectors. For legs, cut cookie sticks into 3 in. lengths. Wrap sticks with foil and secure with glue. For leg connectors, shape three balls of red clay to ½ in. dia. Turn cakes flat side down and attach balls with melted candy. Immediately insert legs at angle, ½ in. deep, into cake. Turn cakes upright, making sure each is level. Turn back to flat side to set.

STEP 4 For grate, roll and position logs of gray clay, ⅛ in. dia. x 3¼ in. long. For grill rim, roll and position a log of red clay, ¼ in. dia. x 10 in. long.

STEP 5 Shape two brown burgers, ¾ in. On parchment paper, roll out yellow clay. Cut square for cheese, ½ in. Position burgers and cheese.

STEP 6 For hot dogs, combine red clay with a little brown. Shape and position two hot dogs, 1¼ in. For wheels, shape two black clay disks, ½ in. Attach to legs with melted candy.

COVERED WITH GLORY FLAG CAKE

Show your true colors! Create a flag-waving cake topped with a bottle-rocket display of sparkling cookies.

RECIPES:

Roll-Out Cookies (p. 183)

Yellow, White or Chocolate Cake (p. 176-177)

Buttercream Icing (p. 181)

INGREDIENTS:

Icing Colors: Christmas Red, Royal Blue

Colored Sugars: Red, Blue

White Candy Melts Candy

TOOLS:

4-Pc. Stars Nesting Metal Cutter Set

Cookie Sheet

Cooling Grid

8 in. x 2 in. Round Pan

13 in. Angled Spatula

Cake Dividing Chart

12 in. Disposable Decorating Bags

Decorating Tips: 12, 16, 13

Plastic ruler

9 in. Tapered Spatula

11¾ in. Lollipop Sticks

White curling ribbon

TECHNIQUES:

Tip Techniques (p. 204)

SERVES: 20.

INSTRUCTIONS:

STEP 1 Prepare and roll out dough following recipe directions. Cut dough using two smallest star cutters from set. Bake and cool cookies.

STEP 2 Bake and cool 2-layer cake. Prepare buttercream icing following recipe directions. Tint portions red and blue; reserve some white. Ice cake smooth with white icing. Divide cake into fourths using cake dividing chart. Use tip 12 to outline flag pole at division marks. Mark 3 in. to the right of each pole for blue field.

STEP 3 In each division, starting from the bottom of cake, pipe six rows of tip 16 stars (p. 212), alternating red and white rows. Use tip 16 to pipe blue stars in marked area. Continue piping alternating rows of tip 16 red and white stars to top of cake, ending with red rows. Use tip 13 to pipe white stars on blue field. Use tip 12 to pipe a ball (p. 204) on top of each flag pole.

STEP 4 Ice cookies smooth with white icing. Immediately sprinkle with sugars.

STEP 5 Melt Candy Melts candy according to package directions. Attach lollipop sticks to backs of cookies with melted candy. Let set.

STEP 6 Cut eight 30 in. lengths of curling ribbon. Curl ribbon and tie to lollipop sticks. Insert cookies in cake.

FRUIT 'N FIREWORKS CANDY-COATED TREATS

A fresh twist on a red-white-and-blue dessert! Tri-color candy-dipped strawberries nestle among blueberries and watermelon stars.

INGREDIENTS:

Fresh strawberries, blueberries and watermelon

Candy Melts Candy: White, Blue (2 pks. cover 30 to 35 medium-size strawberries)

Primary Colors Candy Color Set (blue used)

Silver Stars Edible Accents

TOOLS:

10 in. x 14 in. Cake Boards

Parchment Paper

4-Pc. Stars Nesting Metal Cutter Set

Knife

Serving dish

TECHNIQUES:

Candy/Pop Making Techniques (p. 230)

INSTRUCTIONS:

STEP 1 Melt Candy Melts candy according to package directions. Tint blue a darker shade using candy color from set. Dip strawberries in melted white candy. Chill on parchment paper-covered board until firm. Dip strawberries one third deep in melted blue candy. Immediately sprinkle with edible accents. Chill until firm.

STEP 2 Cut watermelon into ¾ in. thick slices. Cut stars using second smallest star cutter from set. Place blueberries, watermelon stars and strawberries in serving dish.

OUR FLAG WAS STILL THERE CUPCAKES

Add patriotic punch to your next July 4th picnic. Creative piping makes a delicious fireworks starburst backdrop for the flag.

RECIPES:

Yellow or Chocolate Cupcakes (p. 178)

Buttercream Icing (p. 181)

INGREDIENTS:

Icing Colors: Royal Blue, Christmas Red

TOOLS:

Patriotic-Themed Baking Cups

Standard Muffin Pan

Cooling Grid

12 in. Disposable Decorating Bags

Decorating Tip: 233

Stars and Stripes Party Picks

TECHNIQUES:

Tip Techniques (p. 204)

INSTRUCTIONS:

STEP 1 Bake and cool cupcakes.

STEP 2 Prepare buttercream icing following recipe directions. Tint portions blue and red; reserve some white. For fireworks, use tip 233 and blue icing to pipe ring of fringe around rim of cupcake. Use same tip with white icing to pipe a concentric circle. Finish by piping red icing fringe in the center and insert a flag pick.

SUNDAES ON A STICK CAKE POPS

Anyone with a sweet tooth will love these cake pops that look like delicious sundaes! The scrumptious candy coating pairs well with the cinnamon drop "cherry."

RECIPES:

Basic Cake Ball Pops (p. 180)

INGREDIENTS:

Candy Melts Candy: White (2 pks.), **Orange, Yellow, Red, Blue**

Garden Candy Color Set (pink, green, violet used)

Vegetable shortening

Rainbow Nonpareils

Cinnamon Drops Sprinkles

TOOLS:

9 in. x 13 in. x 2 in. Sheet Pan

6 in. Lollipop Sticks

Chocolate Pro Melting Pot

Pops Decorating Stand

15 in. Parchment Triangles

Knife

TECHNIQUES:

Candy/Pop Making Techniques (p. 230)

INSTRUCTIONS:

STEP 1 Prepare medium cake balls and insert sticks following recipe directions. Chill until firm 10 to 15 minutes. Melt Candy Melts candy according to package directions. Tint portions of melted white candy pink, green and violet with candy colors from set. Dip in melted candy. Place in decorating stand and chill until firm 10 to 15 minutes.

STEP 2 Thin ¼ cup melted white candy by adding ½ teaspoon shortening. Working with one cake pop at a time, use melted white candy and a cut parchment bag to pipe topping and drips. Immediately sprinkle on nonpareils and position cinnamon drop. Chill until firm 3 to 5 minutes.

PARFAIT PERFECTION CUPCAKES

Cupcakes have never been cooler or more colorful! They're sitting atop a rainbow of creamy gelatin, and crowned by an icing swirl, rainbow sprinkles and a cherry.

RECIPES:

Creamy Gelatin (p. 188)

Yellow Cupcakes (p. 178)

Buttercream Icing (p. 181)

INGREDIENTS:

Rainbow Sparkling Sugar

Maraschino cherries

TOOLS:

12 in. Disposable Decorating Bags

5 in. tall champagne flutes

Standard Muffin Pan

White Standard Baking Cups

Cooling Grid

Decorating Tip: 1M

TECHNIQUES:

Tip Techniques (p. 204)

INSTRUCTIONS:

STEP 1 Prepare gelatin. Make three or more creamy gelatin recipes, using different gelatin flavors and colors. Chill until slightly thickened. Place gelatin, separately, into cut disposable decorating bags. Pipe three different colors into each flute, stopping ½ in. below rim. Chill until firm.

STEP 2 Bake and cool desired number of cupcakes following recipe directions. Remove baking cups. Position cupcake in flute on top of gelatin.

Prepare buttercream icing following recipe directions. Use tip 1M and buttercream icing to cover tops with a swirl (p. 204). Sprinkle with sparkling sugar. Position cherry on top.

GO BERRY PICKING STRAWBERRY MINI CAKES

Nothing says summer like fresh strawberries! Dipped in melted candy and crowned with fondant leaves, these cake treats are perfect at a barbecue, garden party, brunch or tea.

RECIPES:

Lemon Pound Cake (p. 177)

INGREDIENTS:

Candy Melts Candy: Red, Light Cocoa, Yellow

White Ready-To-Use Rolled Fondant
  (¼ oz. per treat)

Leaf Green Icing Color

TOOLS:

10.5 in. x 15.5 in. x 1 in. Jelly Roll Pan

Cooling Grid

Cut-Outs Fondant Cutters: Heart, Leaf

6 in. Cookie Treat Sticks

Chocolate Pro Melting Pot

Parchment Paper

10 in. x 14 in. Cake Boards

15 in. Parchment Triangles

Scissors

9 in. Fondant Roller

Roll-N-Cut Mat

Decorator Brush Set

TECHNIQUES:

Candy/Pop Making Techniques (p. 230)

Using Rolled Fondant (p. 217)

INSTRUCTIONS:

STEP 1 Bake and cool cake. Cut hearts using largest Cut-Out. Melt Candy Melts candy according to package directions. Dip stick in melted candy and push into top indent. Chill. Dip cake in melted red candy. Set on side on parchment paper-covered board. Chill until firm. Dip bottom third in light cocoa candy. Set on parchment paper-covered board. Chill until set.

STEP 2 Use melted yellow candy in cut parchment bag to pipe seeds. Let set.

STEP 3 Tint fondant green. Roll out ⅟₁₆ in. thick. Use smallest cutter to cut five leaves for each berry. Attach using damp brush. Roll log, ⅛ in. x ⅜ in. long, for stem. Attach on stick using melted candy.

CAKE POP KABOBS

These sweet kabobs really stack up to party success. You choose the toppings for these cake balls and your guests will choose to come back for more.

RECIPES:

Basic Cake Ball Pops (p. 180)

INGREDIENTS:

Candy Melts Candy: Light Cocoa, White

Toppings, such as chopped nuts, coconut, mini chocolate chips

TOOLS:

9 in. x 13 in. x 2 in. Sheet Pan

4 in. Lollipop Sticks

Chocolate Pro Melting Pot

Pops Decorating Stand

15 in. Parchment Triangles

Scissors

11¾ in. Lollipop Sticks

Plastic ruler

INSTRUCTIONS:

STEP 1 Prepare small and medium cake balls (two of each size per kabob) following recipe directions. Insert a 4 in. stick in each following recipe. Chill until firm.

STEP 2 Melt Candy Melts candy according to package directions. Dip pops in melted candy. Roll in various toppings. Place in stand and let set.

STEP 3 Use melted candy and a cut parchment bag to pipe a candy ring about 4 in. from top on 11¾ in. sticks. Chill until firm. Overpipe. Let set. Chill 3 to 5 minutes.

STEP 4 Twist balls off of 4 in. sticks and slide onto 11¾ in. sticks, alternating sizes. Secure top and bottom treats with melted candy.

Spectacular Wedding Cakes

SAY "I DO" TO LAVISHLY BEAUTIFUL CAKES AND TREATS FOR WEDDING AND ANNIVERSARY CELEBRATIONS

• •

SWIRL TOPPED PETIT FOURS

A curlicue of candy is the crowning glory on these petite cakes.

RECIPES:

Lemon Pound Cake (p. 177), Yellow Cake or
  Chocolate Cake (p. 176)

Buttercream Icing (p. 181)

Quick-Pour Fondant Icing (p. 183)

INGREDIENTS:

Light Cocoa Candy Melts Candy

Icing Colors: Creamy Peach, Kelly Green, Yellow

White Sugar Pearls

TOOLS:

Dessert Accents Candy Mold

9 in. x 13 in. x 2 in. Sheet Pan

Knife

Plastic ruler

9 in. Straight Spatula

Cooling Grid

Cookie Sheet

12 in. Disposable Decorating Bags

Decorating Tip: 21

TECHNIQUES:

Candy/Pop Making Techniques (p. 230)

Tip Techniques (p. 204)

INSTRUCTIONS:

STEP 1 In advance, make one swirl accent for each treat. Melt Candy Melts candy according to package directions. Use melted candy and dessert accents mold. Chill until firm.

STEP 2 Bake and cool 1-layer cake.

STEP 3 Cut cooled cake into 1½ in. x 2½ in. pieces. Prepare buttercream icing following recipe directions. Tint portions light peach, green and yellow; reserve majority white. Lightly ice with white icing. Place cakes on cooling grid set over a cookie sheet. Prepare Quick-Pour Fondant Icing following recipe directions. Tint portions light peach, green and yellow. Cover with tinted poured fondant icing. Add Sugar Pearls. Let set.

STEP 4 Use tip 21 to pipe rosette (p. 210) on top. Position candy swirl accents.

GARDEN TERRACES CAKE

Cascades of flowers dress up this curvaceous cake. Delicate floral trims accent all three levels to make a wedding extra special.

RECIPES:

Gum Glue Adhesive (p. 189)

Yellow, White or Chocolate Cake (p. 176-177)

Buttercream Icing (p. 181)

Royal Icing (p. 181)

INGREDIENTS:

Ready-To-Use Gum Paste

Icing Colors: Rose*, Violet*, Black

Ready-To-Use Rolled Fondant: White (144 oz.), **Black** (36 oz.)

Piping Gel

Cornstarch

TOOLS:

Storage Board

Round Cut-Outs Fondant Cutters

Fondant Rollers: 9 in., 20 in.

Brush Set

Fondant Shaping Foam Set

10-Pc. Gum Paste/Fondant Tool Set

Gum Paste Wire and Tape (2 pks.)

20 in. x 30 in. foam core board (½ in. thick)

3-Pc. Paisley Pan Set

Fanci-Foil Wrap

Roll-N-Cut Mat

Fondant Smoother

Cooling Grid

13 in. Angled Spatula

Parchment Paper

Toothpicks

12 in. Disposable Decorating Bags

Decorating Tips: 1, 5

Plastic Dowel Rods

Fresh Flower Spikes

Scissors or wire cutters

Knife

PATTERNS:

Garden Greenery (p. 239)

TECHNIQUES:

Fondant and Gum Paste Decorating Techniques (p. 220)

Using Rolled Fondant (p. 217)

Tiered Construction (p. 227)

Tip Techniques (p. 204)

SERVES: 94.**

 *Combine Violet with Rose for violet shown.

**The top tier is often saved for the first anniversary. The number of servings given does not include the top tier.

INSTRUCTIONS:

STEP 1 Several days in advance, cut 26-gauge green wires into 4 in. lengths. Make 75 gum paste ruffled fantasy flowers on cut wires (p. 226).

STEP 2 One day in advance, prepare base board. Cut foam core board 2 in. larger than largest paisley pan. Wrap with foil. Brush with piping gel. Roll out black fondant ⅛ in. thick. Cut piece 2 in. larger than board. Cover board with fondant. Smooth with fondant smoother.

STEP 3 Bake and cool 2-layer cakes. Prepare buttercream icing following recipe directions. Prepare cakes for fondant by icing in buttercream. Cover cakes with fondant. Smooth with fondant smoother. Prepare for stacked construction (p. 228).

STEP 4 Trace greenery pattern onto parchment paper. Hold against cake sides and use toothpick as a stylus to outline and imprint designs on fondant. Prepare royal icing following recipe directions. Tint black. Use tip 1 to cover designs with outlines. Add random tip 1 dots (p. 206). Stack cakes. Use tip 5 to pipe bead bottom borders (p. 205).

STEP 5 Arrange flowers into two medium (20 flowers each) and one large (30 flowers) crescent-shaped sprays by wrapping stems together with florist tape.

STEP 6 Cut a plastic dowel rod to 5½ in. Insert in top cake, 1 in. from back left edge. Position one medium floral spray by inserting stems into dowel rod. Position remaining floral sprays using fresh flower spikes.

ROMANTIC ROUNDS VIOLET CAKE

Say "I do" to purple violets! Simply elegant tiers are supported by flower-covered globes.

RECIPES:

Royal Icing (p. 181)

Yellow, White or Chocolate Cake (p. 176-177)

Buttercream Icing (p. 181)

INGREDIENTS:

Ready-To-Use Gum Paste (16 oz.)

Icing Colors: Violet*, Rose*, Moss Green

Cornstarch

White Pearl Dust

White Ready-To-Use Rolled Fondant (276 oz.)

Piping Gel

TOOLS:

Fondant Rollers: 9 in., 20 in.

Roll-N-Cut Mat

Gum Paste Flower Cutter Set

Fondant Shaping Foam

10-Pc. Gum Paste/Fondant Tool Set

Parchment Paper

Cake Circles: 8 in., 10 in., 12 in., 14 in., 16 in.

12 in. Disposable Decorating Bags

Decorating Tips: 3, 5

Brush Set

3 in. Globe Pillar Set

2½ in. Globe Pillar Set (2 pks.)

Knife

18 in. dia. foam core board (½ in. thick)

Fanci-Foil Wrap

Fondant Smoother

Round Pans: 8 in. x 2 in., 12 in. x 2 in., 16 in. x 2 in.

Cooling Grid

Decorator Preferred Smooth-Edge Plates: 8 in., 10 in., 16 in.

13 in. Angled Spatula

⅜ in. wide violet satin ribbon (4 yards)

Double Hearts Cake Pick

TECHNIQUES:

Fondant and Gum Paste Decorating Techniques (p. 220)

Using Rolled Fondant (p. 217)

Tiered Construction (p. 227)

Tip Techniques (p. 204)

SERVES: 156.**

 *Combine Violet with Rose for violet shown.

**The top tier is often saved for the first anniversary. The
number of servings given does not include the top tier.

INSTRUCTIONS:

STEP 1 Three days in advance, make flowers. Tint gum
paste violet. Roll out ¹⁄₁₆ in. thick. Cut 1,000 flowers using
medium blossom cutter from set. Place flowers on thick
foam and cup centers using round end of thick modeling
stick from tool set. Make extras to allow for breakage.
Let dry on cornstarch-dusted circle. Prepare royal icing
following recipe directions. Use tip 3 to pipe dot (p. 206)
centers. Let dry overnight. Brush flowers with Pearl Dust.
Store in a covered container to prevent fading.

STEP 2 Prepare globes. Tint 24 oz. fondant green to cover
one set of 3 in. globes and two sets of 2½ in. globes. Roll
out fondant ⅛ in. thick. Cut 9½ in. x 3 in. rectangles for
3 in. globes and 8 in. x 2½ in. rectangles for 2½ in. globes.
Lightly brush globes with piping gel. Attach rectangles.
Smooth with hand and cut fondant away from open holes.
Reserve remaining green fondant. Attach flowers using tip
3 and icing. Let dry overnight.

STEP 3 Prepare base boards. Cut double-thick 9 in. and
13 in. cake circles and 17 in. circle from ½ in. foam core
board. Cover with foil and brush with piping gel. Cover
with fondant. Smooth with fondant smoother. Use 18 oz.
fondant for 9 in., 20 oz. for 13 in., and 34 oz. for 17 in.

STEP 4 Bake and cool 2-layer 8 in., 12 in. and 16 in. cakes.
Prepare buttercream icing following recipe directions.
Prepare cakes for fondant by icing in buttercream. Cover
cakes with fondant. Smooth with fondant smoother.
Position cakes on prepared boards, then separator plates.
Attach ribbon around center of cakes with tip 3 and dots
of royal icing. Attach flowers to ribbon using tip 5 and
buttercream icing. Use tip 5 to pipe bead (p. 205) bottom
border on all tiers. Trim hidden pillars to position into cakes
with globes over pillars. For the 8 in. cake topper, insert
cake pick. Shape mound of green fondant, 5 in. dia. x 1½ in.
high. Attach with damp brush. Attach flowers to mounds
with tip 3 dots of icing.

STEP 5 At reception, assemble cakes on globe bases
and pillars.

SINGLE ROSE MINI CAKES

Everyone loves a personal touch at the table. Make a special occasion even more special with these rose-topped mini cakes.

RECIPES:

Candy Clay (p. 189)

Yellow or Chocolate Cupcakes (p. 178)

Buttercream Icing (p. 181)

INGREDIENTS:

Candy Melts Candy: Pink, Green, White, Light Cocoa

Solid vegetable shortening

Real non-toxic leaves (rose or lemon)

TOOLS:

Decorator Brush Set

Standard Muffin Pan

Mini Muffin Pan

Cake Release Pan Coating

Cooling Grid

Cookie Sheet

Parchment Paper

Parchment Triangles

TECHNIQUES:

Candy/Pop Making Techniques (p. 230)

Tip Techniques (p. 204)

INSTRUCTIONS:

STEP 1 One day in advance, make Candy Clay following recipe directions using pink Candy Melts candy. Start candy clay rose with the base and mold a cone about 1½ in. high from a ¾ in. dia. ball of modeling candy.

Flatten a ⅜ in. dia. ball of clay into a circular petal ¼ in. thick on one side and the diameter of a dime. Make several petals this size. Wrap first petal around point of cone to

form bud. Press three more petals around base. Gently pinch edges of petals. Make five more petals using slightly larger balls of clay. Flatten and thin edge with finger and cup petals.

Continue adding petals, placing them in between and slightly lower than previous row. For a fuller flower, continue adding petals.

STEP 2 To make leaves, thoroughly wash and dry rose or lemon leaves. Melt Candy Melts candy according to package directions. Lighten melted green candy with a little melted white candy. Paint back of leaf using decorator brush. Set aside until firm. Peel off leaf from candy.

STEP 3 Coat standard and mini muffin pans with Cake Release pan coating. Bake and cool standard and mini cupcakes without baking cups.

STEP 4 Place upside down on cooling grid positioned over cookie sheet. Cover with melted candy. Gently tap grid to evenly distribute candy. Set cakes on parchment paper. Chill until firm. Stack cakes. Attach with melted candy.

STEP 5 Use melted light cocoa candy and a cut parchment bag to pipe bead (p. 205) bottom borders. Use melted white candy and a cut parchment bag to pipe dots (p. 206) on side of cake.

STEP 6 Attach rose and leaf to top of cake with melted candy.

BUDDING ROMANCE MINI CAKES

Celebrate a budding romance with these dainty cakes, topped with a budding rose. Reminiscent of a wedding cake tier and topped with fresh flowers, these individual cakes are perfect for an engagement party or a wedding shower.

RECIPES:

Lemon Pound Cake (p. 177), Yellow Cake or
  Chocolate Cake (p. 176)

Buttercream Icing (p. 181)

INGREDIENTS:

White Ready-To-Use Rolled Fondant (24 oz. covers 4 cakes)

Icing Colors: Lemon Yellow*, Golden Yellow*

TOOLS:

12 in. x 18 in. x 1 in. Jelly Roll Pan

Cooling Grid

Round Comfort-Grip Cutter

9 in. Straight Spatula

20 in. Fondant Roller

Roll-N-Cut Mat

Fondant Smoother

Square Cut-Outs Fondant Cutters

Brush Set

12 in. Disposable Decorating Bags

Decorating Tips: 3, 6

Fresh Flower Spikes

Fresh flowers

TECHNIQUES:

Using Rolled Fondant (p. 217)

Tip Techniques (p. 204)

*Combine Lemon Yellow with Golden Yellow for yellow shown.

INSTRUCTIONS:

STEP 1 Bake and cool cake.

STEP 2 Using Comfort-Grip cutter, cut out two circles for each cake. Prepare buttercream icing following recipe directions. Stack two cakes. Prepare for fondant by icing in buttercream. Cover cakes with white fondant.

STEP 3 Tint 4 oz. fondant yellow. Roll out yellow fondant ⅛ in. thick and cut approximately 28 squares for each cake using smallest Cut-Out.

STEP 4 Attach squares to cake sides in diamond fashion using damp brush, starting on top and trimming bottom diamond as needed.

STEP 5 Use tip 3 to pipe dots (p. 206) at meeting points. Use tip 6 to pipe ball (p. 204) bottom border.

STEP 6 Insert flower spike at an angle in cake top. Position flower just before serving.

A PEDESTAL OF PETALS CAKE

This giant cupcake is beautifully detailed with fondant flowers and violet buttercream hearts.

RECIPES:

Thinned Fondant Adhesive (p. 189)

Yellow, White or Chocolate Cake (p. 176-177)

Buttercream Icing (p. 181)

INGREDIENTS:

Gum-Tex

White Ready-To-Use Rolled Fondant (8 oz.)

Cornstarch

White Pearl Dust

White Sugar Pearls

Icing Colors: Violet*, Pink*

TOOLS:

Roll-N-Cut Mat

9 in. Fondant Roller

Flower Cut-Outs Fondant Cutters

Candy Melting Plate

Brush Set

Dimensions Large Cupcake Pan

Cooling Grid

Knife

12 in. Disposable Decorating Bags

Decorating Tips: 6, 45, 2

Plastic ruler

13 in. Angled Spatula

Our Day Figurine

TECHNIQUES:

Tip Techniques (p. 204)

SERVES: 12.

*Combine Violet with Pink for violet shown.

INSTRUCTIONS:

STEP 1 Several days in advance, make flowers. Knead ½ teaspoon Gum-Tex into 8 oz. fondant. Roll out ⅟₁₆ in. thick. Cut 80 flowers using medium flower Cut-Out. Make extras to allow for breakage. Let dry in candy melting plate dusted with cornstarch. Brush flowers with Pearl Dust. Use thinned fondant adhesive to attach Sugar Pearl centers.

STEP 2 Bake and cool large cupcake. Place on serving plate. Stack top and bottom; level a 2 in. circle area on top where ornament will sit. Prepare buttercream icing following recipe directions. Tint portion violet; reserve some white. Use tip 6 and violet icing to pipe two vertical lines into each indentation of cupcake bottom. Use tip 45 and white icing to pipe vertical center line. Use tip 2 and violet icing to pipe bead hearts (p. 205), about ½ in. apart on white lines.

STEP 3 Ice top of cupcake smooth with white icing. Use tip 6 and white icing to attach large flowers, beginning at bottom edge and working upward. Leave center open for ornament.

STEP 4 At reception, position ornament.

ANNIVERSARY FLAIR CAKE

After so many years of marriage, celebrate with anniversary flair. The top tier of this cake is decorated simply with fondant bows, and the bottom tier is adorned with delicate icing lacework.

RECIPES:

Royal Icing (p. 181)

Yellow, White or Chocolate Cake (p. 176-177)

Buttercream Icing (p. 181)

INGREDIENTS:

Meringue Powder

Ready-To-Use Gum Paste (4 oz.)

Ready-To-Use Rolled Fondant: Pink (24 oz.), **White**

Icing Colors: Rose, Leaf Green

Cornstarch

TOOLS:

Parchment Paper

12 in. Disposable Decorating Bags

Decorating Tips: 4, 1

22-gauge white cloth-covered wire (18 in. needed)

18 in. White Pearl Beading (6 mm.)

Lollipop Sticks

Hot glue gun

Stepsaving Rose Bouquets Flower Cutter Set

Fondant Rollers: 9 in., 20 in.

Roll-N-Cut Mat

Toothpicks

10-Pc. Gum Paste/Fondant Tool Set

Fondant Shaping Foam

Wave Flower Former Set

Fondant Trimmer

Plastic ruler

Knife

Brush Set

Cake Circles: 6 in., 10 in.

Round Pans: 6 in. x 2 in., 10 in. x 2 in.

Cooling Grid

13 in. Angled Spatula

Fondant Smoother

Dowel Rods

TECHNIQUES:

Tip Techniques (p. 204)

Using Rolled Fondant (p. 217)

Fondant and Gum Paste Decorating Techniques (p. 220)

PATTERNS:

Numeric Pattern (p. 236)

SERVES: 50.

INSTRUCTIONS:

STEP 1 Two days in advance, make "25" topper. Prepare royal icing following recipe directions. Trace "25" pattern on parchment paper with tip 4 and royal icing. While still wet, bend wire in shape of numbers and place in traced icing. Use tip 4 to cover wire with icing. Immediately position pearl beading. Let dry 24 to 36 hours. When completely dry, peel off parchment paper. Attach lollipop sticks to back with hot glue.

STEP 2 Tint 3 oz. gum paste rose and 1 oz. green. Follow instructions in flower cutter set to make one large full-bloom rose and three small roses, all on toothpicks instead of wires.

STEP 3 Use leaf cutter from set to make eight to 10 green leaves. Let dry on convex side of small flower formers.

STEP 4 To make five bows, roll out 6 oz. pink fondant ⅛ in. thick. Cut 10 to 12 strips, 1 in. x 3 in., reserving excess fondant. Fold strips in half. Brush ends with damp brush. Pinch ends together. Set on edge on cornstarch-dusted

board to dry. When dry, trim ends and press two loops together to form bow. Roll out pink fondant ⅛ in. thick and cut strips, ½ in. wide, for streamers and center knot. Attach knot strip around bow with damp brush. Set aside. Store in a dark place to avoid fading.

STEP 5 Bake and cool 2-layer cakes. Prepare buttercream icing following recipe directions. Prepare cakes for fondant by icing in buttercream. Cover cakes with fondant.

Smooth with fondant smoother. Prepare cakes for stacked construction (p. 228). Place on serving platter.

STEP 6 Cover 10 in. cake with tip 1 cornelli lace (p. 206). Use tip 4 to pipe bead (p. 205) bottom border on both tiers. Position streamers, then bows on 10 in. cake. Insert numbers on top tier. Attach roses and leaves with tip 4 dots of icing.

FORMAL FARE TUXEDO CUPCAKES

All dressed up with somewhere to go! A candy tuxedo puts these chocolate-iced cupcakes in formal attire.

RECIPES:

Yellow or Chocolate Cupcakes (p. 178)

Chocolate Buttercream Icing (p. 181)

INGREDIENTS:

Candy Melts Candy: White, Light Cocoa

TOOLS:

Transparent cellophane tape

10 in. x 14 in. Cake Boards

Parchment Paper

15 in. Parchment Triangles

White Standard Baking Cups

Standard Muffin Pan

9 in. Angled Spatula

PATTERNS:

Bow Tie, Shirt/Lapels (p. 241)

INSTRUCTIONS:

STEP 1 In advance, make shirt/lapels and bow tie. Trace patterns on parchment paper and tape onto cake board. Cover with parchment paper.

STEP 2 Melt Candy Melts candy according to package directions. Use melted candy and cut parchment bags to pipe in pattern areas. Chill until firm 5 to 10 minutes.

STEP 3 Pipe dot buttons and chill until firm.

STEP 4 Prepare chocolate buttercream icing following recipe directions. Ice cupcakes smooth with icing. Position shirt and lapels. Attach bow tie with melted candy.

FLORAL FROST CAKE

Topped with gum paste roses and bedecked with blossoms, this lovely cake will astound your wedding guests. Artfully displayed, this cake creates a stunning centerpiece.

RECIPES:

Royal Icing (p. 181)

Yellow, White or Chocolate Cake (p. 176-177)

Buttercream Icing (p. 181)

INGREDIENTS:

Ready-To-Use Gum Paste (3 pks.)

White Pearl Dust

Cornstarch

White Ready-To-Use Rolled Fondant (108 oz.)

Gum Glue Adhesive

TOOLS:

Gum Paste Flower Cutter Set

Storage Board

9 in. Fondant Roller

10-Pc. Fondant/Gum Paste Tool Set

22-gauge white cloth-covered wire (24-6 in. pcs.)

26-gauge white cloth-covered wire (18-6 in. pcs.)

24-gauge white cloth covered wire (21-6 in. pcs.)

White florist tape

Fondant Shaping Foam

Wave Flower Former Set

Craft block

12 in. Disposable Decorating Bags

Decorating Tips: 2, 4

Scissors

3-Tier Pillar Cake Stand Set

Parchment Paper

Transparent cellophane tape

Roll-N-Cut Mat

4-Pc. Heart Nesting Plastic Cutter Set

Knife

Round Pans: 8 in. x 2 in., 10 in. x 2 in., 12 in. x 2 in.

Bubble wrap

Plastic wrap

Cooling Grid

Cake Circles: 8 in., 10 in., 12 in.

13 in. Angled Spatula

20 in. Fondant Roller

Fondant Smoother

Fresh Flower Spikes

Brush Set

TECHNIQUES:

Fondant and Gum Paste Decorating Techniques (p. 220)
Using Rolled Fondant (p. 217)

SERVES: 94.*

*The top tier is often saved for the first anniversary. The
 number of servings given does not include the top tier.

INSTRUCTIONS:

STEP 1 At least one week in advance, make gum paste roses and stephanotis, blossoms and leaves following instructions from flower cutter set. Make 24 roses on 22-gauge wires using smallest rose cutter and 18 leaves on 26-gauge wires using smallest rose leaf cutter. Make 21 stephanotis on 24-gauge wires using small calyx cutter. Also make 308 small blossoms and 196 medium blossoms using ejector cutter. Make extras to allow for breakage. Prepare royal icing following recipe directions. Use tip 2 to pipe dot (p. 206) centers on all blossoms. Let dry 48 hours. Brush flowers with Pearl Dust.

STEP 2 Also one week in advance, make draped hearts. Cover plates from 3-Tier Pillar Cake Stand Set and outside of cake pans with parchment paper. Secure pans to corresponding plates with royal icing dots. Roll ⅜ in. thick fondant logs, long enough to wrap around bottom of each cake pan. Wrap logs in plastic wrap then secure in position with icing dots. Roll out gum paste ⅛ in. thick. Cut 28 hearts using second largest cutter from nesting set. Use dots of icing to attach hearts around prepared pans, with heart points hanging about 1½ in. below plates. Position 11 hearts around 12 in. pan, nine around 10 in. pan. Position eight hearts around 8 in. pan, trimming one heart in back to fit. Use royal icing to decorate hearts with tip 2 scrolls. Attach three small and five medium blossoms to each heart with tip 4 dots of icing. Let dry for several days.

STEP 3 Carefully remove hearts and store on large bubble wrap until reception. Reserve plastic-wrapped fondant logs for assembling cake.

STEP 4 Bake and cool 2-layer cakes. Prepare buttercream icing following recipe directions. Prepare cakes for fondant by icing in buttercream. Cover cakes with fondant. Smooth with fondant smoother. Position cakes on tier stand plates. Remove plastic wrap from fondant logs used for setting up draped hearts and attach at base of each cake with icing dots. Assemble three bouquets with florist tape using eight roses, seven stephanotis and six leaves for each. Insert into fresh flower spikes filled with fondant. Insert in cakes.

STEP 5 At reception, assemble cakes on stand. Attach draped hearts around 12 in. cake with dots of royal icing. Use tip 4 dots of icing to attach additional small blossoms in garland shape, 1½ in. deep, starting 2 in. from top edge of cake. Attach a medium blossom below each garland point. Add a tip 2 dot above each small blossom in garland. Repeat with 10 in. and 8 in. cakes.

Ghoulish Goodies

MAKE HALLOWEEN MAGICAL FOR YOUR LITTLE MONSTERS WITH TASTY TRICKS AND SPOOKY TREATS

CLAWING HIS WAY BACK HALLOWEEN CUPCAKES

It's alive! These spooky Halloween cupcakes will grab your Halloween guests' attention with a candy hand clawing its way out of a cupcake and buttercream "grave."

RECIPES:

Yellow or Chocolate Cupcakes (p. 178)

Buttercream Icing (p. 181)

INGREDIENTS:

Icing Colors: Leaf Green*, Lemon Yellow*, Black

Halloween Pumpkin Mix Sprinkles

Large chocolate nougat candies

Fruit jelly discs

Granulated sugar

Light Cocoa Candy Melts Candy

TOOLS:

Halloween-Themed Baking Cups

Standard Muffin Pan

Cooling Grid

12 in. Disposable Decorating Bags

Decorating Tips: 233, 3

9 in. Fondant Roller

Parchment Paper

Knife

TECHNIQUES:

Tip Techniques (p. 204)

*Combine Leaf Green with Lemon Yellow for green shown.

INSTRUCTIONS:

STEP 1 Bake and cool cupcakes.

STEP 2 Prepare buttercream icing following recipe directions. Tint green and black. Cover cupcake top with tip 233 pull-out grass (p. 207). Position sprinkles. Insert nougat candy in center of cupcake.

STEP 3 Roll out fruit disc on granulated sugar-covered parchment paper. Cut hand shape. Use tip 3 to pipe black nails. Melt Candy Melts candy according to package directions. Attach hand to arm with melted candy.

CANDY CORN BROWNIE BITES

Use buttercream icing and melted Candy Melts candy to turn brownies into so-cute candy corn bites. They'll be surefire hits at fall classroom parties and bake sales.

RECIPES:

Cake Brownies or Fudgy Brownies (p. 179)

Buttercream Icing (p. 181)

INGREDIENTS:

Candy Melts Candy: White, Orange (1 pk. of each covers 4 to 5 treats), **Yellow** (1 pk. covers 6 to 8 treats)

TOOLS:

Round Pops Silicone Mold

Cookie Sheet

Cooling Grid

12 in. Disposable Decorating Bags

Decorating Tip: 12

9 in. Angled Spatula

Parchment Paper

10 in. x 14 in. Cake Boards

15 in. Parchment Triangles

TECHNIQUES:

Candy/Pop Making Techniques (p. 230)

INSTRUCTIONS:

STEP 1 Bake and cool brownies in silicone mold supported by cookie sheet. Prepare buttercream icing following recipe directions. Use tip 12 to pipe icing to build up point. Smooth with spatula. Set on parchment paper-covered board. Freeze until icing is firm.

STEP 2 Melt Candy Melts candy according to package directions. Ice bottoms with melted white candy. Chill until firm. Stand on cooling grid set over cookie sheet. Cover with melted white candy. Chill until firm. Bring to room temperature.

STEP 3 Hold brownie by tip and dip to coat with melted orange candy, leaving top third white. Set on cooling grid. Tap to settle and chill until firm. Dip to coat bottom third with melted yellow candy. Set on cooling grid. Tap to settle and chill until firm.

DRAC'S COOKIE POPS

Sink your fangs into a crunchy cookie vampire, decorated with Candy Melts candy in screaming colors.

RECIPES:
Roll-Out Cookies (p. 183)

INGREDIENTS:
Candy Melts Candy: Vibrant Green, Black, White

Primary Candy Color Set (red used)

TOOLS:
12 in. Rolling Pin

3-Pc. Halloween Cutter Set

Knife

Cookie Sheet

Cooling Grid

Parchment Paper

10 in. x 14 in. Cake Board

15 in. Parchment Triangles

8 in. Cookie Treat Sticks

TECHNIQUES:
Candy/Pop Making Techniques (p. 230)

INSTRUCTIONS:

STEP 1 Prepare and roll out dough following recipe directions. Cut dough using pumpkin cutter from set. Cut off stem. Bake and cool cookies.

STEP 2 Melt green Candy Melts candy according to package directions. Cover cookies with melted green candy (p. 232). Let set 10 to 15 minutes.

STEP 3 Place cookies on parchment paper-covered board to decorate. Melt white and black Candy Melts candy according to package directions. Tint portion of melted white candy red using candy color from set.

STEP 4 Use melted candy and cut parchment bags to pipe hair, eyebrows, nose, eyes, mouth and cheeks. Let set.

STEP 5 Use melted candy and cut parchment bags to add dot pupils and pipe in fangs and tongue.

STEP 6 Pipe ears on side of cookie with melted candy. Chill to set. Attach cookie stick to back of cookie with melted candy. Chill to set 5 to 10 minutes.

A CHUMMY MUMMY COOKIE

Everyone, especially kids, will love to drizzle the yummy mummy "wrapping" on these chocolate cookies.

RECIPES:

Chocolate Roll-Out Cookies (p. 184)

INGREDIENTS:

White Cookie Icing

Candy-coated chocolates

Black Decorating Icing-Tube

TOOLS:

12 in. Rolling Pin

Gingerbread Boy Metal Cutter Set

Cookie Sheet

Cooling Grid

Decorating Tip: 3

Coupler Ring Set

INSTRUCTIONS:

STEP 1 Prepare and roll out dough following recipe directions. Cut cookies using largest gingerbread boy cutter from set. Bake and cool cookies.

STEP 2 Drizzle cookie icing over cookies. Position candy-coated chocolate for eyes.

STEP 3 Use tube icing to pipe tip 3 dot (p. 206) pupils.

EYEBALL CUPCAKE

Looking for a way to serve up some spooky fun? The creepy peepers cupcakes are sure to be a Halloween party favorite.

RECIPES:

Yellow or Chocolate Cupcakes (p. 178)

Buttercream Icing (p. 181)

INGREDIENTS:

Icing Colors: Christmas Red*, Red-Red*, Violet, Black

Cornstarch

TOOLS:

Halloween-Themed Baking Cups

Standard Muffin Pan

Cooling Grid

9 in. Angled Spatula

12 in. Disposable Decorating Bags

Decorating Tips: 12, 2, 4

TECHNIQUES:

Tip Techniques (p. 204)

*Combine Christmas Red with Red-Red for red shown.

INSTRUCTIONS:

STEP 1 Bake and cool cupcakes.

STEP 2 Prepare buttercream icing following recipe directions. Tint portions red, violet and black; reserve some white. Ice cupcakes smooth with white icing.

STEP 3 For iris, use tip 12 to pipe ball (p. 204) 1½ in. dia.

STEP 4 For veins, use tip 2 to pipe strings around iris.

STEP 5 For pupil, use tip 4 to pipe dot (p. 206) in center of iris. Flatten and smooth with finger dipped in cornstarch.

BAT CUPCAKES

Instantly increase your batting average at your next Halloween party. Wacky, wicked treats combine cookie wings and cupcake bodies for a spooky sweet with bite!

RECIPES:

Chocolate Roll-Out Cookies (p. 184)

Yellow or Chocolate Cupcakes (p. 178)

Chocolate Buttercream Icing (p. 181)

Buttercream Icing (p. 181)

INGREDIENTS:

Icing Colors: Black, Leaf Green*, Lemon Yellow*

Cornstarch

Chocolate chips

TOOLS:

12 in. Rolling Pin

Leaves and Acorns Nesting Metal Cutter Set

Cookie Sheet

Cooling Grid

Halloween-Themed Baking Cups

Standard Muffin Pan

9 in. Angled Spatula

12 in. Disposable Decorating Bags

Decorating Tips: 5, 3

*Combine Leaf Green with Lemon Yellow for green shown.

INSTRUCTIONS:

STEP 1 Prepare and roll out dough following recipe directions. Cut two wings for each cupcake using smallest oak leaf cutter from set. Bake and cool cookies.

STEP 2 Bake and cool cupcakes. Prepare chocolate buttercream icing following recipe directions. Tint portion black; reserve rest. Ice smooth with chocolate icing.

STEP 3 Prepare buttercream icing following recipe directions. Tint portion green; reserve some white. Use tip 5 to pipe ball (p. 204) eyes and dot (p. 206) pupils. Flatten and smooth with finger dipped in cornstarch. Use tip 3 to pipe outline mouth and pull-out fangs. Use tip 5 to pipe ball nose. Flatten and smooth.

STEP 4 Insert cookie wings. Attach chocolate chip ears with dots of icing.

WITCHES' FINGER COOKIES

These gnarly fingers will lend a creepy hand to your Halloween festivities. Wild colors, bold sprinkles, assorted Candy Melts candy and sugars give these cookies just the spark they need for this haunting occasion.

RECIPES:

Sugar Cookies for Pan-Shaped Cookies (p. 185)

INGREDIENTS:

Candy Melts Candy: Yellow, Orange, Black

Sparkle Gels: Orange, Light Green

Assorted Sprinkles, Sugars and Jimmies, such as Orange, Lavender and Black Colored Sugars; Halloween Pumpkin Mix, Silver Stars Edible Accents and White Sugar Pearls

TOOLS:

Monster Fingers Non-Stick Cookie Pan
Cooling Grid

INSTRUCTIONS:

STEP 1 Prepare dough following recipe directions. Press into pan cavities. Bake and cool cookies.

STEP 2 Decorate cookies with icing gels, melted Candy Melts candy, sprinkles and sugars as desired.

WITCH CAKE

Your Halloween party guests will love her, warts and all! This bewitching cake, covered with buttercream decorations, is sure to cast a spell!

RECIPES:

Yellow, White or Chocolate Cake (p. 176-177)

Buttercream Icing (p. 181)

INGREDIENTS:

Icing Colors: Violet*, Rose*, Orange, Leaf Green*, Lemon Yellow*, Black, Red-Red

Cornstarch

TOOLS:

Star Pan

Cooling Grid

Toothpicks

12 in. Disposable Decorating Bags

Decorating Tips: 3, 12, 1, 16, 21

TECHNIQUES:

Tip Techniques (p. 204)

PATTERNS:

Witch Face, Witch Hat (p. 244)

*Combine Violet with Rose for violet shown. Combine Leaf Green with Lemon Yellow for green shown.

SERVES: 12.

INSTRUCTIONS:

STEP 1 Bake and cool cake. Prepare buttercream icing following recipe directions. Tint portions violet, orange, green, rose, black and red; reserve small amount white. Ice sides smooth with yellow icing.

STEP 2 Use patterns to mark face and hat. Use tip 3 to pipe mouth, tongue and teeth. Pat smooth with finger dipped in cornstarch. Use tip 12 to build up areas for nose, cheeks and whites of eyes. Pat smooth.

STEP 3 Use tip 3 to outline (p. 208) and fill in pupils. Pat smooth. Use tip 1 to pipe outline veins. Use tip 3 to outline face. Cover with tip 16 stars (p. 212). Add tip 3 dot (p. 206) wart on nose.

STEP 4 Use tip 12 to outline and fill in hatband and buckle. Pat smooth. Use tip 3 to outline hat. Cover with tip 16 stars. Overpipe hat brim with more tip 16 stars. Use tip 16 to pipe lines for hair. Finish with tip 21 star bottom border.

WACKY WEBSPINNER SPIDER BROWNIES

Get caught in the web with these leggy treats! They're sure to spin a few heads!

RECIPES:

Cake Brownies or Fudgy Brownies (p. 179)

INGREDIENTS:

Black Icing Color

White Ready-To-Use Decorator Icing

Pretzel sticks

Mini candy-coated chocolates

Chocolate nougat candy

TOOLS:

Mini Ball Pan

Cooling Grid

12 in. Disposable Decorating Bags

Decorating Tips: 5, 2

TECHNIQUES:

Tip Techniques (p. 204)

INSTRUCTIONS:

STEP 1 Bake and cool brownies following recipe directions. Remove from pan.

STEP 2 Tint portion of white icing black; reserve some white. Use tip 5 to pipe dot (p. 206) eyes with white icing. Attach mini candy-coated chocolate pupils and nose. Use tip 2 to pipe outline (p. 208) mouth with black icing and pull-out fangs with white icing. Insert pretzel sticks for upper portion of legs. Insert nougat on stick. Insert pretzel sticks for ends of legs.

JACK-O-LANTERN CAKE POPS

These pumpkins are a scream! With comical faces, petite pumpkin pops will have Halloween party guests laughing their heads off.

RECIPES:

Basic Cake Ball Pops (p. 180)

INGREDIENTS:

Candy Melts Candy: White, Black, Orange

Primary Candy Color Set (orange used)

Candy Eyeballs

Small green spice drops

TOOLS:

9 in. x 13 in. x 2 in. Sheet Pan

6 in. Cookie Treat Sticks

Chocolate Pro Melting Pot

Pops Decorating Stand

12 in. Disposable Decorating Bags

Decorating Tip: 1

15 in. Parchment Triangles

INSTRUCTIONS:

STEP 1 Prepare medium cake balls and insert sticks following recipe directions. Chill until firm. Melt Candy Melts candy according to package directions. Tint melted orange candy darker using orange candy color from set. Dip cake balls in melted orange candy. Place in decorating stand. Chill until firm.

STEP 2 Use tip 1 to pipe noses, mouths, cheeks and eye sockets with melted candy. Attach candy eyeballs and spice drop half for stem using melted candy. Chill until firm 5 to 10 minutes.

HAIR-RAISING FUN MONSTER CAKE

On Halloween, this bride says, "I Boo." Sure to set the party scene, Mrs. Monster will bring some hair-raising fun.

RECIPES:

Yellow, White or Chocolate Cake (p. 176-177)

Buttercream Icing (p. 181)

INGREDIENTS:

Icing Colors: Lemon Yellow*, Leaf Green*, Black*

Black shoestring licorice

Pink wafer candies

Black spice drops

TOOLS:

Long Loaf Pan

Cooling Grid

13 in. x 19 in. Cake Board

Fanci-Foil Wrap

Transparent cellophane tape

Scissors

11 in. Straight Spatula

Plastic ruler

12 in. Disposable Decorating Bags

Decorating Tips: 12, 8, 3, 10, 2B (2 needed)

TECHNIQUES:

Tip Techniques (p. 204)

SERVES: 18.

*Combine Lemon Yellow with Leaf Green for green shown. Combine a small amount of Black with white icing for gray shown.

INSTRUCTIONS:

STEP 1 Bake and cool cake. Wrap cake board with foil (p. 192). Position cake vertically on prepared board. Prepare buttercream icing following recipe directions. Tint portions green and gray; reserve some white. Ice 6 inches of top and sides of cake smooth with green icing.

STEP 2 Use tip 12 to pipe ball (p. 204) eyeballs, tip 8 to pipe ball nose and tip 3 to pipe string mouth, eyebrows, green eyelids and dot (p. 206) pupils.

STEP 3 Cut 1 in. pieces of licorice and insert into eyeballs for lashes. Use tip 10 to pipe curved outline (p. 208) ears and overpipe with tip 10.

STEP 4 Attach black spice drops to sides of neck and wafers to cheeks with dots of icing.

STEP 5 For hair, fit two decorating bags with tip 2B. Fill one bag with white icing and the other with gray.

Begin at bottom border on cake side and pipe tip 2B wavy hair, alternating white and gray icing. Continue over the cake. On top edge of cake, pipe tip 2B pull-out stars (p. 212).

Bountiful Thankgiving Harvest

TOP OFF YOUR THANKSGIVING FEAST WITH BEAUTIFUL AUTUMN SWEETS AND ADORABLE TURKEY DAY TREATS

• •

AUTUMN LEAVES MINI CAKE POPS

Your guests will want to jump right into this pile of leaves! Candy-covered leaf-shaped mini cakes make for festive fall fun.

RECIPES:

Lemon Pound Cake (p. 177)

INGREDIENTS:

Candy Melts Candy: Green, Orange, Red, Yellow, Light Cocoa

Shredded coconut

Brown Icing Color

TOOLS:

10.5 in. x 15.5 in. x 1 in. Jelly Roll Pan

Cooling Grid

Knife

Plastic ruler

9-Pc. Leaves and Acorns Nesting Metal Cutter Set

6 in. Cookie Treat Sticks

Chocolate Pro Melting Pot

Pops Decorating Stand

15 in. Parchment Triangles

Scissors

Resealable plastic food storage bag

4 in. x 4 in. x 3 in. craft foam block

Basket

TECHNIQUES:

Candy/Pop Making Techniques (p. 230)

INSTRUCTIONS:

STEP 1 Bake and cool cake. Level to 1 in. high.

STEP 2 Cut assorted leaves using smallest cutters from set. Melt Candy Melts candy according to package directions. Dip cookie sticks in melted candy and insert into cakes. Chill until firm.

STEP 3 Dip cakes in melted candy. Place in decorating stand and chill until firm. Use contrasting colors of melted candy in cut parchment bags to pipe veins. Chill until firm.

STEP 4 Place a small amount of coconut in plastic bag. Add a little brown icing color. Close bag and knead to tint. Insert craft block in basket and cover with coconut. Insert pops.

GOBBLE 'EM UP TURKEY CAKE POPS

Just when Thanksgiving guests think they can't eat another bite, these adorable turkey cake ball pops waddle onto the scene. Flashing their finest fondant feathers, these turkey day treats will have partygoers saying, "What pie?"

RECIPES:
Basic Cake Ball Pops (p. 180)

INGREDIENTS:
Gum-Tex

White Ready-To-Use Rolled Fondant (4 oz. for 2 treats)

Icing Colors: Christmas Red*, Red-Red*, Lemon Yellow*, Golden Yellow*, Brown*, Orange

Light Cocoa Candy Melts Candy

Garden Candy Color Set (black used)

TOOLS:
9 in. Fondant Roller

Roll-N-Cut Mat

Oval Cut-Outs Fondant Cutters

9 in. x 13 in. x 2 in. Sheet Pan

6 in. Cookie Treat Sticks

Chocolate Pro Melting Pot

Pops Decorating Stand

Plastic ruler

Knife

Brush Set

15 in. Parchment Triangles

TECHNIQUES:
Using Rolled Fondant (p. 217)

Candy/Pop Making Techniques (p. 230)

*Combine Christmas Red with Red-Red for red shown.
 Combine Lemon Yellow with Golden Yellow for yellow shown.
 Combine Brown with Red-Red for brown fondant shown.

INSTRUCTIONS:

STEP 1 One day in advance, make tail feathers. Knead ½ teaspoon Gum-Tex into 4 oz. fondant. Divide into four portions and tint red, yellow, brown and orange. Roll out ⅛ in. thick. Cut red, yellow and orange ovals using medium Cut-Out. Move cutter ½ in. in and cut 1¼ in. x ½ in. for feathers. Reserve brown and excess fondant. Let dry 24 hours.

STEP 2 Prepare large cake balls and insert sticks following recipe directions. Chill until firm. Melt Candy Melts candy according to package directions. Tint small portion black using candy color from set; reserve majority light cocoa. Dip cake balls in melted light cocoa candy. Place in decorating stand and chill until firm. Roll out brown fondant ⅛ in. thick. Cut wings, 1¼ in. x ¾ in. wide. Shape neck and head, 1½ in. high. Trim to shape using knife. Attach using melted candy.

STEP 3 Shape beak and wattle from reserved fondant. Attach with damp brush. Use melted black candy and a cut parchment bag to pipe dot eyes. Attach tail feathers using melted candy.

FALL FAVORITE CUPCAKES

See how a classic cupcake can blossom with the addition of a colorful gum paste mum! Pair the warm colors of fall's signature flower with a rich chocolate icing for a treat that greets the season.

RECIPES:

Gum Glue Adhesive (p. 189)

Yellow Cupcakes (p. 178)

Chocolate Buttercream Icing (p. 181)

INGREDIENTS:

Ready-To-Use Gum Paste

Icing Colors: Creamy Peach, Golden Yellow, Leaf Green

TOOLS:

Dusting Pouch

Roll-N-Cut Mat

Toothpicks

9 in. Fondant Roller

Cut-Outs Fondant Cutters: Daisy, Leaves

Storage Board

Fondant Shaping Foam

10-Pc. Gum Paste/Fondant Tool Set

Flower Forming Cups

Foam cup

Brush Set

White Standard Baking Cups

Standard Muffin Pan

Cooling Grid

9 in. Angled Spatula

TECHNIQUES:

Fondant and Gum Paste Decorating Techniques (p. 220)

INSTRUCTIONS:

STEP 1 Three days in advance, make mums (p. 225). Tint gum paste peach and yellow. Make one mum for each cupcake.

STEP 2 Make leaves (p. 222). Tint gum paste green. Roll out less than ¹⁄₁₆ in. thick. Cut one leaf for each cupcake using medium leaf Cut-Out. Make extras of all to allow for breakage. Let dry.

STEP 3 Bake and cool cupcakes. Prepare chocolate buttercream icing following recipe directions. Ice smooth with icing. Position mums and leaves on cupcakes.

THE FIRST THANKSGIVING CAKE

Commemorate the first Thanksgiving as you gather to feast. Pilgrim and Native American cookies pray at a cake table, topped with tiny fondant yams, corn, pumpkins and even a turkey.

RECIPES:

Roll-Out Cookies (p. 183)

Royal Icing (p. 181)

Yellow, White or Chocolate Cake (p. 176-177)

Buttercream Icing (p. 181)

INGREDIENTS:

White Ready-To-Use Rolled Fondant (57 oz.)

Icing Colors: Golden Yellow*, Lemon Yellow*, Leaf Green*, Kelly Green, Orange*, Black*, Red-Red*, Brown*, Copper, Royal Blue

Meringue Powder

Cornstarch

TOOLS:

Plastic ruler

10-Pc. Gum Paste/Fondant Tool Set

Knife

Brush Set

12 in. Rolling Pin

101 Cookie Cutter Set

Cookie Sheet

Cooling Grid

12 in. Disposable Decorating Bags

Decorating Tips: 6, 2A, 2, 1

13 in. x 19 in. Cake Boards

Fanci-Foil Wrap

9 in. x 5 in. Loaf Pan

11 in. Straight Spatula

20 in. Fondant Roller

Roll-N-Cut Mat

Fondant Smoother

TECHNIQUES:

Using Rolled Fondant (p. 217)

Fondant and Gum Paste Decorating Techniques (p. 220)

Tip Techniques (p. 204)

SERVES: 24.

*Combine Golden Yellow with Lemon Yellow for yellow shown. Combine Leaf Green with Lemon Yellow for lighter green in corn. Combine Orange with Red-Red and Black for yams. Combine Brown with Red-Red, Orange and Black for turkey. Combine Brown with Red-Red for other brown shades shown.

INSTRUCTIONS:

STEP 1 In advance, make food for table. Tint fondant 3 oz. yellow, 3 oz. green, 1 oz. lighter green, 4 oz. orange, 3 oz. gray, 1 oz. light brown, 1 oz. dark brown, 2 oz. orange for yams, 3 oz. brown for turkey. Reserve remaining white fondant.

FOR YAMS: Use 2 oz. orange fondant to shape balls, ½ in. dia., into random ovals. Make indentations with small end of veining tool.

FOR CORN: For ears, roll yellow logs, ⅜ in. dia. x 1½ in. Score kernel lines with small paring knife. For corn husks, knead together small portions of yellow, light and dark green and brown to marbleize. Roll out marbleized fondant ⅛ in. thick. Cut various size elongated husk strips. Attach with damp brush to each ear, pinching together at bottom to shape. For corn silk, cut strips, ¼ in. x ¾ in. in brown; cut partial slits ¹⁄₁₆ in. apart. Roll and attach to top of corn. Cut some very thin strips to randomly tuck inside husks.

FOR TURKEY: Roll out brown fondant into teardrop shape, about 2¼ in. x 1¾ in. x 1 in. high. Flatten bottom. Use small end of veining tool to score top and add dots

for texture. Roll logs, ¼ in. dia. x 1 in. and shape into wings. Marbleize brown with white and shape log, ¼ in. dia. x 1 in. for bone. Flatten end and score with tool. Wrap with a brown log, 1 in. x ½ in. and taper for drumstick. Attach pieces with damp brush.

STEP 2 Make cookies. Prepare and roll out dough following recipe directions. Cut figures using large gingerbread boy cutter from set. For easels, use large Christmas tree from set to cut one large tree for each character. Trim off trunk and cut in half to form two triangle easels. Bake and cool cookies.

STEP 3 Decorate cookies with royal icing. Prepare royal icing following recipe directions. Tint portions yellow, brown, dark brown, red, black, blue and gray; reserve some white. Use tip 6 to outline and fill in clothes and faces. Pat smooth with finger dipped in cornstarch. Pipe tip 2A arms with tip 6 hands. Pipe tip 2 swirls and lines for hair, tip 6 dot nose and tip 1 outline mouth and eyes.

FOR PILGRIM WOMAN: Shape top of hat and brim from fondant. Attach with icing. Use tip 2 to pipe collar and cuffs.

FOR PILGRIM MAN: Use fondant to make top of hat. Attach with icing. Cut fondant strips, ¼ in. for hatband, small yellow square for buckle and smaller white square for center. Attach all. Cut fondant strip, ¼ in. for hat brim. Attach. Use tip 2 with icing to outline and fill in collar.

FOR NATIVE AMERICANS: Cut fondant strips, ¼ in. for headbands and fondant, 1 in. for feathers. Attach with icing. Use tip 2 and icing to add feather details, hair ties and stripes on shirts.

Use tip 6 and icing to attach pilgrim cookies and Native American cookies to easel backs. Let dry overnight.

STEP 4 Wrap cake board with foil. Bake and cool two loaf cakes and position end to end on prepared board. Prepare buttercream icing following recipe directions. Prepare cake for fondant by icing in buttercream. Roll out white fondant ⅛ in. thick. Cover cake with fondant. Smooth top only with fondant smoother, allowing sides to drape for tablecloth effect.

STEP 5 Roll out gray fondant ⅛ in. thick. Cut plates using smallest circle cutter from set. Cut serving plate for yams using medium circle from set. Cut a strip, ¼ in. Attach for raised rim.

STEP 6 Use football cutter from set to cut serving plate for corn. Trim ends to round off. Cut a strip, ¼ in. Attach for raised rim. Cut a rectangle, 2 in. x 3½ in. for turkey platter. Position plates and food on table. Position cookie people in back.

THANKSGIVING COOKIE POPS

The first Thanksgiving was surely a historic gathering. These cookie pop characters represent the Native Americans, Pilgrims and "guest of honor" you might welcome to your holiday table.

RECIPES:

Roll-Out Cookies (p. 183)

INGREDIENTS:

Copper Icing Color (for light skin tone shown)

Cocoa powder

Colored Sugars: Red, Yellow, Orange

Candy Melts Candy: White, Light Cocoa

Candy Color Sets: Garden (green, pink and black used), **Primary** (yellow, orange and red used)

Black shoestring licorice

Orange spice drops

TOOLS:

12 in. Rolling Pin

101 Cookie Cutter Set

9-Pc. Leaves and Acorns Nesting Metal Cutter Set

Cookie Sheet

Cooling Grid

Parchment Paper

15 in. Parchment Triangles

Scissors

Cordial Cups Candy Mold

12 in. Disposable Decorating Bags

TECHNIQUES:

Using Rolled Fondant (p. 217)

Candy/Pop Making Techniques (p. 230)

INSTRUCTIONS:

STEP 1 Make cookies. Prepare cookie dough. Reserve small amount of plain cookie dough. Tint half of remaining dough skin tone. Tint other half of dough light brown by adding 1 to 2 teaspoons cocoa powder and kneading into dough.

Roll out tinted doughs ⅛ in. thick. Cut out heads using medium circle cutter from set. Roll out plain dough ⅛ in. thick. Cut turkey feathers using second largest maple leaf cutter from set. Sprinkle feathers with colored sugars. Bake and cool all cookies.

STEP 2 Melt Candy Melts candy according to package directions. Tint portions of melted white candy black, red, light pink, yellow, green and orange using candy colors from sets.

STEP 3 Mold oak leaf for headband feathers. Place smallest oak leaf cutter from set on parchment paper-covered cookie sheet. Fill cutter ⅛ in. deep with combination of green and yellow melted candy to marbleize. Tap to settle and chill until firm. Pipe leaf vein using melted candy in cut parchment bag. Chill until firm.

STEP 4 Decorate cookie faces using melted candy and a cut parchment bag. Pipe dot eyes and cheeks, and pipe string mouths and hair.

STEP 5 Make pilgrim girl hat. Place large and medium circle cutters on parchment paper-covered cookie sheet. Fill with melted candy and chill until firm. Cut 1⅛ in. from bottom of large circle for brim. Attach medium circle to brim with melted candy.

STEP 6 Make pilgrim boy hat. Pipe a 2½ in. dia. candy circle on parchment paper for brim. Mold a cordial cup for hat and chill until firm. Attach hat to brim with melted candy. Pipe band and buckle with melted candy. Chill until firm.

STEP 7 Make Native American boy and girl. Pipe headband directly on cookie using melted candy and a cut parchment bag. For each of girl's braids, cut three

½ in. licorice strings. Twist together and trim to 2½ in. Attach bottom pieces together with melted black candy.

STEP 8 Make bows. Roll out spice drops and cut with scissors in bow shape. Attach to braids with melted candy.

STEP 9 Make turkey. Use melted light cocoa candy and a cut parchment bag to pipe 1¼ in. oval body and ball head on cookies. Chill until firm. Pipe beak, eyes, wattle and wings with melted candy. Pipe feet on parchment paper and chill until firm. Carefully remove and attach to turkey with melted candy.

STEP 10 Attach hats, headband feathers, leaves, braids and sticks to cookies with melted candy.

GOBBLE IT UP TURKEY CAKE

Bake and decorate a fun Thanksgiving centerpiece cake and your guests will Gobble It Up!

RECIPES:

Lemon Pound Cake (p. 177)

Buttercream Icing (p. 181)

Chocolate Buttercream Icing (p. 181)

INGREDIENTS:

White Ready-To-Use Rolled Fondant (18 oz.)

Icing Colors: Lemon Yellow, Black, Red-Red

Cornstarch

Red Color Mist Food Color Spray

White Candy Melts Candy

TOOLS:

9 in. Fondant Roller

Roll-N-Cut Mat

9-Pc. Leaves and Acorns Nesting Metal Cookie Set

10 in. x 14 in. Cake Boards

8 in. Lollipop Sticks

3-D Rubber Ducky Pan

Cooling Grid

12 in. Cake Circle

Fanci-Foil Wrap

12 in. Disposable Decorating Bags

Decorating Tips: 3, 5, 18, 2A

TECHNIQUES:

Using Rolled Fondant (p. 217)

Fondant and Gum Paste Decorating Techniques (p. 220)

Tip Techniques (p. 204)

SERVES: 12.

INSTRUCTIONS:

STEP 1 Two days in advance, make leaves. Tint 18 oz. fondant yellow. Roll out ⅛ in. thick and cut about 20 leaves using largest maple leaf cutter from set. Let dry on cornstarch-dusted board 48 hours. Spray lower part of leaves with food color spray, gradually fading toward tops. (It is best to spray several light coats rather than one heavy coat.) Let dry 10 minutes. Melt Candy Melts candy according to package directions. Attach lollipop sticks to backs of leaves with melted candy. Set aside.

STEP 2 Bake and cool rubber ducky cake. Trim down beak area to form a point. Place on cake board. Prepare buttercream icing and chocolate buttercream icing following recipe directions. Tint portions of white icing yellow, black and red; reserve a small portion white.

STEP 3 Ice beak smooth with yellow icing. Use tip 3 to pipe horizontal line for mouth. Use tip 5 to pipe dot (p. 206) eyes and tip 3 pupils. Flatten and smooth with finger dipped in cornstarch. Use tip 18 and chocolate icing to cover cake with stars (p. 212). Use tip 18 to pipe pull-out stars on sides for wings. Use tip 2A to pipe wattle. Start with light pressure at top of beak and then increase pressure as you pipe bottom of wattle. Cut sticks on leaves to various lengths. Insert in ascending order on back of turkey.

AUTUMN LEAVES CAKE

The Autumn Leaves Cake is perfect for a chilly fall afternoon or any autumn celebration.

RECIPES:

Yellow, White or Chocolate Cake (p. 176-177)

Buttercream Icing (p. 181)

INGREDIENTS:

White Ready-To-Use Decorator Icing

Ready-To-Use Rolled Fondant: White (24 oz.),
   Primary Colors Multi Pack, Natural Colors Multi Pack

Icing Colors: Orange, Kelly Green, Golden Yellow

Pure Lemon Extract

TOOLS:

10 in. Cake Circle

Fanci-Foil Wrap

13 in. Angled Spatula

9 in. x 2 in. Round Pan

Cooling Grid

20 in. Fondant Roller

Roll-N-Cut Mat

Fondant Smoother

Leaf Cut-Outs Fondant Cutters

Brush Set

TECHNIQUES:

Using Rolled Fondant (p. 217)

Fondant and Gum Paste Decorating Techniques (p. 220)

SERVES: 24.

INSTRUCTIONS:

STEP 1 Wrap cake circle with foil. Bake and cool 2-layer cake. Prepare buttercream icing following recipe directions. Prepare cake for fondant by icing in buttercream. Cover cake with white fondant. Smooth with fondant smoother. Place on prepared circle.

STEP 2 Create leaves. Roll out colored fondant ⅛ in. thick, combining colors to create new colors or marbling two or more colors. Use the largest leaf cutter Cut-Out to cut out three or four leaves at a time in various colors.

STEP 3 Position leaves on cake, attaching with damp brush. Smooth edges with fingers. Continue adding leaves to cover entire cake.

STEP 4 For border, roll out colored fondant ⅛ in. thick. Use smallest leaf Cut-Out to cut out leaves in various colors. Attach to bottom of cake using damp brush.

STEP 5 Add veins to leaves. For some of the leaves, roll ¹⁄₁₆ dia. colored fondant ropes and trim to fit on leaves. Attach with damp brush. For remaining leaves, paint vein lines using an icing color/lemon extract mixture.

WISE GUY PIE

Whooo doesn't like pumpkin pie?! Especially one with our wise friend owl perched on top and surrounded by pie crust maple leaves.

RECIPES:

Your favorite pumpkin pie

INGREDIENTS:

Additional single pie crust

Color Dust: Orange, Brown, Spruce Green, Periwinkle Blue, White

Pure Lemon Extract

TOOLS:

9 in. x 1.5 in. Pie Pan

12 in. Rolling Pin

Knife

6-Pc. Harvest Mini Metal Cutter Set

Cookie Sheet

Cooling Grid

Brush Set

TECHNIQUES:

Pearl Dust and Color Dust
  Color Effects (p. 226)

PATTERNS:

Owl (p. 243)

SERVES: 8.

INSTRUCTIONS:

STEP 1 Bake and cool pie following recipe directions.

STEP 2 Roll out extra pie crust dough ⅛ in. thick. Use pattern and knife to cut one owl. Use mini maple leaf cutter to cut 25 leaves. Bake owl and leaf pieces separately until edges are light golden brown. Cool completely.

STEP 3 Mix orange and white Color Dust for orange shown. Mix spruce green and periwinkle blue Color Dust for green shown. Paint details on owl and leaves using Color Dust/lemon extract mixture (p. 226). Let dry 10 to 15 minutes.

STEP 4 Arrange leaves on pie.

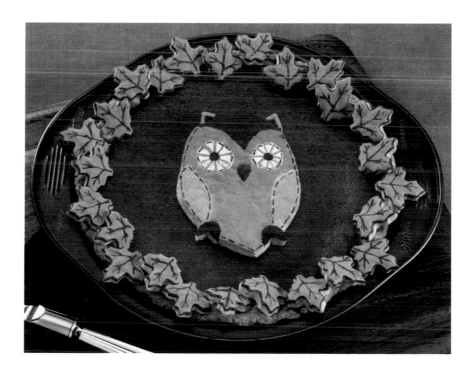

Ring in the Holiday Season

CREATE MAGICAL CHRISTMAS MEMORIES WITH BEAUTIFULLY DECORATED COOKIES AND FESTIVE YULETIDE CAKES

• •

HOLIDAY HEAD HONCHO BROWNIES

These cute little brownie Santas and elves are a great holiday treat.

RECIPES:
Cake Brownies or Fudgy Brownies (p. 179)

INGREDIENTS:
Candy Melts Candy: White, Green, Red, Dark Cocoa
Primary Candy Color Set (orange used for skin tone)
Sugar ice cream cones

TOOLS:
Round Pops Mold
Cookie Sheet
Cooling Grid
Knife
15 in. Parchment Triangles
Scissors
Parchment Paper
10 in. x 14 in. Cake Boards
Plastic ruler

TECHNIQUES:
Candy/Pop Making Techniques (p. 230)

INSTRUCTIONS:

STEP 1 Bake and cool brownies in silicone mold supported by cookie sheet. Unmold and trim bottoms if necessary for flat surface.

STEP 2 Melt white Candy Melts candy according to package directions. Use orange candy color from set to tint a portion skin tone. Reserve remaining white candy. Cover brownies with melted candy (p. 232). Let set 10 to 15 minutes. Cover with second coat. Let set 10 to 15 minutes. Use melted candy and a cut parchment bag to cover bottoms to seal. Let set on parchment paper-covered board.

STEP 3 Melt green and red Candy Melts candy, separately, according to package directions. Cut cones to 2 in. high. Set on cooling grid. Cover with melted candy. Let set on parchment paper-covered board 10 to 15 minutes.

STEP 4 Melt dark cocoa Candy Melts candy according to package directions. Use all melted candy and cut parchment bags to assemble and decorate brownies. Attach hats to heads. Use melted white candy and a cut parchment bag to pipe Santa's swirl beard, mustache, both hat brims and pompoms. Pipe dot eyes and fill-in mouths. Pipe Santa's dot nose, elf's dot cheeks, pull-out nose and ears.

SPRITZ COOKIE EXTRAVAGANZA

Pressed Spritz cookies are a holiday tradition! Assorted disks let you create a variety of cookies from just one cookie recipe. Decorating is fast, too, with colored icing and holiday sprinkles!

RECIPES:

Classic Spritz Cookies (p. 185)

INGREDIENTS:

Cookie Icings: Red, White, Green

Red Colored Sugar

White Sugar Pearls

TOOLS:

Comfort-Grip Cookie Press

Cookie Sheet

Cooling Grid

INSTRUCTIONS:

STEP 1 Prepare dough following recipe directions. Fill cookie press with dough according to package directions.

STEP 2 Press an assortment of cookie shapes onto cookie sheet. Bake and cool cookies.

STEP 3 Use cookie icings to decorate cookies. For flower cookie, cover petals with colored sugar.

STEP 4 Add dots or Sugar Pearls in centers of cookies with cookie icings. Let set.

WHITE CHRISTMAS TREE COOKIES

Ready to pick out the Christmas tree? Select one made using cookie dough and decorated with ornaments and garland.

RECIPES:

Roll-Out Cookies (p. 183)

Color Flow Icing (p. 182)

INGREDIENTS:

Color Flow Mix

Decorating Gel-Tubes: Green, Red

TOOLS:

12 in. Rolling Pin

Christmas Tree Comfort-Grip Cutter

Cookie Sheet

Cooling Grid

12 in. Disposable Decorating Bags

INSTRUCTIONS:

STEP 1 Prepare and roll out dough following recipe directions. Cut dough using tree cutter. Bake and cool cookies.

STEP 2 Prepare Color Flow icing following recipe directions. Place cookies on cooling grid over cookie sheet. Cover cookies using thinned white icing (p. 233). Let dry 24 hours.

STEP 3 Use green decorating gel to outline (p. 208) garlands. Use red decorating gel to add dot (p. 206) ornaments.

SNUGGLY SNOWMAN COOKIE POPS

This cheerful snowman cookie pop will take the chill out of any winter day. Iced smooth and accented with a scarf, he's a frosty friend who will bring cheer to any holiday gathering.

RECIPES:

Roll-Out Cookies (p. 183)

Royal Icing (p. 181)

INGREDIENTS:

Meringue Powder

Icing Colors: Sky Blue*, Royal Blue*, Black, Orange

White Candy Melts Candy

Cornstarch

Large marshmallows

Primary Colors Fondant Multi Pack (½ oz. blue per cookie)

TOOLS:

12 in. Rolling Pin

18-Pc. Holiday Cutter Set

Round Comfort-Grip Cutter

Cookie Sheet

Cooling Grid

12 in. Disposable Decorating Bags

Decorating Tips: 2, 5, 1

8 in. Cookie Treat Sticks

Knife

Plastic ruler

9 in. Fondant Roller

Roll-N-Cut Mat

Brush Set

TECHNIQUES:

Tip Techniques (p. 204)

*Combine Sky Blue with Royal Blue for blue shades shown.

INSTRUCTIONS:

STEP 1 Prepare and roll out dough following recipe directions. Use Santa hat cutter from set and round Comfort-Grip cutter to cut cookies. Bake and cool cookies.

STEP 2 Prepare royal icing following recipe directions. Tint portions light blue, dark blue, black and orange; reserve some white. Place cookies on cooling grid positioned over cookie sheet. Cover round cookies with thinned white icing and hat cookies with thinned light blue icing (p. 233). Immediately use tip 2 and thinned dark blue icing to pipe stripes on hat cookies. Let dry 24 hours.

STEP 3 Melt Candy Melts candy according to package directions. Use melted candy to attach hat cookie to front of round cookie and stick to back. Chill until firm 3 to 5 minutes. Decorate cookies with full-strength icing. Use tip 5 and white icing to pipe swirl pompom and cuff on hat. Use tip 2 to pipe black dot (p. 206) eyes. Use tip 1 to pipe black outline (p. 208) mouth. Use tip 5 to pipe orange pull-out nose and white dot cheeks. Flatten and smooth cheeks with finger dipped in cornstarch.

STEP 4 Use knife to cut marshmallow to ½ in. thick. Cut in half and wrap around stick for neck. Roll out blue fondant ⅛ in. thick. For scarf, cut a strip, ½ in. x 3 in. Use damp brush to attach around marshmallow. For tails, cut strips, ½ in. x 1½ in. and ½ in. x 2 in. Use damp brush to attach. For knot, use wide end of any tip to cut a circle. Attach. Let dry overnight.

ROOFTOP DROP-OFF COOKIE POPS DISPLAY

What's that you hear up on the rooftop? The echo of reindeer hooves will make party guests' hearts beat with anticipation as you serve a chimney full of cookie pops.

RECIPES:

Roll-Out Cookies (p. 183)

Chocolate Roll-Out Cookies (p. 184)

Royal Icing (p. 181)

INGREDIENTS:

Meringue Powder

Icing Colors: Brown, Black, Christmas Red*, Red-Red*, Kelly Green, Lemon Yellow*, Golden Yellow*, Copper
(for skin tone shown)

White Candy Melts Candy

TOOLS:

12 in. Rolling Pin

18-Pc. Holiday Cutter Set

Cookie Sheet

Cooling Grid

12 in. Disposable Decorating Bags

Decorating Tips: 3, 5, 2

9 in. Angled Spatula

Parchment Paper

11¾ in. Lollipop Sticks

3 in. x 3 in. x 4 in. high craft foam block

3½ in. x 3½ in. x 5½ in. high container

Wrapping paper

1 in. wide white ribbon (15 in.)

Transparent cellophane tape

Scissors

Curling ribbon

TECHNIQUES:

Tip Techniques (p. 204)

*Combine Christmas Red with Red-Red for red shown. Combine Lemon Yellow with Golden Yellow for yellow shown.

INSTRUCTIONS:

STEP 1 Prepare and roll out regular and chocolate dough following recipe directions. Cut eight chocolate reindeer cookies, one gingerbread boy and one sleigh cookie using cutters from set. Bake and cool cookies.

STEP 2 Prepare royal icing following recipe directions. Tint portions brown, black, red, green, yellow and copper; reserve some white. For reindeer, use tip 3 to pipe outline (p. 208) antlers. Use tip 5 to pipe outline harness. Use tip 2 to pipe dots (p. 206) on harness. Use tip 3 to pipe dot eyes, nose and hooves. Use tip 5 to pipe pull-out tail.

STEP 3 Use spatula and green icing to ice sleigh smooth. Use tip 5 and red icing to outline runners. Use tip 5 and white icing to pipe swirl trim. Let dry overnight.

STEP 4 Use spatula to ice Santa suit and face smooth. Position Santa on parchment paper. Use tip 3 to pipe pull-out hair. Use tip 3 to pipe green gloves, black belt and yellow buckle. Use tip 3 to pipe swirl hair, beard and hat trim. Use tip 3 to pipe dot nose. Use tip 2 to pipe dot eyes and mouth. Let dry overnight.

STEP 5 Melt Candy Melts candy according to package directions. Using melted candy, attach sleigh cookie onto Santa cookie. Attach sticks to all cookies with melted candy. Let set. Insert craft block in container. Wrap container with wrapping paper. Use tape to attach white ribbon to top rim. Insert cookies into craft block; trim sticks as needed. Position curling ribbon.

CHRISTMAS COOKIE TREE

Decorating a tree for Christmas is easy, especially when it's made with delicious roll-out cookies!

RECIPES:

Roll-Out Cookies (p. 183)

Color Flow Icing (p. 182)

INGREDIENTS:

Color Flow Mix

Kelly Green Icing Color

Piping Gel

Light Green Colored Sugar

TOOLS:

12 in. Rolling Pin

Christmas Cookie Tree Cutter Kit

Cookie Sheet

Cooling Grid

15 in. Parchment Triangles

Brush Set

Cake plate

¼ in. wide red ribbon (11 in. long)

Scissors

INSTRUCTIONS:

STEP 1 One day in advance, prepare and roll out dough following recipe directions. Use cutters from kit to cut two stars of each size. Bake and cool cookies.

STEP 2 Prepare three batches of Color Flow Icing following recipe directions. Tint 1½ cups dark green and the remainder light green. Use full-strength light green icing in a cut parchment bag to outline stars. Let set 1 to 2 hours. Decorate cookies one at a time from this point.

STEP 3 Use thinned light green icing in cut parchment bag to flow in. Immediately use thinned dark green icing in cut parchment bag to pipe lines from middle of star to points and to pipe branch lines in a V shape from center line. Let dry 24 hours.

STEP 4 Brush cookie edges with piping gel. Cover with light green sugar. Assemble tree on a cake plate, stacking from largest to smallest, staggering star points and securing with dots of full-strength icing. Make a bow and attach to treetop with dots of icing.

SPARKLING STAR STOCKING COOKIES

This Christmas stocking has all of its treats on the outside. Kids of all ages will have fun decorating these favorites.

RECIPES:

Roll-Out Cookies (p. 183)

Color Flow Icing (p. 182)

INGREDIENTS:

Color Flow Mix

Christmas Red Icing Color

White Nonpareils Sprinkles

TOOLS:

12 in. Rolling Pin

4-Pc. Jolly Shapes Cutter Set

Cookie Sheet

Cooling Grid

15 in. Parchment Triangles

Decorating Tip: 3

Scissors

TECHNIQUES:

Tip Techniques (p. 204)

INSTRUCTIONS:

STEP 1 Prepare and roll out dough following recipe directions. Use stocking cutter from set to cut cookies. Bake and cool cookies.

STEP 2 Prepare Color Flow icing following recipe directions. Tint portion red; reserve some white. Use tip 3 and full-strength red icing to outline red area of stocking. Use tip 3 and full-strength white icing to outline toe and cuff area. Let dry 1 to 2 hours. Flow in stocking with thinned red icing in cut parchment bag. Let dry 1 to 2 hours. Flow in toe and cuff with thinned white icing in cut parchment bag. Immediately sprinkle with white nonpareils. Let dry 24 hours.

STEP 3 Use tip 3 and full-strength white icing to pipe lines and dots for stars. Let dry 1 to 2 hours.

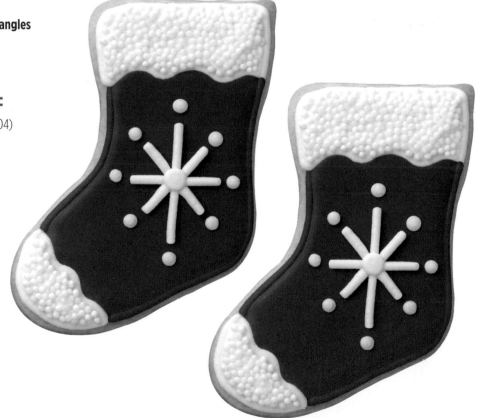

EASY GINGERBREAD BOY COOKIES

This holiday cookie makes a great family project! The kids can help cut out the cookies and even beginners can pipe on the easy dot and squiggle details.

RECIPES:

Grandma's Gingerbread Cookies (p. 186)

Royal Icing (p. 181)

INGREDIENTS:

Meringue Powder

Icing Colors: Christmas Red, Kelly Green

TOOLS:

12 In. Rolling Pin

Gingerbread Boy Comfort-Grip Cutter

Cookie Sheet

Cooling Grid

12 in. Disposable Decorating Bags

Decorating Tips: 3, 5

TECHNIQUES:

Tip Techniques (p. 204)

INSTRUCTIONS:

STEP 1 Prepare and roll out dough following recipe directions. Cut dough using gingerbread boy cutter. Bake and cool cookies.

STEP 2 Prepare royal icing following recipe directions. Tint portions red and green; reserve some white. Use tip 3 and white icing to pipe dot (p. 206) and outline (p. 208) facial features and zigzag (p. 215) trim on arms and legs.

STEP 3 Use tip 3 and red icing to pipe in bow tie and dot knot. Use tip 5 and green icing to add dot buttons.

REINDEER COOKIES

Adorable reindeer cookies will be the "bells" of your holiday ball. Cookies covered in melted Candy Melts candy, sporting pretzel antlers, deliver the perfect present: salty-sweet delight! These treats will fly off the dessert table.

RECIPES:

Roll-Out Cookies (p. 183)

INGREDIENTS:

Candy Melts Candy: White, Dark Cocoa, Light Cocoa
   (12 oz. covers 40 to 50 treats)

Mini pretzel twists

Mini chocolate chips

TOOLS:

12 in. Rolling Pin

12-Pc. Holiday Mini Cutter Set

Knife

Cookie Sheet

Cooling Grid

Parchment Paper

10 in. x 14 in. Cake Boards

15 in. Parchment Triangles

Scissors

TECHNIQUES:

Candy/Pop Making Techniques (p. 230)

Tip Techniques (p. 204)

INSTRUCTIONS:

STEP 1 Prepare and roll out dough following recipe directions. Cut dough using bell cutter from set. Trim off clappers with knife. Bake and cool cookies.

STEP 2 Melt Candy Melts candy according to package directions. Lighten melted light cocoa candy with some melted white candy for a lighter shade. Place cookies on cooling grid positioned over cookie sheet. Cover with melted candy. Chill until set 10 to 15 minutes.

STEP 3 Cut pretzels for antlers. Position heads on parchment paper-covered board. Use melted candy and a cut parchment bag to attach antlers and chocolate chip ears. Pipe outline (p. 208) smile, dot (p. 206) eyes and nose. Chill until set 5 to 10 minutes.

EAR-RESISTIBLE SNOWMEN CAKE POPS

Holiday party guests won't be able to muffle their squeals of delight when you serve these suave snowmen cake pops. Licorice and spice drop ear muffs top off these dandy dudes.

RECIPES:

Basic Cake Ball Pops (p. 180)

INGREDIENTS:

White Candy Melts Candy

Garden Candy Color Set (black used)

Spice drops

Black shoestring licorice

TOOLS:

9 in. x 13 in. x 2 in. Sheet Pan

6 in. Cookie Treat Sticks

Pops Decorating Stand

15 in. Parchment Triangles

Scissors

Knife

Plastic ruler

TECHNIQUES:

Candy/Pop Making Techniques (p. 230)

INSTRUCTIONS:

STEP 1 Prepare small cake balls and insert sticks following recipe directions. Chill until firm 5 to 10 minutes. Melt Candy Melts candy according to package directions. Tint small portion black using candy color from set. Dip pops in melted white candy. Place in decorating stand. Chill until firm 5 to 10 minutes.

STEP 2 Use melted candy and a cut parchment bag to pipe dot (p. 206) eyes and outline (p. 208) mouth.

STEP 3 Use knife to cut a cone-shaped piece of spice drop for nose. Use melted white candy to attach.

STEP 4 For ear muffs, cut spice drop halves and 2 in. licorice strings. Insert licorice in spice drops. Use melted white candy to attach.

SUGAR CANE CAKE POPS

Throw holiday guests a curve with candy cane-shaped cake ball pops. These treats earn their stripes with cuteness.

RECIPES:

Basic Cake Ball Pops (p. 180)

INGREDIENTS:

Candy Melts Candy: White, Red

Red Colored Sugar

TOOLS:

9 in. x 13 in. x 2 in. Sheet Pan

Plastic Dowel Rods (cut to 4 in.)

Plastic ruler

6 in. Cookie Treat Sticks

9 in. Angled Spatula

Parchment Paper

10 in. x 14 in. Cake Boards

Cooling Grid

Cookie Sheet

12 in. Disposable Decorating Bags

Knife

15 in. Parchment Triangles

Scissors

TECHNIQUES:

Candy/Pop Making Techniques (p. 230)

INSTRUCTIONS:

STEP 1 Prepare cake ball mixture following recipe directions. Pack firmly into plastic dowel rods. Insert cookie treat stick 2½ in. into dowel rod. Chill completely, then push up stick to release. Gently shape top curve of cane. Chill until firm 5 to 10 minutes.

STEP 2 Melt white Candy Melts candy according to package directions. Use spatula to ice back with melted candy. Set on parchment paper-covered board. Chill until firm 10 to 15 minutes. Place on cooling grid over parchment paper-covered cookie sheet. Cover with melted candy using cut disposable bag (p. 232). Tap to settle. Chill until firm 10 to 15 minutes.

STEP 3 Melt red Candy Melts candy according to package directions. Use melted red candy and a cut parchment bag to pipe ½ in. wide stripes. Immediately sprinkle on red sugar. Chill until firm 3 to 5 minutes.

MERRY MITTEN COOKIES

Count on a big round of applause when you serve these cute mitten cookies. A sweet traditional design sets these apart from the rest. Fun to make and eat, everyone will want to give you a hand!

RECIPES:

Roll-Out Cookies (p. 183)

Color Flow Icing (p. 182)

INGREDIENTS:

Color Flow Mix

Icing Colors: Moss Green*, Leaf Green*

TOOLS:

12 in. Rolling Pin

18-Pc. Holiday Metal Cutter Set

Cookie Sheet

Cooling Grid

15 in. Parchment Triangles

Decorating Tip: 3

TECHNIQUES:

Tip Techniques (p. 204)

*Combine Moss Green with Leaf Green for green shown.

INSTRUCTIONS:

STEP 1 Prepare and roll out dough following recipe directions. Use mitten cutter from set to cut cookies. Bake and cool.

STEP 2 Prepare Color Flow icing following recipe directions. Tint portion green; reserve some white. Outline mitten with tip 3 and full-strength icing. Flow in cookie with thinned icing in a cut parchment bag. Let dry 24 hours. Use tip 3 and full-strength white icing to pipe lines, snowflakes, dots (p. 206) and zigzag (p. 215) cuffs on mittens. Let dry 1 to 2 hours.

NORTH POLE PENGUIN CAKE

He may look chilly, but he'll warm your heart! This cute cake is pure penguin fun!

RECIPES:

Yellow, White or Chocolate Cake (p. 176-177)

Buttercream Icing (p. 181)

INGREDIENTS:

White Ready-To-Use Rolled Fondant (48 oz.)

Icing Colors: Lemon Yellow*, Golden Yellow*, Black, Red-Red*, Christmas Red*

TOOLS:

Plastic ruler

20 in. Fondant Roller

Roll-N-Cut Mat

Brush Set

Scissors

6 in. Lollipop Sticks

3-Pc. Paisley Pan Set

Cooling Grid

13 in. Angled Spatula

Fondant Smoother

12 in. Disposable Decorating Bags

Decorating Tips: 17, 10

PATTERNS:

Penguin Body, Wings, Feet, Beak (p. 240)

SERVES: 17.

*Combine Lemon Yellow with Golden Yellow for yellow shown. Combine Red-Red with Christmas Red for red shown.

INSTRUCTIONS:

STEP 1 In advance, prepare fondant details. Tint 6 oz. fondant yellow. Use patterns as a guide to shape two feet (1 in. thick) and one beak (taper from ¾ in. to ½ in. thick at tip). Indent feet using brush handle. Cut beak open using scissors. Cut lollipop sticks to 3 in. Insert into beak and feet, leaving 2 in. exposed. Roll out white fondant ¼ in. thick. Use pattern to cut one full and one partial wing.

STEP 2 Bake and cool cakes, one layer 9 in. x 6 in. x 2 in. and another 12.75 in. x 9 in. x 2 in. Turn smaller cake over for hat. Trim 2 in. off wide end to match curve of head. Tint 10 oz. fondant red. Prepare buttercream icing following recipe directions. Tint portions yellow and black; reserve some white. Prepare cakes for fondant by icing in buttercream. Cover cakes with fondant. Smooth with fondant smoother. Use pattern to mark black areas on body. Cover with tip 17 stars (p. 212). Position wings. Cover with tip 17 stars. Pipe tip 10 dot (p. 206) eyes. Insert beak and feet.

STEP 3 Position hat cake. For hat trims, roll out white fondant ⅛ in. thick. For base, cut a strip, ¾ in. x 9 in. Attach over gap where cakes meet using damp brush. For fringe, cut about 15 strips, 1 in. x 4 in. Use scissors to cut partial slits, ¾ in. deep, ⅛ in. apart, across one edge. Brush uncut edge with damp brush and roll up, pinching bottom edge to form tufts. Fluff cut ends. Trim bottom level. Attach. For pompom, repeat as above using a strip, 1½ in. x 10 in. Insert stick in hat tip leaving ¾ in. extended. Attach pompom over stick.

A VERY MERRY-GO-ROUND GINGERBREAD BOY CAKE

Complete your holiday party with gingerbread cookie border around each of the two tiers of this cake. Seasonal treats complete the decorations.

RECIPES:

Royal Icing (p. 181)

Yellow, White or Chocolate Cake (p. 176-177)

Chocolate Buttercream Icing (p. 181)

Buttercream Icing (p. 181)

INGREDIENTS:

White Ready-To-Use Rolled Fondant (24 oz.)

Icing Colors: Brown*, Red-Red*, Kelly Green

Cornstarch

Meringue Powder

Spice drops

Rainbow Nonpareils Sprinkles

Small candy canes

6 in. candy canes (five needed)

TOOLS:

9 in. Fondant Roller

Roll-N-Cut Mat

4-Pc. Gingerbread Boys Nesting Cutter Set

10 in. x 14 in. Cake Boards

12 in. Disposable Decorating Bags

Decorating Tips: 2, 1M

Hidden Pillars

Brush Set

Round Pans: 6 in. x 2 in., 10 in. x 2 in.

Cooling Grid

Cake Circles: 6 in., 10 in.

Knife or **Cake Leveler**

13 in. Angled Spatula

3-Pc. Icing Comb Set

Decorator Preferred Smooth-Edge Separator Plate
  (8 in. used)

TECHNIQUES:

Using Rolled Fondant (p. 217)

Tiered Construction (p. 227)

Tip Techniques (p. 204)

SERVES: 40.

*Combine Brown with Red-Red for brown shown.

INSTRUCTIONS:

STEP 1 Tint fondant 12 oz. brown, 6 oz. red; reserve remaining white. Roll out ⅛ in. thick. Use brown fondant and second smallest cutter from set to cut 14 gingerbread boys. Let dry on cornstarch-dusted cake board 24 hours.

STEP 2 Prepare royal icing following recipe directions. Tint portions red and green; reserve some white. Use tip 2 to pipe dot (p. 206) and outline (p. 208) facial features and trim on gingerbread boys.

STEP 3 Roll out red and white fondant ⅛ in. thick. Use knife to cut ¼ in. strips of each color. Wrap around top 3 in. of hidden pillars, attaching with damp brush. Set aside.

STEP 4 Bake and cool 2-layer cakes. Trim layers 1½ in. high for a 3 in. cake. Prepare chocolate buttercream icing following recipe directions. Ice cakes smooth in chocolate icing, ½ in. thick on sides. Immediately comb sides using icing comb with ridged comb edge.

STEP 5 Prepare for push-in pillar construction (p. 228). Insert hidden pillars into 10 in. cake so that fondant strips rest just above cake. Position 6 in. cake on separator plate.

STEP 6 Pipe tip 1M rosette (p. 210) top and bottom borders. Cover top tier with tip 1M rosettes, adding a second row in center.

STEP 7 Position spice drop and sprinkle nonpareils on each rosette.

STEP 8 Position gingerbread boys and small candy canes around cakes. Insert large candy canes.

ALL SMILES SANTA CAKE

Santa just keeps on giving with this sweet centerpiece cake. With a beard and hat made of buttercream, he's sure to make your party jolly and bright.

RECIPES:

Yellow, White or Chocolate Cake (p. 176-177)

Buttercream Icing (p. 181)

INGREDIENTS:

Icing Colors: Christmas Red, Black, Copper
  (for light skin tone shown)

Cornstarch

TOOLS:

10 in. x 14 in. Cake Boards

Fanci-Foil Wrap

Scissors

Transparent cellophane tape

3-Pc. Paisley Pan

Toothpicks

12 in. Disposable Decorating Bags

Decorating Tips: 3, 18, 32

TECHNIQUES:

Tip Techniques (p. 204)

SERVES: 14.

INSTRUCTIONS:

STEP 1 Cut cake board to fit cake. Wrap board with foil. Bake and cool 1-layer cake in 12.75 in. x 9 in. x 2 in. pan. Place on prepared board,

STEP 2 Use toothpick to mark details. Prepare buttercream icing following recipe directions. Tint portions red, black and copper; reserve some white. Use tip 3 to outline (p. 208) eyes and outline and fill in mouth. Pat smooth with finger dipped in cornstarch. Use tip 18 to cover hat and face with stars (p. 212); overpipe nose for dimension. Use tip 18 to pipe elongated reverse shell (p. 211) beard, curved outline mustache and outline eyebrows. Pipe tip 32 rosettes (p. 210) on hat brim and tip.

SNOWMAN-TOPPED CAKE

This detailed cake needs little more than a dusting of confectioners' sugar and some holiday colors to impress.

RECIPES:

Sugar Cookies for Pan-Shaped Cookies (p. 185)

Yellow, White or Chocolate Cake (p. 176-177)

INGREDIENTS:

White Ready-To-Use Rolled Fondant (14 oz.)

Icing Colors: Kelly Green, Brown*, Orange, Red-Red*

Piping Gel

White Candy Melts Candy

Confectioners' sugar

TOOLS:

12-Cavity Non-Stick Mini Holiday Cookie Shapes Pan

Cooling Grid

Dimensions Belle Pan

9 in. Fondant Roller

Roll-N-Cut Mat

Knife

15 in. Parchment Triangles

Scissors

Plastic ruler

6 in. Cookie Sticks

TECHNIQUES:

Using Rolled Fondant (p. 217)

SERVES: 12.

*Combine Brown with Red-Red for brown shown.

INSTRUCTIONS:

STEP 1 In advance, make cookie. Prepare dough following recipe directions. Press into pan. Bake and cool cookie.

STEP 2 Bake and cool cake.

STEP 3 For snowman cookie, tint fondant 1 in. dia. ball green, ¼ in. dia. ball brown and ¼ in. dia. ball orange (for nose). Roll out white fondant ⅛ in. thick. Use cookie pan as guide to cut snowman shape. Attach to cookie with piping gel in cut parchment bag.

Roll out green fondant ⅛ in. thick and cut strips for hat and scarf. Attach with piping gel, trimming to fit. Roll small cone shape using orange fondant for nose and roll small brown fondant balls for eyes and buttons. Attach with piping gel. Let dry.

STEP 4 Melt Candy Melts candy according to package directions. Attach stick to cookie back with melted candy. Let set 10 to 15 minutes.

STEP 5 Tint 5 oz. fondant red. Roll 5 oz. white and red fondant ropes, ⅜ in. dia. and 27 in. long. Twist both colors together (p. 222). Wrap around base of cake, attaching with piping gel. Sprinkle cake with confectioners' sugar.

STEP 6 Roll a small ball of fondant and place in center of cake. Insert snowman on stick.

TREE-MENDOUSLY GENEROUS PETITS FOURS

An entire tree made of presents? Who wouldn't want to wake up to that on Christmas morning?

RECIPES:

Lemon Pound Cake (p. 177), Yellow Cake or Chocolate Cake (p. 176)

INGREDIENTS:

Primary Colors Fondant Multi Pack

Cornstarch

White Candy Melts Candy (7 pks.)

Garden Candy Color Set (green used)

TOOLS:

9 in. Fondant Roller

Roll-N-Cut Mat

Knife

Plastic ruler

10 in. x 14 in. Cake Boards

6-Pc. Star Nesting Plastic Cutter Set

Brush Set

12 in. x 18 in. x 2 in. Sheet Pan

Cooling Grid

Parchment Paper

Paring knife

6 in. Lollipop Sticks

TECHNIQUES:

Candy/Pop Making Techniques (p. 230)

INSTRUCTIONS:

STEP 1 One day in advance, make fondant loops and star. Roll out various colors of fondant ⅛ in. thick. For bow loops, cut strips, ¼ in. x 2 in.; cut 60 loops each in red, blue, green and yellow. Pinch ends together to form loops; let dry on side on cornstarch-dusted board. Cut star from yellow fondant using second smallest star cutter from set. Cut ⅛ in. wide yellow strips for star swirl and lines. Shape swirl and attach along with lines with damp brush. Let dry overnight.

STEP 2 Bake and cool 1-layer cake. Cut into 47 squares, each 2 in., with paring knife. Melt Candy Melts candy according to package directions. Tint green using candy color from set. Cover squares with melted candy. Chill until firm on parchment paper-covered cake boards 10 to 15 minutes. For cake ribbons, roll out various colors of fondant ⅛ in. thick. Cut ¼ in. wide strips to fit across top and sides of cakes. Attach with damp brush.

STEP 3 Stack cakes in tree shape on serving plate, placing 21 for bottom layer, 14 for second layer, seven for third layer, four for fourth layer and one for top layer. Attach loops to package and stick to back of star with melted candy. Insert star on top.

SANTA'S SURPRISE! CAKE

A detailed alternative to a gingerbread house! This fun holiday design assures there will be plenty of dessert to go around.

RECIPES:

Royal Icing (p. 181)

Lemon Pound Cake (p. 177), Yellow Cake or Chocolate Cake (p. 176)

Buttercream Icing (p. 181)

INGREDIENTS:

Meringue Powder

Sugar ice cream cones

Icing Colors: Kelly Green, Brown, Lemon Yellow, Red-Red, Black, Rose, Royal Blue, Violet, Copper (for light skin tone)

Jumbo Rainbow Nonpareils Sprinkles

Jumbo spice drops

Granulated sugar

White Ready-To-Use Rolled Fondant (30 oz.)

Piping Gel

Cornstarch

Square caramels

Mini jelly candies

TOOLS:

Knife

Plastic ruler

12 in. Disposable Decorating Bags

Decorating Tips: 17, 3, 4, 1, 2, 7, 45

Star Cut-Outs Fondant Cutters

18 in. x 13 in. foam core board (½ in. thick)

Fanci-Foil Wrap

Transparent cellophane tape

20 in. Fondant Roller

Roll-N-Cut Mat

Brush Set

Pastry Wheel

Stand-Up House Pan

Cooling Grid

9 in. Angled Spatula

Toothpick

TECHNIQUES:

Tip Techniques (p. 204)

Using Rolled Fondant (p. 217)

PATTERNS:

Fireplace, Staircase Riser (p. 242)

SERVES: 24.

INSTRUCTIONS:

STEP 1 In advance, make four small and six large trees. For small trees, cut sugar cones to 1¾ in., 2 in., 2½ in. and 3 in. high. Prepare royal icing following recipe directions. Tint green.

For each large tree, stack three sugar cones and secure with royal icing. Beginning at bottom, cover trees with tip 17 pull-out stars (p. 212). Attach nonpareils as you pipe branches to treetop.

For stars, roll out yellow spice drop on surface sprinkled with granulated sugar. Cut two stars using medium Cut-Out. Attach with tip 3 dots (p. 206) of royal icing.

STEP 2 Cover foam core base with foil. Using pan as a guide, mark base where house cakes will be positioned, creating a 30° angle where house fronts meet. Mark floor area by drawing a line from corner of house backs to corner of base.

For floor, tint 8 oz. fondant brown. Roll out ⅛ in. thick; cut an 18 in. x 7 in. piece. Brush base from house backs to edge of base lightly with piping gel. Attach fondant, trimming at markings. Using ruler and straight-edge wheel of pastry wheel, score lines for floorboards. First, mark horizontal lines ⅜ in. apart. Next, mark floorboards 3 in. and 3½ in. long to stagger joints.

For snow area, roll out remaining white fondant ⅛ in. thick. Brush base from house fronts to edge of base lightly with piping gel; cover area with fondant. Trim to fit.

STEP 3 Bake and cool cakes. Trim bottoms of two house cakes to stand level on board. Position on base. Prepare buttercream icing following recipe directions. Tint portions yellow, light and dark brown, green, red, black, gray, rose, blue, violet and copper; reserve some white. On both house fronts, mark with toothpick and ice smooth 1½ in. square top windows.

STEP 4 Decorate house fronts (outside of houses). On door house, mark and ice smooth a 2 in. square top window and a 1¾ in. x 3¼ in. door with a ½ in. square top window.

On chimney house, mark and ice smooth a 2 in. x 3 in. bottom window.

On both house fronts and sides, use tip 4 to pipe ½ in. x ¼ in. high bricks, staggering ends to create a brickwork pattern. Smooth with finger dipped in cornstarch. Use tip 1 to outline (p. 208) windowpanes. Use tip 3 to pipe pull-out window and door garland trim, wreath, bushes and tree in front window. Attach nonpareils.

On wreath, use tip 2 to pipe dot berries and outline bow. Use tip 3 to pipe doorknob and pull-out icicles on windowsills. For chimney, cut four caramels on an angle to fit roof peak; attach two on each side of peak with icing. Attach a second row of four caramels. Ice rooftops fluffy with spatula. Use tip 7 to pipe icicles along eaves.

STEP 5 Decorate house backs (inside of houses). Ice walls on both houses smooth with yellow icing. Use tip 45 to pipe trim on peak of both houses.

On chimney house, mark a 1½ in. dia. circle for wreath. Use tip 3 to pipe dot wreath and bow. Mark fireplace using pattern, starting 1 in. from left edge of wall. Ice inside area smooth. Use tip 3 with heavy pressure to pipe bricks. Smooth with finger dipped in cornstarch. Use tip 3 to outline mantel, candles and dot garland. Use tip 2 to pipe dot flames.

STEP 6 For Santa, use tip 7 to outline and pipe in head. Pat smooth with finger dipped in cornstarch. Use tip 4 to outline and pipe in suit, hat and boots and pat smooth. Use tip 2 to pipe facial features. Use tip 3 to pipe zigzag (p. 215) fur trim, swirl beard and pompom, pull-out mustache and dot mittens. Pipe tip 3 dot garland along bottom of trim.

STEP 7 On house, mark inside door 1¾ in. x 3¼ in. high. Outline and pipe in. Pat smooth with finger dipped in cornstarch. Use tip 3 to outline and pipe in a ½ in. square window; add dot doorknob. Mark upstairs railing, with top beam 2¾ in. from house peak and bottom 1 in. below top beam. Use tip 3 to outline beams with vertical posts 1 in. apart.

STEP 8 For family, use tip 7 to outline and pipe in heads and pat smooth. Use tip 4 to outline and pipe in clothing and pat smooth. Use tip 2 to pipe dot facial features and hands. Use tip 3 to outline or pipe zigzag (p. 215) hair. Use tip 3 to pipe garland on staircase and railing.

For staircase, mark and pipe in riser pattern; mark banister 1½ in. above riser, following angle. Pipe tip 3 outline banister with vertical posts 1 in. apart.

For gifts, trim jumbo spice drops into squares and roll in granulated sugar. Pipe tip 2 outline ribbons and bows.

STEP 9 Ice white portion of prepared board fluffy, leaving walkway clean. Attach mini jelly candies for walkway. Position cone trees and packages.

PINWHEEL CANDY LOLLIPOPS

Two fun candy molds make one merry lollipop! Use the pinwheel mold to create the classic Christmas candy backdrop for the cute candy kids.

INGREDIENTS:

Candy Melts Candy: White, Red, Green, Light Cocoa

TOOLS:

Pinwheel Lollipop Mold

15 in. Parchment Triangles

Scissors

6 in. Lollipop Sticks

Bite-Size Gingerbread Boy Mold

TECHNIQUES:

Tip Techniques (p. 204)

Candy/Pop Making Techniques (p. 230)

INSTRUCTIONS:

STEP 1 Melt Candy Melts candy according to package directions. Mold pinwheel lollipops using piping method (p. 230). Chill until firm 15 to 20 minutes. Mold gingerbread boys in silicone mold, filling cavities ¼ in. deep. Chill until firm 15 to 20 minutes.

STEP 2 Use melted candy and a cut parchment bag to add dot (p. 206), zigzag (p. 215) and outline (p. 208) details. Attach gingerbread boys to pinwheels with melted candy. Let set 5 to 10 minutes.

PEARLED PRESENT COOKIES

Let your guests unwrap something delicious with these pearly present cookies.

RECIPES:

Roll-Out Cookies (p. 183)

Color Flow Icing (p. 182)

INGREDIENTS:

Color Flow Mix

Icing Colors: Kelly Green, Christmas Red*, Red-Red*, Violet*, Rose*, Lemon Yellow*, Golden Yellow*, Sky Blue

White Pearl Dust

White Sugar Pearls

TOOLS:

12 in. Rolling Pin

18-Pc. Holiday Cutter Set

Cookie Sheet

Cooling Grid

15 in. Parchment Triangles

Decorating Tip: 3

Scissors

Brush Set

*Combine Christmas Red with Red-Red for red shown. Combine Violet with Rose for violet shown. Combine Lemon Yellow with Golden Yellow for yellow shown.

INSTRUCTIONS:

STEP 1 Prepare and roll out dough following recipe directions. Use gift cutter from set to cut cookies. Bake and cool cookies.

STEP 2 Prepare Color Flow icing following recipe directions. Tint portions green, red, violet, yellow, and blue; reserve some white. Outline cookies with tip 3 and full-strength icing in desired color. Flow in with thinned icing in same color in cut parchment bag. Let dry 24 hours. Brush with Pearl Dust.

STEP 3 Use tip 3 and full-strength white icing to pipe in bow. Use tip 3 and full-strength white icing to attach Sugar Pearls to bow area in desired patterns with dots and lines. Let dry 1 to 2 hours.

CANDY-FILLED SNOWMAN FRIENDS

There must have been some magic in that fondant top hat, because this candy snowman hides a belly full of candy.

INGREDIENTS:

White Ready-To-Use Rolled Fondant (2 oz. per treat)

Icing Colors: Black, Violet*, Rose*, Leaf Green, Royal Blue

Cornstarch

White Candy Melts Candy

Assorted mini candies

White Pearl Dust

TOOLS:

12 in. Disposable Decorating Bags

Decorating Tips: 2A, 7, 8

9 in. Fondant Roller

Roll-N-Cut Mat

Brush Set

Parchment Paper

10 in. x 14 in. Cake Boards

4-Pc. Circles Nesting Metal Cutter Set

Cookie Sheet

Dessert Dome Mold

9 in. Angled Spatula

15 in. Parchment Triangles

Scissors

Knife

Plastic ruler

TECHNIQUES:

Candy/Pop Making Techniques (p. 230)

Tip Techniques (p. 204)

*Combine Violet with Rose for violet shown.

INSTRUCTIONS:

STEP 1 In advance, make hat. Tint fondant ½ oz. black and ¼ oz. violet.

Dust inside of tip 2A with cornstarch. Fill with black fondant. Remove. Trim off narrow end to leave 1 in. high hat.

Roll out black and violet fondant ⅛ in. thick. Cut hat base using wide end of tip 2A. Reserve excess fondant. Attach top to base using damp brush. Cut violet strip, 2 in. x ⅛ in. wide. Attach around hat with damp brush. Let dry on parchment paper-covered board 2 to 3 hours.

STEP 2 Also in advance, make candy base and snowman sections. Melt Candy Melts candy according to package directions. To make base, set second largest circle cutter on cookie sheet. Fill ¼ in. deep with melted candy. Tap to settle. Chill until firm 15 to 20 minutes.

Mold candy shell snowman sections using dessert dome mold and melted white candy. Make two of each size for each section. Chill until firm 15 to 20 minutes. Smooth edges if needed on a warm cookie sheet or warming tray. Fill bottom halves with assorted mini candies. Run top halves over warm surface to slightly melt candy. Attach halves and hold until set. Smooth seams. Position vertically. Slightly flatten top and bottom of large and medium globes and bottom only of small globe by running over warm surface. Let set 2 to 3 minutes.

STEP 3 Use spatula to spread melted candy "snow" over candy base. Immediately position largest globe. Hold until set. Attach next two globes with melted candy. Hold until set.

STEP 4 Use melted candy and a cut parchment bag to pipe dot (p. 206) nose. Brush snowman and snow with Pearl Dust. Tint fondant ¼ oz. green and ⅛ oz. blue. Roll out green, blue and reserved black ⅛ in. thick. Cut eyes using narrow end of tip 7. For smile, cut curve using tip 2A. Move down ⅛ in. and cut again. Trim to ⅝ in. long. Cut scarf, 5 in. x ¼ in. Cut buttons using narrow end of tip 8. Attach fondant trims using damp brush. Attach hat using melted candy.

Recipes

Yellow Cake

INGREDIENTS:

3 cups sifted cake flour

2½ teaspoons baking powder

½ teaspoon salt

⅔ cup (10⅓ tablespoons) butter, softened

1¾ cups granulated sugar

2 eggs

1½ teaspoons Wilton Pure Vanilla Extract

1¼ cups milk

INSTRUCTIONS:

STEP 1 Preheat oven to 350°F. Spray two 8 in. round pans with vegetable pan spray.

STEP 2 In medium bowl, stir together flour, baking powder and salt.

STEP 3 In large bowl, beat butter and sugar with electric mixer until light and fluffy. Add eggs and vanilla; mix well. Add flour mixture alternately with milk, beating well after each addition. Continue beating 1 minute. Pour into prepared pans.

STEP 4 Bake 30 to 35 minutes or until toothpick inserted into center comes out clean. Cool 10 minutes on cooling grid; remove from pans and cool completely.

MAKES: 5 cups batter.

Chocolate Cake

INGREDIENTS:

2½ cups all-purpose flour

1 teaspoon baking soda

½ teaspoon salt

6 ounces semi-sweet chocolate

¾ cup (1½ sticks) butter, softened

1½ cups granulated sugar

3 eggs

2 teaspoons Wilton Pure Vanilla Extract

1½ cups milk

INSTRUCTIONS:

STEP 1 Preheat oven to 350°F. Spray two 9 in. round pans with vegetable pan spray.

STEP 2 In medium bowl, stir together flour, baking soda and salt.

STEP 3 In large microwavable bowl, melt chocolate and butter on HIGH for 1 minute. Stir and continue to melt at 50% power until smooth. (Mixture can also be melted on stove top in heavy saucepan over low heat.) Transfer to large bowl; add sugar and beat with electric mixer until well blended. Add eggs, one at a time, and vanilla; mix well. Add flour mixture alternately with milk, beating until well blended after each addition. Pour into prepared pans.

STEP 4 Bake 28 to 32 minutes or until toothpick inserted into center comes out clean. Cool 10 minutes on cooling grid; remove from pans and cool completely.

MAKES: 5½ cups batter.

Classic White Cake

INGREDIENTS:

3 cups sifted cake flour

1 tablespoon baking powder

½ teaspoon salt

¾ cup (1½ sticks) butter, softened

1¾ cups granulated sugar

1 teaspoon Wilton Imitation Clear Vanilla Extract

1 cup milk

6 egg whites

INSTRUCTIONS:

STEP 1 Preheat oven to 350°F. Spray two 9 in. round pans with vegetable cooking spray.

STEP 2 In medium bowl, sift together flour, baking powder and salt.

STEP 3 In large bowl, beat butter and sugar with electric mixer until light and fluffy. Add vanilla; beat well. Add flour mixture to butter mixture alternately with milk, beating until well blended after each addition. In separate bowl, beat egg whites until stiff but not dry; gently fold into batter. Pour into prepared pans.

STEP 4 Bake 33 to 38 minutes or until toothpick inserted into center comes out clean. Cool 10 minutes on cooling grid; remove from pans and cool completely.

MAKES: 5½ cups batter.

For Cupcakes: Line muffin pan with baking cups. Fill cups two-thirds full with batter. Bake 17 to 19 minutes or until toothpick inserted into centers comes out clean. Cool cupcakes in pan on cooling grid 5 minutes. Remove from pan; cool completely.

MAKES: 5½ cups batter.

Lemon Pound Cake

INGREDIENTS:

2¾ cups all-purpose flour, plus additional for dusting pan

2 teaspoons baking powder

½ teaspoon salt

2 cups (4 sticks) butter, softened

2 cups granulated sugar

6 eggs

1 tablespoon Wilton Pure Lemon Extract

2 teaspoons grated lemon zest

1 teaspoon Wilton Pure Vanilla Extract

INSTRUCTIONS:

STEP 1 Preheat oven to 350°F. Prepare pan following pan instructions.

STEP 2 In medium bowl, combine flour, baking powder and salt.

STEP 3 In large bowl, beat butter and sugar with electric mixer until light and fluffy. Add eggs, one at a time, scraping bottom and sides of bowl often. Add lemon extract, lemon zest and vanilla; beat until combined. Add flour mixture and beat at low speed until flour is just combined. Pour batter into prepared pan.

STEP 4 Bake and cool cake according to pan instructions.

MAKES: 6½ cups batter.

Yellow Cupcakes

INGREDIENTS:

3 cups sifted cake flour

2½ teaspoons baking powder

½ teaspoon salt

⅔ cup (10⅓ tablespoons) butter, softened

1¾ cups granulated sugar

2 eggs

1½ teaspoons Wilton Pure Vanilla Extract

1¼ cups milk

INSTRUCTIONS:

STEP 1 Preheat oven to 350°F. Line muffin pan with baking cups.

STEP 2 In medium bowl, combine flour, baking powder and salt.

STEP 3 In large bowl, beat butter and sugar with electric mixer until light and fluffy. Add eggs and vanilla; mix well. Add flour mixture alternately with milk, beating well after each addition. Continue beating 1 minute. Fill baking cups two-thirds full with batter.

STEP 4 Bake 18 to 20 minutes or until toothpick inserted into centers comes out clean. Cool cupcakes in pan on cooling grid 5 minutes. Remove from pan; cool completely.

MAKES: 24 cupcakes.

Chocolate Cupcakes

INGREDIENTS:

1 box (about 16½ oz.) chocolate cake mix

1⅓ cups water

1 cup mayonnaise

3 eggs

⅓ cup unsweetened cocoa powder

INSTRUCTIONS:

STEP 1 Preheat oven to 350°F. Line muffin pan with baking cups.

STEP 2 In large bowl, combine cake mix, water, mayonnaise, eggs and cocoa powder. Beat with electric mixer at low speed 30 seconds, scraping bowl frequently. Beat at medium speed 2 minutes. Fill baking cups two-thirds full with batter.

STEP 3 Bake 18 to 20 minutes or until toothpick inserted into centers comes out clean. Cool cupcakes in pan on cooling grid 5 minutes. Remove from pan; cool completely.

MAKES: 24 cupcakes.

Cake Brownies

INGREDIENTS:

1½ cups cake flour

¾ teaspoon baking powder

¼ teaspoon salt

4 ounces unsweetened chocolate, coarsely chopped

¾ cup (1½ sticks) unsalted butter, softened

1½ cups granulated sugar

3 eggs

2 teaspoons Wilton Pure Vanilla Extract

INSTRUCTIONS:

STEP 1 Preheat oven to 350°F. Spray 8 in. x 2 in. or 9 in. x 2 in. square pan with vegetable pan spray.

STEP 2 In small bowl, combine flour, baking powder and salt.

STEP 3 In medium microwavable bowl, melt chocolate in microwave on high for 1 minute. Stir and continue to melt at 50% power for an additional 30 to 45 seconds until completely melted. Let cool slightly. In large bowl, beat butter and sugar with electric mixer until light and fluffy. Add eggs, vanilla and melted chocolate; mix well. Stir in flour mixture with wooden spoon until just combined. Spread batter into prepared pan.

STEP 4 Bake 30 to 35 minutes or until toothpick inserted into center comes out almost clean. Cool completely in pan on cooling grid before cutting.

MAKES: about 16 brownies.

Fudgy Brownies

INGREDIENTS:

1½ cups all-purpose flour

½ teaspoon baking soda

½ teaspoon salt

⅔ cup (10⅓ tablespoons) unsalted butter

1½ cups granulated sugar

¼ cup water

4 cups (24 oz.) semi-sweet chocolate chips, divided

2 teaspoons Wilton Pure Vanilla Extract

4 eggs

INSTRUCTIONS:

STEP 1 Preheat oven to 350°F. Spray 9 in. x 13 in. x 2 in. sheet pan with vegetable pan spray.

STEP 2 In medium bowl, combine flour, baking soda and salt.

STEP 3 In small saucepan, melt butter and sugar with water; stir until sugar is dissolved. Add 2 cups chocolate chips; stir until melted. Remove from heat. Stir in vanilla.

STEP 4 In large bowl, beat eggs with electric mixer. Add chocolate mixture; mix well. Add flour mixture; stir until just combined. Stir in remaining 2 cups chocolate chips. Spread batter in prepared pan.

STEP 5 Bake 25 to 30 minutes or until toothpick inserted into center comes out almost clean. Cool completely in pan on cooling grid before cutting.

MAKES: about 24 brownies.

Basic Cake Ball Pops

INGREDIENTS:

1 box (about 16½ oz.) cake mix

1 box (3.4 oz.) instant pudding and pie filling mix

4 eggs

1 cup water

⅓ cup vegetable oil

½ cup Wilton White Ready-To-Use Decorator Icing

1 package (12 oz.) Wilton Candy Melts Candy

Wilton Lollipop Sticks or Cookie Treat Sticks

INSTRUCTIONS:

STEP 1 Preheat oven to 350°F. Spray 9 in. x 13 in. x 2 in. sheet pan or two 8 in. or 9 in. round pans with vegetable pan spray.

STEP 2 In large bowl, combine cake mix, pudding mix, eggs, water and oil. Beat with electric mixer at medium speed 2 minutes. Pour into prepared pan.

STEP 3 Bake 35 to 40 minutes for sheet pan, 30 to 35 minutes for round pans, or until toothpick inserted into center comes out clean. Cool in pan 10 minutes. Remove from pan to cooling grid; cool completely. Divide cake in half; freeze one half for future use.

STEP 4 In large bowl, use hands to crumble cake until no large chunks remain. Add icing; mix with fingers until well combined. Form mixture into cake balls. Chill in refrigerator at least 2 hours. Melt Candy Melts candy according to package directions. Dip sticks into melted candy and insert into cake balls; let set. Wait until candy is completely firm before dipping the pops completely in melted candy.

MAKES:

For SMALL pops, 1 tablespoon makes a 1¼ in. dia. ball. One recipe makes 48 small cake balls.

For MEDIUM pops, 2 tablespoons make a 1½ in. dia. ball. One recipe makes 24 medium cake balls.

For LARGE pops, 3 tablespoons make a 1¾ in. dia. ball. One recipe makes 16 large cake balls.

Crisped Rice Cereal Treat

INGREDIENTS:

¼ cup (½ stick) butter or margarine

4 cups miniature marshmallows

6 cups crisped rice cereal

INSTRUCTIONS:

STEP 1 Spray 9 in. x 13 in. x 2 in. sheet pan and rubber spatula or wooden spoon with vegetable pan spray.

STEP 2 In large saucepan, melt butter; add marshmallows. Cook and stir until melted. Add cereal; mix well. Spread into prepared pan.

STEP 3 When cool to touch, cut into bars or shapes designated in specific projects.

MAKES: about 24 (2 in. x 2 in.) bars.

Buttercream Icing

This recipe makes medium consistency icing.

INGREDIENTS:

½ cup solid vegetable shortening

½ cup (1 stick) butter, softened

1 teaspoon Wilton Imitation Clear Vanilla Extract

4 cups sifted confectioners' sugar (about 1 lb.)

2 tablespoons milk

INSTRUCTIONS:

STEP 1 In large bowl, beat shortening and butter with electric mixer until creamy. Add vanilla. Gradually add sugar, 1 cup at a time, beating well at medium speed. Scrape sides and bottom of bowl often.

STEP 2 When all sugar has been mixed in, icing will appear dry. Add milk and beat at medium speed until light and fluffy.

STEP 3 Keep bowl covered with a damp cloth until ready to use. For best results, keep icing bowl in refrigerator when not in use. Refrigerated in an airtight container, this icing can be stored 2 weeks. Bring to room temperature and rewhip before using.

MAKES: about 2¼ cups.

For thin (spreading) consistency icing: Add 1 to 2 tablespoons light corn syrup, water or milk.

Chocolate Buttercream Icing: Add ¾ cup cocoa powder (or three 1 oz. squares unsweetened chocolate, melted) and an additional 1 to 2 tablespoons milk to buttercream icing. Mix until well blended.

Chocolate Mocha Icing: Substitute strong brewed coffee for milk in Chocolate Buttercream Icing.

Darker Chocolate Icing: Add an additional ¼ cup cocoa powder (or 1 additional 1 oz. square unsweetened chocolate, melted) and 1 additional tablespoon milk to Chocolate Buttercream Icing.

Royal Icing

INGREDIENTS:

4 cups sifted confectioners' sugar (about 1 lb.)

6 tablespoons water

3 tablespoons Wilton Meringue Powder

INSTRUCTIONS:

In large bowl, beat all ingredients with electric mixer at low speed 7 to 10 minutes (10 to 12 minutes at high speed for portable mixer) until icing forms peaks.

MAKES: about 2¾ cups.

For Thinned Royal Icing: To thin for pouring, add 1 teaspoon water per cup of royal icing. Use grease-free spoon or spatula to slowly stir in ½ teaspoon water at a time until you reach proper consistency.

Color Flow Icing

This recipe makes full-strength icing for outlining.

INGREDIENTS:

4 cups sifted confectioners' sugar (about 1 lb.)

¼ cup plus 1 teaspoon water

2 tablespoons Wilton Color Flow Mix

Wilton Icing Colors

INSTRUCTIONS:

In large bowl, beat all ingredients with electric mixer at low speed 5 minutes using grease-free utensils. If using hand mixer, use high speed. Stir in desired Wilton Icing Color. Color Flow icing "crusts" quickly, so keep bowl covered with a damp cloth while using.

MAKES: about 2 cups.

For Thinned Color Flow: To fill in an outlined area, the recipe above must be thinned with ½ teaspoon water per ¼ cup icing (add just a few drops at a time as you near proper consistency). Use grease-free spoon or spatula to stir slowly. Color Flow is ready for filling in outlines when a small amount dropped into the mixture takes a count of 10 to disappear.

Note: Color Flow designs take a long time to dry, so plan to do your Color Flow piece at least 48 to 72 hours in advance. Let outlines that will be filled in with the same color dry a few minutes. Let outlines that will be filled in with a different color dry 1 to 2 hours. Let thinned icing dry 48 hours.

Confectioners' Sugar Glaze Icing

INGREDIENTS:

3 tablespoons milk

1¼ cups confectioners' sugar

½ teaspoon Wilton Imitation Clear Vanilla Extract

INSTRUCTIONS:

In medium bowl, stir milk into sugar. Add vanilla. May be thickened with confectioners' sugar or thinned with milk or other flavored liquids.

MAKES: about ½ cup.

Quick-Pour Fondant Icing

INGREDIENTS:

6 cups sifted confectioners' sugar (about 1½ lbs.)

½ cup water

2 tablespoons light corn syrup

1 teaspoon Wilton Imitation Almond Extract

Wilton Icing Colors

INSTRUCTIONS:

STEP 1 Place sugar in saucepan. Combine water and corn syrup in small bowl. Add to sugar and stir until well mixed. Place over low heat. Don't allow temperature to exceed 100°F. Remove from heat; stir in extract and desired icing color.

STEP 2 To cover, place cake or cookies on cooling grid over a parchment paper-lined cookie sheet. Pour fondant into center and work towards edges. Touch up bare spots with spatula. Let set. Excess fondant can be reheated.

Note: Before covering with Quick-Pour Fondant Icing, cakes should be covered with a thin coating of buttercream icing. Let set 15 minutes before covering with fondant.

MAKES: about 2½ cups.

Roll-Out Cookies

INGREDIENTS:

2¾ cups all-purpose flour

1 teaspoon baking powder

1 teaspoon salt

1 cup (2 sticks) unsalted butter, softened

1½ cups granulated sugar

1 egg

1½ teaspoons Wilton Imitation Clear Vanilla Extract

½ teaspoon Wilton Imitation Almond Extract

INSTRUCTIONS:

STEP 1 Preheat oven to 350°F.

STEP 2 In medium bowl, combine flour, baking powder and salt. In large bowl, beat butter and sugar with electric mixer until light and fluffy. Beat in egg and extracts. Add flour mixture to butter mixture, 1 cup at a time, mixing after each addition. Do not chill dough. Divide dough into two balls.

STEP 3 On floured surface, roll each ball into a circle approximately 12 in. dia. and ⅛ in. thick. Dip cookie cutter in flour before each use.

STEP 4 Bake cookies on ungreased cookie sheet 8 to 11 minutes or until cookies are lightly browned. Remove cookies to cooling grid; cool completely.

MAKES: about 3 dozen 3 in. cookies.

Chocolate Roll-Out Cookies

INGREDIENTS:

2¾ cups all-purpose flour

1 teaspoon baking powder

1 teaspoon salt

1 cup (2 sticks) unsalted butter, softened

1½ cups granulated sugar

1 egg

1½ teaspoons Wilton Imitation Clear Vanilla Extract

3 squares (3 oz.) unsweetened chocolate, melted and cooled

INSTRUCTIONS:

STEP 1 Preheat oven to 350°F.

STEP 2 In medium bowl, combine flour, baking powder and salt. In large bowl, beat butter and sugar with electric mixer until light and fluffy. Beat in egg, vanilla and melted chocolate. Add flour mixture to butter mixture, 1 cup at a time, mixing after each addition. Do not chill dough. Divide dough into two balls.

STEP 3 On floured surface, roll each ball into a circle approximately 12 in. dia. and ⅛ in. thick. Dip cookie cutter in flour before each use.

STEP 4 Bake cookies on ungreased cookie sheet 8 to 11 minutes or until cookies are lightly browned. Remove cookies to cooling grid; cool completely.

MAKES: about 3 dozen 3 in. cookies.

Shortbread Cookies

INGREDIENTS:

1½ cups (3 sticks) butter, softened

1 cup granulated sugar

½ teaspoon salt

6 egg yolks

2 teaspoons Wilton Pure Vanilla Extract

4 cups all-purpose flour

INSTRUCTIONS:

STEP 1 In large bowl, beat butter, sugar and salt with electric mixer until light and fluffy. Add egg yolks, one at a time, mixing well after each addition. Add vanilla. Add flour; mix just until combined. Divide dough in half. Press dough to flatten; wrap with plastic wrap. Refrigerate at least 2 hours or overnight.

STEP 2 Preheat oven to 375°F.

STEP 3 Work with one dough disk at a time. Let chilled dough stand at room temperature 10 minutes. Lightly flour work surface and roll dough ⅛ in. to ¼ in. thick. Cut into desired shapes. Carefully transfer cookies to ungreased cookie sheet.

STEP 4 Bake 14 to 16 minutes or until edges are lightly browned. Remove cookies to cooling grid; cool completely.

MAKES: about 4 dozen 3 in. cookies.

Vanilla Sugar Cookies on a Stick

INGREDIENTS:

2¾ cups all-purpose flour

1 teaspoon salt

1 cup (2 sticks) unsalted butter, softened

1½ cups granulated sugar

1 egg

1½ teaspoons Wilton Imitation Clear Vanilla Extract

½ teaspoon Wilton Imitation Almond Extract

INSTRUCTIONS:

STEP 1 Preheat oven to 350°F. Lightly spray pan cavities with vegetable pan spray.

STEP 2 In medium bowl, combine flour and salt. In large bowl, beat butter and sugar with electric mixer at medium speed until well blended. Beat in egg and extracts; mix well. Add flour mixture to butter mixture. Beat until well blended. Press dough into cavities, filling half full. Position stick in pan. Press dough into pan cavities, filling three-fourths full.

STEP 3 Bake 10 to 12 minutes or until cookies are light brown around edges. Cool in pan 10 minutes. Remove cookies from pan. Cool completely on cooling grid.

MAKES: about 1 dozen 4 in. cookies.

Sugar Cookies for Pan-Shaped Cookies: Preheat oven to 350°F. Lightly spray pan or mold cavities with vegetable pan spray. Prepare dough as for Vanilla Sugar Cookies on a Stick. Press dough into prepared pan or mold, filling to ¼ in. deep. Bake 12 to 15 minutes or until light brown around edges. Cool in pan 10 minutes. Carefully remove cookies. Cool completely on cooling grid. Makes about 3 dozen cookies.

Classic Spritz Cookies

INGREDIENTS:

3½ cups all-purpose flour

1 teaspoon baking powder

1½ cups (3 sticks) butter, softened

1 cup granulated sugar

1 egg

2 tablespoons milk

1 teaspoon Wilton Imitation Clear Vanilla Extract

½ teaspoon Wilton Imitation Almond Extract

INSTRUCTIONS:

STEP 1 Preheat oven to 350°F.

STEP 2 In medium bowl, combine flour and baking powder.

STEP 3 In large bowl, beat butter and sugar with electric mixer until light and fluffy. Add egg, milk and extracts; mix well. Gradually add flour mixture to butter mixture, mixing to make a smooth dough. Do not chill. Place dough into cookie press and press cookies onto ungreased cookie sheet.

STEP 4 Bake 10 to 12 minutes or until lightly browned around edges. Remove cookies from cookie sheet; cool completely on cooling grid.

MAKES: 7 to 8 dozen cookies.

Chocolate Ganache

INGREDIENTS:

1 package (12 oz.) Wilton Dark or Light Cocoa Candy Melts Candy

⅓ cup heavy whipping cream

INSTRUCTIONS:

Chop candy (you can use food processor). Heat whipping cream in saucepan just to boiling point. Do not boil. Remove from heat and add chopped candy. Stir until smooth and glossy.

MAKES: about 1¾ cups.

For Whipped Ganache: Follow recipe directions using ⅔ cup whipping cream. Allow mixture to set and cool to room temperature (mixture will have the consistency of pudding, this may take 1 to 2 hours). Whip on high speed with an electric mixer until light and soft peaks form. Refrigerate until ready to serve.

Basic Truffle Candy Center

INGREDIENTS:

1 package (12 oz.) Wilton White Candy Melts Candy, coarsely chopped

⅓ cup heavy whipping cream

INSTRUCTIONS:

STEP 1 In medium microwavable bowl, combine candy with cream. Heat at 50% power or defrost setting 1 minute. Stir thoroughly. Continue to microwave and stir at 30-second intervals until smooth and completely melted. Let stand 15 minutes. Pour into shallow pan. Refrigerate 1 to 2 hours or until firm but pliable.

STEP 2 Roll into 1 in. dia. balls. Dip into additional melted candy.

MAKES: 2 dozen (1 in.) balls.

Note: For stove top preparation, combine candy with cream in saucepan or double boiler. Heat over low heat, stirring constantly, until candy is melted.

Creamy Gelatin

INGREDIENTS:

1 package (3 oz.) favorite flavor gelatin mix

1 cup hot water

½ cup cold water

½ cup frozen non-dairy whipped topping, thawed

INSTRUCTIONS:

STEP 1 In large bowl, prepare gelatin mix following package directions, using 1 cup hot water and ½ cup cold water. Chill until slightly thickened.

STEP 2 Gently fold whipped topping into gelatin until combined. Pipe or spoon mixture into serving glasses following project instructions. Chill at least 3 hours.

Candy Clay

INGREDIENTS:

1 package (12 oz.) Wilton Candy Melts Candy

¼ cup light corn syrup

INSTRUCTIONS:

Melt Candy Melts candy following package directions. Add corn syrup and stir to blend. Turn out mixture onto parchment paper and let set at room temperature to dry. Wrap well and store at room temperature until needed. Candy clay handles best if hardened overnight.

To Use: Candy clay will be very hard at the start; knead a small portion at a time until workable. If candy clay gets too soft, set aside at room temperature or refrigerate briefly. When rolling out candy clay, sprinkle work surface with cornstarch or cocoa powder (for cocoa clay) to prevent sticking. Roll to approximately ¼ in. thick.

To Tint: White candy clay may be tinted using Wilton Candy Color or Icing Color. Knead in color until well blended.

To Store: Prepared candy clay will last for several weeks at room temperature in an airtight container.

Thinned Fondant Adhesive

INGREDIENTS:

1 oz. Wilton White Ready-To-Use Rolled Fondant (1½ in. dia. ball)

¼ teaspoon water

INSTRUCTIONS:

Knead water into fondant until it becomes soft and sticky. To attach a fondant decoration, place mixture in decorating bag fitted with a small round tip, or brush on back of decoration. Recipe may be doubled.

Gum Glue Adhesive

INGREDIENTS:

¼ teaspoon Wilton Gum Paste

1 tablespoon water

INSTRUCTIONS:

Break gum paste into very small pieces. Dissolve pieces in water. Let rest about 1 hour. Mixture will be ready to use even if some pieces have not dissolved. To use, just brush it on to your decorations. Store unused portions covered in the refrigerator for up to 1 week.

Techniques

● ●

CAKE PREPARATION

The best cakes for decorating have a light, golden brown surface. Here is how to bake, level, torte and ice consistently great cakes.

BAKING A CAKE

PREPARE THE PAN

Use Bake Easy! non-stick spray or Cake Release pan coating and a pastry brush—no flour needed. Or, use solid vegetable shortening and flour.

To bake a cake without forming a crown, use Wilton Bake-Even Strips. Just saturate with water, run fingers down strips to remove excess moisture and wrap around the sides of your pan. See wilton.com for more information.

MIX THE BATTER

Preheat your oven to temperature specified in recipe for 10 to 15 minutes.

Measure ingredients before you begin.

For liquids, measure at eye level in clear standard liquid measuring cups. For dry ingredients, spoon into measuring cups for dry ingredients and level off. Avoid packing in cup.

Scrape the sides and bottom of the bowl for even mixing.

FILL THE PAN

Fill prepared pan half to ⅔ full.

Bake immediately after mixing as near to the center of the oven as possible.

Allow at least 1 in. of space on all sides and between pans if baking more than one cake.

Avoid opening the oven door during the first 20 minutes of baking.

TEST FOR DONENESS

To test, insert the Wilton Cake Tester or toothpick near the center of the cake. The cake is done if the cake tester comes out clean.

Remove cake from oven and cool in pan for 10 minutes on a cooling grid unless specified otherwise in recipe instructions.

REMOVE CAKE FROM PAN

Place parchment paper over the cake.

Place a second cooling grid on top of the cake and invert the cake while sandwiched between the two grids.

Remove top grid and cake pan. Cool completely on remaining grid. The paper prevents the grid from breaking the crust or leaving imprints.

● ●

USING CAKE BOARDS

You'll want your cake board to be 2 in. larger than your cake to allow room for borders, unless specified otherwise in project instructions. For example, for an 8 in. round cake, use a 10 in. cake circle.

ROUND CAKES

Simply use a Wilton Cake Circle sized 2 in. larger than your cake.

SHAPED CAKES

Use a Wilton Cake Board and cut to fit. Turn the pan upside down and trace outline onto board. Cut board with a craft knife, leaving ¼ in. extra around outline. Since shaped pans have an extra rim around the edge, your board will already be sized to allow room for borders.

SHEET AND SQUARE CAKES

Either use a Wilton Cake Board as is or cut the board to fit using a craft knife.

WRAPPING A CAKE BOARD

Trace your board onto Fanci-Foil Wrap. For a shaped cake, place board face down on underside of Fanci-Foil Wrap and make the outline 3 in. to 4 in. larger than the board. For round, square and sheet cakes, make the outline about 2 in. larger than the board. Cut Fanci-Foil Wrap along the outline.

Place board, white side down, on top of cut foil. Cut deep slits at several points along foil edge, creating tabs of foil to wrap neatly around the board. Tape tabs to back of board. To hold cake in place, spread a thin layer of icing on wrapped board before positioning cake.

LEVELING AND TORTING A CAKE

After cooling the cake and before decorating, you'll need to level the top. You might also want to cut the cake into layers to add a tasty filling. This is called torting. Either task can be done using a Wilton Cake Leveler or a serrated knife.

USING A CAKE LEVELER

Position ends of the cutting wire (or feet on ULTIMATE Cake Leveler, not pictured) into the notches at desired height.

For leveling, with legs standing on the work surface, cut into the crusted edge using an easy sawing motion, then gently glide wire or blade through the cake. For torting, reposition the height of your leveler as needed. For 2 in. high cakes, you can divide in half for two equal layers.

USING A SERRATED KNIFE

For leveling, place the cake on a cake board, then place on a Trim-N-Turn Plus Cake Turntable. While slowly rotating the turntable, move knife back and forth across the top to remove the crown. Keep knife level.

For torting, divide cake sides and mark equal horizontal points with dots of icing or toothpicks all around. Place cake on board and then on cake turntable. While slowly rotating the turntable, move knife back and forth to cut the cake along the measured marks. Repeat for each additional layer.

SEPARATING TORTED LAYERS

To separate the torted layers, carefully slide the top layer onto a cake board to keep it rigid and safe from breakage. Repeat for each additional layer.

FILLING A TORTED CAKE

Use a large round tip, like tip 12, with your decorating bag, or simply use the coupler without a tip. Fill the bag with medium consistency buttercream icing.

Start with the bottom layer, torted side up. Pipe a dam of icing just inside the edge of the cake (about ¾ in. high and ¼ in. from the outside edge). Fill with icing, preserves or pudding.

Place next layer on top and repeat. Finish with top layer, torted side down.

• •

ICING A CAKE

For the best-looking iced cakes, you need to keep crumbs out of the icing. Follow these guidelines to make it easy:

- Thin your icing with 1 to 2 tablespoons of light corn syrup, water or milk for easier spreading.

- Never allow the spatula to touch the cake surface or to pull icing from the cake surface.

- Try "crumb coating": Lightly ice the cake first, allow a light crust to form, then add a top icing cover.

- Try the Wilton Icing Smoother. It's sized specifically for standard cake heights to easily smooth icing with comfort and control.

USING A SPATULA

Place the cake on its cake board on a decorating turntable. Place a large amount of thin consistency icing on the center of the cake.

Spread icing across the top, pushing toward edges.

Cover cake sides with icing. Smooth sides by holding the spatula upright with the edge against the icing, slowly spinning the turntable without lifting the spatula from the icing's surface. Return excess icing to the bowl and repeat until sides are smooth.

Smooth cake top last using the edge of the spatula. Sweep the spatula edge from the rim of the cake to its center. Lift off and remove excess icing. Rotate the cake slightly and repeat the procedure, starting from a new point on the rim until you have covered the entire top.

MORE HINTS

- For easier smoothing, dip spatula in hot water, wipe dry and glide across entire surface.

- Set the cake aside and let icing crust over for at least 15 minutes before decorating. When crusted, place parchment paper on the cake top and gently smooth with the palm of your hand.

USING TIP 789

This extra-wide tip works fast—especially on cake sides!

Trim a 16 in. Featherweight bag to fit tip 789. Fill bag halfway with icing. Place the cake on its cake board on a decorating turntable. Hold bag at a 45° angle and lightly press tip against cake. Squeeze a ribbon of icing in a continuous spiral motion to cover cake top, with the last ribbon forcing icing over edge.

To ice the sides, squeeze icing as you turn the cake slowly. Repeat until the entire cake side is covered.

Smooth sides and top with spatula (see Using a Spatula p. 191).

CAKE BAKING AND SERVING GUIDES

The following guides are based on baking recommendations from the Wilton Test Kitchen. Your results may vary depending on oven performance or altitude in your area. Always check for doneness at the shortest bake time listed.

For any pans 3 in. deep and 12 in. dia. or larger, we recommend using a Wilton Heating Core to ensure even baking. Use two cores for 18 in. pans. Baking times in these charts are based on heating core use.

Serving amounts are based on party-size portions of 1½ in. x 2 in. or smaller wedding-size portions of approximately 1 in. x 2 in. Cakes from 3 in. to 6 in. high, baked in the same size pan, would yield the same number of servings because they follow the same pattern of cutting. Cakes shorter than 3 in. would yield half the number of servings indicated for that pan. Number of servings are intended as a guide only.

Icing amounts are very general and will vary with consistency, thickness applied and tips used. Icing amounts allow for top and bottom borders.

• •

4 IN. HIGH CAKES

The figures for 4 in. high cakes are based on using 2 in. deep pans to make a 2-layer, 4 in. high cake. Fill pans half to ⅔ full.

Square

Size	Number of Servings (Party)	Number of Servings (Wedding)	Cups Batter (1 Layer, 2 in.)	Baking Temp. (F)	Baking Time (Minutes)	Approx. Cups Icing to ice and decorate cake
6 in.	12	18	3	350°	40-45	3½
8 in.	20	32	6	350°	45-50	4½
10 in.	30	50	9	350°	50-55	6
12 in.	48	72	11½	325°	55-60	7½
14 in.	63	98	16	325°	55-60	9
16 in.	80	128	22	325°	60-70	11½

Round

Size	Number of Servings (Party)	Number of Servings (Wedding)	Cups Batter (1 Layer, 2 in.)	Baking Temp. (F)	Baking Time (Minutes)	Approx. Cups Icing to ice and decorate cake
4 in.	8	8	¾	350°	22-26	1½
6 in.	12	12	2¼	350°	35-40	2½
8 in.	20	24	4	350°	37-42	3½
9 in.	24	32	5	350°	40-45	4
10 in.	28	38	6	350°	40-45	5
12 in.	40	56	8	350°	45-50	6
14 in.	63	78	11½	325°	50-55	8½
16 in.	77	100	16	325°	55-60	9½

Heart

Size	Number of Servings (Party)	Number of Servings (Wedding)	Cups Batter (1 Layer, 2 in.)	Baking Temp. (F)	Baking Time (Minutes)	Approx. Cups Icing to ice and decorate cake
6 in.	8	14	2	350°	30-35	3
8 in.	18	22	4	350°	40-45	4
9 in.	20	28	4¼	350°	40-45	5½
10 in.	24	38	6½	350°	45-50	7
12 in.	34	56	9¼	325°	55-60	8½
14 in.	48	72	13½	325°	55-60	9½
16 in.	64	94	17	325°	60-65	13

Hexagon

Size	Number of Servings (Party)	Number of Servings (Wedding)	Cups Batter (1 Layer, 2 in.)	Baking Temp. (F)	Baking Time (Minutes)	Approx. Cups Icing to ice and decorate cake
6 in.	10	12	2	350°	35-40	2½
9 in.	20	26	4½	350°	40-45	4
12 in.	34	40	8	350°	50-55	5½
15 in.	48	70	14	350°	55-60	7

Petal

Size	Number of Servings (Party)	Number of Servings (Wedding)	Cups Batter (1 Layer, 2 in.)	Baking Temp. (F)	Baking Time (Minutes)	Approx. Cups Icing to ice and decorate cake
6 in.	6	8	1½	350°	30-35	3
9 in.	14	18	3¾	350°	35-40	4½
12 in.	38	40	7¼	350°	45-50	6
15 in.	48	64	10⅔	325°	55-60	8

Oval

Size	Number of Servings (Party)	Number of Servings (Wedding)	Cups Batter (1 Layer, 2 in.)	Baking Temp. (F)	Baking Time (Minutes)	Approx. Cups Icing to ice and decorate cake
7.75 in. x 5.5 in.	9	13	2¾	350°	30-35	2½
10.75 in. x 7.8 in.	20	26	5	350°	40-44	4
13.5 in. x 9.8 in.	30	45	8¼	325°	50-55	5½
16.5 in. x 12.4 in.	44	70	13¼	325°	50-55	7½

Paisley

Size	Number of Servings (Party)	Number of Servings (Wedding)	Cups Batter (1 Layer, 2 in.)	Baking Temp. (F)	Baking Time (Minutes)	Approx. Cups Icing to ice and decorate cake
9 in. x 6 in.	9	13	2¾	350°	35-40	4½
12.5 in. x 9.5 in.	28	38	7	350°	45-50	7
16.5 in. x 12.5 in.	40	56	10½	325°	55-60	9

Sheet

Size	Number of Servings (Party)	Number of Servings (Wedding)	Cups Batter (1 Layer, 2 in.)	Baking Temp. (F)	Baking Time (Minutes)	Approx. Cups Icing to ice and decorate cake
7 in. x 11 in.	24	32	5½	350°	40-45	5
9 in. x 13 in.	36	50	10	350°	45-50	7
11 in. x 15 in.	54	74	11½	325°	50-55	9
12 in. x 18 in.	72	98	16	325°	55-60	11

Diamond

Size	Number of Servings (Party)	Number of Servings (Wedding)	Cups Batter (1 Layer, 2 in.)	Baking Temp. (F)	Baking Time (Minutes)	Approx. Cups Icing to ice and decorate cake
10.25 in. x 7.4 in.	12	18	3	350°	30-35	3
15 in. x 11 in.	20	32	6	350°	45-50	6
19.25 in. x 14.25 in.	42	66	11	325°	55-60	9½

Pillow

Size	Number of Servings (Party)	Number of Servings (Wedding)	Cups Batter (1 Layer, 2 in.)	Baking Temp. (F)	Baking Time (Minutes)	Approx. Cups Icing to ice and decorate cake
6.75 in. x 6.75 in.	13	19	2½	350°	33-38	3
10 in. x 10 in.	30	40	5½	350°	39-44	6½
13.25 in. x 13.25 in.	64	72	10	350°	41-46	9½

• •

3 IN. HIGH CAKES

The figures for 3 in. high cakes are based on using a 3 in. deep pan to make a 1-layer cake that is torted and filled to reach 3 in. high. Fill pans half full.

For any pans 3 in. deep and 12 in. dia. or larger, we recommend using a heating core to ensure even baking. Use two cores for 18 in. pans. For additional pan information, visit wilton.com.

Round

Size	Number of Servings (Party)	Number of Servings (Wedding)	Cups Batter (1 Layer)	Baking Temp. (F)	Baking Time (Minutes)	Approx. Cups Icing to ice and decorate cake
6 in.	12	12	3	350°	45-50	3½
8 in.	20	24	5	350°	55-60	4
10 in.	28	38	8	350°	55-60	4½
12 in.	40	56	10	350°	55-60	5¼
14 in.	63	78	15	325°	70-75	6¼
16 in.	77	100	18	325°	70-75	7
18 in. Half, 3 in. layer	110*	146*	12**	325°	60-65	7½

*Two half rounds.
**For each half round pan.

Contour

Size	Number of Servings (Party)	Number of Servings (Wedding)	Cups Batter (1 Layer)	Baking Temp. (F)	Baking Time (Minutes)	Approx. Cups Icing to ice and decorate cake
9 in.	11	17	5¾	350°	55-60	3

ICING INDEX

Different icings have different qualities, which make them best for certain types of decorating tasks. Here's a rundown of the five main types of icing used in most Wilton decorating projects.

BUTTERCREAM ICINGS

Tasks: Icing cakes smooth, piping borders, writing, flowers, etc.

Qualities: Softer and more spreadable than most icings. The traditional choice for flavor and versatility.

Types:

• Homemade—See Buttercream recipe (p. 181).

• Wilton Ready-To-Use Decorator Icing—Available in white or chocolate.

• Wilton Creamy White Buttercream Icing Mix—Same taste and texture as homemade.

Special Information:

• Buttercream flowers are soft enough to be cut with a knife.

• Wedding white buttercream flowers have a translucent look when air-dried.

• All buttercream icings taste and look great for most decorating.

Consistency: All buttercream icings can be adjusted to the consistency you want. Our buttercream recipes are thin-to-stiff depending on the amount of corn syrup or sugar added (sugar stiffens). Wilton Ready-To-Use Icing in 1 lb. cans is stiff. You can make roses right from the can (thin with corn syrup if desired). Our 4.5 lb. tub is thin-to-medium consistency so you can spread on a cake without thinning.

Coloring: Buttercream icings (except chocolate) yield all colors. Wedding white and white ready-to-use icings may yield truer colors due to their pure white base color. Most colors deepen upon setting. Chocolate buttercream is recommended when black or brown icing is needed.

Storage: Buttercream can be refrigerated in an airtight container for two weeks. Before using, bring icing to room temperature and stir with a spatula. Iced cakes store at room temperature for two to three days.

ROYAL ICING

Tasks: Flower making, figure piping, making flowers on wires. Great for decorating cookies and gingerbread houses.

Qualities: Dries candy-hard for lasting decorations. Great for making decorations ahead of time.

Types:

• Homemade—Made with Wilton Meringue Powder.

• Wilton Ready-To-Use Royal Icing Mix—so convenient; just add water.

Special Information:

• Bowls and utensils must be kept grease-free to maintain stability.

• Cover icing with damp cloth to prevent crusting.

Consistency: Thin-to-stiff, depending on the amount of water added. Thinned royal icing may be used for covering cookies or filling in outlined areas.

Coloring: Yields deep colors. Some colors may fade in bright light. Requires more icing color than buttercream to achieve the same intensity.

Storage: Store at room temperature in an airtight container for two weeks.

ROLLED FONDANT

Tasks: Cover cakes with a perfectly smooth surface. Ideal for creating hand-shaped decorations, stand-up bows, molded borders and more.

Qualities: Flexible, easy-to-shape. Like edible clay for your cake! Light, delicate vanilla or chocolate flavor.

Types:

• Wilton Ready-To-Use Rolled Fondant. Available in white or chocolate, plus a variety of colors.

Special Information:

- When covering cakes with fondant, lightly cover surface with apricot glaze or buttercream icing to seal in moisture.

- Heighten the flavor by kneading in your favorite extract.

Consistency: Dough-like. Roll out before applying to cake or cutting decorations.

Coloring: White produces pastels to deep colors. Wilton pre-colored fondant is available in many shades.

Storage: Excess fondant can be stored two months in an airtight container wrapped in plastic wrap. Do not refrigerate or freeze. Iced cakes store at room temperature for three to four days.

GUM PASTE

Tasks: Making detailed flowers with very thin petals.

Qualities: Can be rolled out very thin yet hold its shape. Dries hard. Gum paste flowers, trims and accents are meant for decoration only.

Types:

- Homemade—Use Wilton Gum-Tex and Glucose.
- Wilton Ready-To-Use Gum Paste.

Special Information:

- Gum paste picks up dust and lint very easily. Be sure your hands and work surfaces are very clean before handling.

- Shortening helps keep gum paste pliable. Before kneading, rub a thin coat of vegetable shortening on your hands and work surface to avoid sticking.

Consistency: Dough-like. Roll out before cutting decorations.

Coloring: White produces pastels to deep colors.

Storage: Gum paste dries out quickly. Keep wrapped in plastic wrap and stored in a plastic bag. Keeps up to two weeks at room temperature. If storing longer, cover with a thin coating of vegetable shortening, wrap tightly with plastic wrap, place in a plastic bag in a covered container and refrigerate.

COLOR FLOW ICING

Tasks: Create detailed icing decorations which can be placed on cakes and cookies.

Qualities: Dries hard with a shiny finish. You can "draw" almost any design by outlining pattern areas with full-strength Color Flow, then filling in with thinned Color Flow.

Type:

- Homemade—Use Wilton Color Flow Mix.

Special Information:

- Moist icings break down Color Flow decorations. Position Color Flow decorations on your cake shortly before serving or place on sugar cubes.

- Color Flow designs take a long time to dry. Allow at least 48 or 72 hours in advance when making decorations.

- Bowls and utensils must be kept grease-free to maintain texture.

- Cover icing with damp cloth to prevent crusting.

Consistency: Thin or full-strength.

Coloring: Produces pastels to deep colors.

Storage: Store at room temperature in an airtight container for two weeks.

COLORING BUTTERCREAM OR ROYAL ICING

You can create virtually any color using Wilton Icing Colors. The concentrated colors won't affect your icing consistency. To get consistent color in the shade you want, keep the hints below in mind.

- Begin with white icing. For dark brown or black buttercream icing, begin with chocolate buttercream icing to reduce the amount of color needed. For large areas of red, use No-Taste Red.

- Icing colors intensify in buttercream about 1 to 2 hours after mixing. Royal icing requires more color than buttercream to achieve the same intensity.

- To maintain color consistency, always mix enough of each icing color to complete your cake, including flowers and borders. It can be difficult to duplicate the exact shade of any color.

Visit wilton.com for more hints, a color mixing chart and bag striping effects.

TO COLOR

Dip a toothpick into the color, then swirl it into the icing.

Add color a little at a time until you achieve the shade you desire.

Always use a new toothpick each time you add color. Avoid getting icing in your jar of color. Blend icing well with a spatula.

It's easy to create a wide variety of skin tones using various Wilton Icing Colors. If you wish to reach a shade lighter or darker than what is indicated, add slightly less or more of the icing color. Color listings for projects in this book reflect skin tone shown; feel free to choose your own shade.

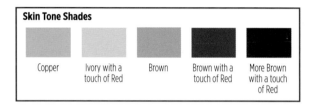

Skin Tone Shades | Copper | Ivory with a touch of Red | Brown | Brown with a touch of Red | More Brown with a touch of Red

USING DECORATING BAGS

The decorating bag is the container that holds the icing and tip together so that you can create amazing decorations. There are three types of bags to choose from:

- Wilton Featherweight Bags are strong and reusable, and made of a flexible coated polyester.

- Wilton Disposable Decorating Bags are made of strong, flexible plastic that can be discarded after each use.

- Wilton Parchment Bags are made from parchment triangles. These disposable bags are used for smaller amounts of icing, flowing in Color Flow icing, and melting and piping Candy Melts candy.

PREPARING A FEATHERWEIGHT BAG TO USE WITHOUT A COUPLER

- Just drop the tip inside the bag with the narrow end pointing down. When using some larger tips, the bag might need to be trimmed. Simply drop the tip into the bag and trim accordingly so that the tip opening is clear.

PREPARING A DISPOSABLE DECORATING BAG TO USE WITHOUT A COUPLER

- Cut ¾ in. off the tip of the bag. Drop the decorating tip into the bag and position to expose ½ in. of the decorating tip. If necessary, trim the bag, bit by bit, until the tip fits correctly.

PREPARING A FEATHERWEIGHT BAG TO USE WITH A COUPLER

1. Remove ring from coupler base. Drop the coupler base, narrow end first, into the bag and push it down as far as it will go.

2. Use a pen or pencil to mark the outside of the bag above the top screw thread (closest to tip).

3. Push the coupler base up into the bag so that you can cut an opening at the mark.

4. Push the coupler down through the opening. One thread should be showing. Place a decorating tip over the part of the coupler base extending from the bag.

5. Put the ring over the tip and twist it on, locking the tip in place.

PREPARING A DISPOSABLE DECORATING BAG TO USE WITH A COUPLER

1. Remove ring from coupler base. Drop the coupler base, narrow end first, into the bag and push it down as far as it will go.

2. Use a pair of scissors to score the bag half way down the smooth part of the coupler base.

3. Pull off the point of bag. Place the decorating tip over the base extending from the bag.

4. Put the ring over the tip and twist it on, locking the tip in place.

- -

FILLING A DECORATING BAG

1. Hold bag with one hand and fold down the top with the other hand to form a generous cuff over your hand. Or, use the Wilton Decorating Bag Sleeve, which makes it easy to fill the bag without holding it.

2. Fill bag about half full with icing. Do not overfill the bag! Icing may squeeze out from the top.

3. Remove icing from the spatula by squeezing the bag with your thumb and fingers against the spatula and pulling the spatula out.

4. Close bag by unfolding the cuff and twisting the bag closed. This forces the icing down into the bag.

5. Use a Wilton Icing Bag Tie to secure the bag and ensure that the icing does not squeeze out of the top.

6. Place the twisted part of the bag between your thumb and forefinger. Close your hand around the bag so that you can squeeze the icing in the bag between your palm and fingers.

MAKING A PARCHMENT BAG

 1. Place parchment triangle on a flat surface with short point facing you.

 2. Curl right side point up and under, bringing it toward you until it meets the center point.

3. The curled edge of the right side point should lie on top of the center point.

 4. Hold both points with your left hand, picking up left side point with your right hand.

5. Wrap left point around to meet the other points in back.

6. All three points align to form one sharp point, which forms the bag's cone.

7. Hold bag with both hands, thumbs inside.

 8. Slide inside and outside points in opposite direction to make an upside down "W" as shown.

 9. Fold points of bag down into bag.

 10. Tear two notches along folded edge and fold notch down.

 11. Tape seam if desired.

FILLING AND CLOSING A PARCHMENT BAG

 1. Hold the bag near the bottom and fill the bag only half full with an angled spatula using about 3 tablespoons of icing at a time.

 2. Remove icing from the spatula by squeezing the bag with your thumb and fingers against the spatula and pulling the spatula out.

 3. Close the bag by first squashing the top of the bag flat above the icing.

 4. Fold in left side, then right side, then the top. Hold the bag just above the fold to prevent icing from coming out of the top of the bag.

TO USE WITH A COUPLER

 1. Drop coupler base, narrow end first, into bag and push it down as far as you can.

2. Hold coupler and bag together in place with one hand and twist on the ring.

3. When secure, tear away tip of parchment bag.

 4. Add tip. Replace ring and twist, locking tip in place.

TO USE WITH A DECORATING TIP AND WITHOUT A COUPLER

1. Cut ¾ in. off end of bag.

2. Drop tip in, narrow end first.

3. Don't be concerned if tip doesn't fit snugly. The icing will hold it in place.

- -

THREE ESSENTIALS OF CAKE DECORATING

Every decoration you make is the result of three things working together: the consistency of your icing, the position of the bag (how you are holding it), and the amount and type of pressure you apply to the bag.

- -

ICING CONSISTENCY

The icing consistency you want depends on what type of decorations you are doing. Just a few drops of liquid in your icing can make a big difference in your decorating results. Many factors can affect your icing consistency, such as humidity, temperature, ingredients and equipment.

For buttercream icing, as a general guideline, if you feel your icing is too thin, add a little more confectioners' sugar. If you feel your icing is too thick, add a little more liquid as directed below. For royal icing, if adding more than ½ cup confectioners' sugar to thicken icing, add 1 to 2 more teaspoons of meringue powder.

OPTION 1: STIFF ICING

Used for decorations, such as flowers with upright petals, like the rose.

Use this test to check the consistency:

- Place 1 cup of icing in a 9 oz. cup, 3¾ in. tall and about 2¾ in. dia.

- Insert a 9 in. straight spatula all the way into the center of the icing and jiggle the cup.

- When the icing is stiff consistency, the spatula will not move.

OPTION 2: MEDIUM ICING

Used to create stars, dimensional decorating, borders and flowers with petals that lie flat.

To convert stiff consistency to medium consistency, add 1 teaspoon of water for each cup of stiff consistency icing (2½ teaspoons of water for the full recipe). Mix until well blended.

- Use the same test as for stiff consistency.

- When the icing is medium consistency, the spatula will move slightly and start to lean when you jiggle the cup.

OPTION 3: THIN ICING

Used for writing and printing, leaves and icing a cake.

To convert stiff consistency to thin consistency, add 2 teaspoons of water for each cup of stiff consistency icing (5 teaspoons of water for the full recipe). Mix until well blended.

- Use the same test as for stiff consistency.

- When the icing is thin consistency, the spatula will fall over when you jiggle the cup.

When making thin consistency icing for writing and printing, add ½ teaspoon of piping gel per cup of thin consistency icing. It will add stretch to the icing to make writing and printing easier.

● ●

BAG POSITION (HOLDING THE BAG)

The way your decorations curl, point and lie depends on the way you hold and move the bag. Bag position is described in terms of both angle and direction.

ANGLE

Angle refers to the position of the bag relative to the work surface. There are two basic angles.

Right-Handed   **Left-Handed**

90° angle is straight up, perpendicular to the work surface. It is used when making stars or drop flowers.

Right-Handed   **Left-Handed**

45° angle is halfway between vertical and horizontal. It is used for writing, borders and many flowers.

BAG DIRECTION

The angle of the bag to the work surface, when holding it at 45°, is only half the story of bag position. The other half is the direction in which the back of the bag is pointed.

Correct bag position is easiest to learn when you think of the back of the bag as the hour hand of a clock. When you hold the bag with the tip in the center of the clock, you can sweep out a circle with the back end of the bag. Pretend the circle you formed in the air is a clock face. The hours on the clock face correspond to the direction you point the back end of the bag.

Right-Handed

3:00   4:30   6:00

Left-Handed

9:00   7:30   6:00

Tip techniques in this chapter will list the correct direction for holding the bag. When the bag direction differs for left-handed decorators, that direction will be listed in parentheses. (Example: When right-handers hold bag at 3:00, left-handers hold bag at 9:00.)

Right-handed decorators always decorate from left to right. Left-handed decorators always decorate from right to left, except for writing.

Most decorating tip openings are the same shape all the way around—so there is no right side or wrong side up when squeezing the bag. For tips such as petal, ruffle, basketweave and leaf, which have irregularly shaped openings, you must watch tip position as well as bag position.

PRESSURE CONTROL (SQUEEZING THE BAG)

The size and uniformity of your decorations depends on the amount of pressure you apply to the bag and the steadiness of the pressure. Learn to apply pressure so consistently that you can move the bag in a free and easy glide while just the right amount of icing flows through the tip.

Light Pressure

Medium Pressure

Heavy Pressure

USING A FLOWER NAIL

The flower nail is a revolving platform you hold in your hand to conveniently build roses and other flowers. It allows you to work close up, to turn for easy piping and to remove your completed flowers to dry without damage.

The key to making a flower on the flower nail is to coordinate the turning of the flower nail with the formation of each petal.

Attach a square of parchment paper or a pre-cut flower square on the flat surface of the flower nail using a dot of icing. Pipe your flower directly on the parchment paper. Hold the flower nail between the thumb and forefinger of your left (right) hand (use other fingers to support flower nail) and roll it slowly counterclockwise (clockwise for lefties) as you press out icing with the decorating bag held in the right (left) hand. Your right (left) hand moves in and out, or up and down, as it holds the decorating bag and tip at just the right angle (in most cases 45°) and keeps the icing flowing at an even speed. After piping, slide the paper square with flower off the nail to dry flat or on flower formers.

TRANSFERRING PATTERNS TO CAKES

Add fun accents to your cakes using patterns. You can apply your patterns either using piping gel or a toothpick. We recommend using the toothpick method for fine detail.

USING PIPING GEL

1. Make a copy of pattern. Turn copy over and trace pattern on back to create a reverse pattern. Tape pattern reverse side up on flat surface.

2. Cover pattern with parchment paper and outline with piping gel.*

*Shown using blue tinted gel for clarity.

3. Carefully lay outlined pattern, gel side down, on iced cake that has crusted. Using a decorator brush, gently trace over gel lines.

4. To remove, lift pattern straight up from cake.

ALTERNATE—USING TOOTHPICK

1. Trace pattern on parchment paper.

2. Cut out pattern and trace the outline of pattern on lightly crusted icing with toothpick.

TIP TECHNIQUES

Technique instructions will list the correct direction for holding the bag. When the bag direction differs for left-handed decorators, that direction will be listed in parentheses. (Example: When right-handers hold at 3:00, left-handers hold bag at 9:00.)

Right-handed decorators always decorate from left to right. Left-handed decorators always decorate from right to left, except for writing.

TIP 1M/ROUND TIP SWIRL

Add a fancier flourish with an elegant spiral of icing.

It takes just minutes to pipe a fancy icing swirl on your cupcake top and it makes all the difference in eye appeal!

1. For a ridged swirl on a standard cupcake, hold tip 1M approximately ½ in. above cupcake top at a 90° angle to cupcake surface. Squeeze out icing to form a star.

2. Without releasing pressure, raise tip slightly as you drop a line of icing around the star in a tight, complete rotation.

3. After completing the first rotation, move tip toward center and up and around to make a second spiral around the inside edge of the first spiral.

4. Release pressure to end spiral at center of cupcake.

For a smooth swirl, follow the same technique using a round tip, such as 1A. Instead of starting with a center star, you will pipe a ball. You will also need to make more rotations than for tip 1M. It's easy to create exciting, multi-colored swirls. After each rotation, attach tip 1A to a different bag of tinted icing and pipe individual circles.

- -

BALL

The ball shape makes bold borders and is the first step to learn for figure piping. Vary the basic look by adding stars, dots or spirals on the ball shapes. Practice with round tip 8 and medium consistency icing.

1. Holding the bag at 90° angle straight up with tip slightly above surface, squeeze the bag, applying a steady, even pressure. As the icing begins to build up, raise the tip with it, but keep the tip buried in the icing.

2. Stop squeezing as you bring the end of the tip to the surface.

3. Lift the tip up and pull away from your piped ball. Use the edge of the tip to shave off any point, so that your ball is nicely rounded.

BEAD

This technique is great for borders, framing decorations or accents for letters. If you can pipe a shell (p. 211), you can pipe a bead, since the movements are similar. Practice with tip 5 and medium consistency icing.

 1. Hold the decorating bag at 45° angle at 3:00 (9:00) with tip slightly above surface. Squeeze as you lift tip slightly so that icing fans out.

 2. Relax pressure as you draw the tip down and bring the bead to a point. Stop squeezing and pull tip away.

 3. To make a bead border, start the next bead a little behind the previous one so that the fanned out end covers the tail of the preceding bead to form an even chain. To pipe a bead heart, simply pipe one bead, then a second next to it, joining the tails. Smooth together using a decorator brush.

BASKETWEAVE

This technique turns any treat into a beautiful basket. Try using different tips to vary the woven effects. Practice with tip 47 and medium consistency icing.

 1. Using tip 47, serrated side up, hold the bag and tip at 45° angle at 6:00 for vertical stripes or at 3:00 (9:00) for horizontal bars. Lightly touch the surface of your cake. Squeeze out a vertical stripe of icing from top to bottom (shown ridged side up).

 2. Squeeze out short horizontal stripes of icing across the vertical stripe. Spacing between stripes should be the same as the width of the tip opening. Squeeze next vertical stripe over ends of horizontal stripes. Start next set of horizontal stripes by burying the tip under the first vertical stripe.

 3. Squeeze next vertical stripe over ends of horizontal stripes. Start next set of horizontal stripes by burying the tip under the first vertical stripe. Squeeze, pulling hand back slowly and lifting tip over vertical stripe and then back down again. Repeat vertical lines then horizontal lines until you achieve basketweave effect. Each new set should fit between the previous set.

CORNELLI LACE

The perfect look for formal presentations, such as wedding and anniversary cupcakes—the precise, lacy design of this freehand technique depends on the continuous curving strings that do not overlap or touch. Practice with tip 1 or 2 and thin consistency icing.

1. Hold the decorating bag at 90° straight up with tip close to cake without scraping cake with tip and without flattening icing strings.

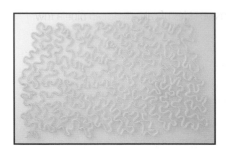

2. Beginning and ending at edges, pipe a continuous string of icing, curve it up, down and around until area is covered. Make certain strings never touch or cross. Don't leave any loose ends in the center area! Stop pressure; pull tip away.

NOTE: Try not to create a repeat pattern design by changing directions often. Try tip 2 for a slightly larger design. It will be easier on your hand, too.

DOT

The dot shape is perfect for flower centers, faces, figure piping and border effects. When making large dots, lift the tip as you squeeze to allow icing to fill out completely. Practice with round tip 3 and medium consistency icing.

1. Hold the decorating bag at 90° angle straight up with tip slightly above the surface. Squeeze bag and keep point of tip buried in icing until the dot is the size you want.

2. Stop pressure, pull tip up and to the side to help prevent points in dots.

PULL-OUT DOT

For pull-out dot, continue squeezing as you life away from surface to desired length and gradually decrease pressure as you pull away. Stop pressure and pull tip away once you're at desired length.

DROP STRINGS

Perfect for swags on sides of cakes, you can pipe a row of single strings or multiple strings in rows of two or three. The trick to beautiful drop strings is to pull the bag toward you as the string drapes down. If you "draw" the string with the tip, you won't achieve a pretty curve and strings tend to break. Practice with round tip 3 and stiff consistency icing slightly thinned with corn syrup.

 1. With a toothpick, mark horizontal divisions on cake in the width you desire. For multiple rows of strings, mark the cake for the deepest row and pipe that row. Hold decorating bag at shoulder level at 4:30 (7:30). Hold tip lightly touching surface to attach strings. Touch tip to first mark and squeeze, pausing momentarily so that icing sticks to the surface.

 2. While squeezing, pull the bag toward you. Continue squeezing to allow the icing to drape naturally into an arc. Icing will drop by itself—do not move the tip down with the string. The end of the tip should be the same distance from the surface as the width from point to point on your cake.

 3. Stop pressure before you touch the tip to the second mark to end string. Repeat on remaining marks, keeping drop strings uniform in length and width.

DOUBLE AND TRIPLE DROP STRINGS

4. For double drop strings, return to the first drop string point. Squeeze the bag and drop a string with a slightly shorter arc than in the first row.

5. Join the end of this string to the end of the corresponding string in the first row. Repeat the process to complete the row. If desired, pipe triple drop strings, with a slightly shorter arc than in the second row. Join the ends of strings to the ends of the corresponding first and second row strings.

PULL-OUT GRASS/FUR

 The grass tip creates one of the most easily accomplished decorations! The serrated edges of the grass tip make ridges in the icing as you squeeze it out. Practice with tip 233 and medium consistency icing.

 1. Hold the decorating bag 90° straight up with tip ⅛ in. above surface.

 **2.** Squeeze bag to form grass. Pull up and away when icing strand is long enough (about ½ in. or longer for each project) stop pressure and pull tip away. Grass will be neatly formed only if you stop squeezing before you pull tip away.

For a more natural look, sometimes pull tip slightly to the right or left instead of straight up. Remember to keep clusters close together so cake does not show through.

LEAVES

A variety of leaves will help give your cakes a more realistic garden feel. Add piping gel to your icing to keep your leaves from breaking. Practice with tips 352, 366 or

Basic Leaf Tip 352

Large Leaf Tip 366

Veined Leaf Tip 67

67 and thin consistency icing. Hold bag at 45° angle at 6:00 with tip lightly touching surface.

1. Squeeze hard to build up the base and, at the same time, lift the tip slightly.

2. Relax pressure as you pull the tip toward you, drawing the leaf to a point.

3. Stop squeezing and lift away.

ATTACHING ROYAL ICING LEAVES TO WIRE STEMS

On a Wilton Pre-Cut Icing Flower Square, using royal icing, pipe a dot base with tip 4. Make a ⅛ in. hook on the end of florist wire and insert hook into the dot base.

Use tip 352 to pipe leaf directly on top of wire. Push the other end of wire into craft block and let dry. Remove icing flower square when dry.

OUTLINE

Characters or designs are often outlined first, then piped in with stars or zigzags. Outlines can also be used for facial features or Color Flow plaques. This technique can be done with round or star tips, depending on whether perfectly round or ridged outlines are desired. Practice with tip 3 and thin consistency icing. Hold bag at 45° angle at 3:00 (9:00) with tip slightly above surface.

1. Touch tip to surface. Lift tip slightly and squeeze and guide tip along surface.

2. Stop squeezing. Touch tip to surface. Pull away.

PRINTING

Personalize a celebration cake with a message written in perfect penmanship! Achieving beautiful results is easier than you might think, following these easy steps. And, practice makes perfect!

Adding piping gel to thinned icing will help your lines flow without breaking. Add ½ teaspoon piping gel per cup of icing. Practice with tip 3 and thin consistency icing. Right handers hold bag at 45° angle al 6:00 for vertical lines, 3:00 for horizontal and curving lines. Left handers hold bag at 45° angle at 6:00 for vertical lines, 45° angle at 9:00 for horizontal and curving lines. Hold tip lightly touching surface.

1. Letters can be piped freehand or after marking with a toothpick or imprinting with a Wilton message press set. With message press, let icing crust slightly before imprinting.

2. Raise tip slightly and with steady even pressure, squeeze out a straight line, lifting the tip off the surface to let the icing string drop.

3. Stop squeezing, touch tip to surface, and pull tip away. Be sure that the end of the tip is clean before you go on to another line.

ROPE

Rope is a wonderful technique for finishing your piped baskets with pretty edging and handles. It is also excellent for western- or nautical-themed cakes. You can make a great looking rope with round or star tips. Practice with tip 21 and medium consistency icing. Hold the decorating bag at 45° angle at 4:30 (7:30). The tip should be lightly touching the surface.

1. Using steady, even pressure, move the tip in a gentle sideways "S" curve. Stop pressure and pull tip away.

2. Insert tip under the bottom curve of the "S" shape.

3. Squeeze the bag with steady pressure as you pull down, then lift the tip. Move up and over the tail of the "S" as you continue to squeeze and form a hook.

4. Keep spacing as even as possible and "S" curves uniform in thickness, length and overall size. Be sure to tuck the tip into the bottom curve of the previous "S" before you begin squeezing, to ensure the clean, continuous look of a rope.

ROSEBUD WITH SIDE PETALS AND CALYX

This flower can be piped directly on a cake or a cupcake in your favorite colors. The outer petals give it a more dimensional look, but rosebuds can be made without them if you want a smaller flower. Practice with tip 104 for petals, round tip 3 for sepals and calyx. Use buttercream—stiff consistency for petals, thin consistency for sepals and calyx. For petals, hold bag at 45° angle at 4:30 (7:30); for sepals and calyx, hold bag at 45° angle at 6:00.

 1. Using tip 104, make the base petal. Keep the narrow end of the tip raised up and slightly to the right (left for left handers). While squeezing, move the tip along the surface away from you in a straight line about ¼ in. long. Pause, then continue squeezing as the icing fans out. Returning the tip to the original position and halfway back, start to release pressure, move tip to starting point, stop pressure and pull tip away.

 2. Using tip 104, make the overlapping petal. Touch the wide end of the tip to the outside edge of completed petal. The bag is positioned as for the base petal at

4:30 (7:30). Hold it steady in this position until the second petal is completed. As you continue squeezing, the icing will catch the edge of the base petal and roll over it naturally. When the second petal looks complete, stop pressure completely, touch the tip back down to the surface and pull tip away. For a rosebud without side petals, move to step 4.

 3. Using tip 104, make the right and left side petals. Touch the wide end of the tip to the left side of rosebud. Raise the tip, then pull back down for a standup look. Repeat for right side petal.

 4. Using tip 3, make the sepals and calyx. Form the middle sepal first by squeezing and letting icing build up. Lift the bag up and away from the flower. Stop pressure as you pull away to form the point of the sepal. Repeat, making a sepal on the left and right sides. For the calyx, insert tip into the base of the center sepal. Squeeze, letting the icing build up. Slowly draw the tip toward you, relaxing pressure as you move away from the flower. Stop pressure and pull away.

• •

ROSETTE

The rosette has the tight, swirling look of a rose, but is achieved in one continuous rotation, rather than with wrapped layers of petals. Single rosettes are also used as candle holders on top of a cake or cupcake. Rosettes can be used in place of piped roses on the side of your cake for the effect of a rose without the work. Try finishing rosettes with a center star or dot. Practice with tip 16 and medium consistency icing. Hold bag at 90° angle straight up with tip slightly above surface.

 1. Squeeze out icing to form a star.

 2. Without releasing pressure, raise tip slightly as you drop a line of icing around the star in a tight, complete rotation. Begin at 9:00 (3:00), move to 12:00, then 3:00 (9:00) and continue to 6:00.

 3. Stop pressure at 6:00 but continue to move the tip back to the starting point to make a complete rotation.

 4. Pull tip away, continuing the circular motion so that the tail maintains the circular shape of the rosette. For a rosette border, pipe a line of uniform rosettes, touching one another.

RUFFLE

Ruffles add a decorative touch to your cakes or cupcakes. Use for borders, garlands and other accent trims. Moving your hand quickly up and down will give you a tight ruffle. For a looser look, move more slowly across the surface. Practice different looks to perfect your pressure control. Practice with tip 104 and medium consistency icing. Hold bag at 45° angle at 3:00 (9:00), with wide end of tip lightly touching surface and narrow end facing away from surface.

 1. As you keep the wide end against the cake, move wrist up to pull up icing.

 2. Move wrist down to complete one curl of the ruffle.

 3. Repeat up and down motion.

 4. Raise and lower the narrow end as you move around the cake. Repeat this motion for the entire ruffle.

SHELL

The shell is the most popular icing technique of all. It's the basis for many borders, fleurs de lis and more. Lift the tip only slightly when piping to avoid a bumpy look. Practice with tip 21 and medium consistency icing. Hold bag at 45° angle at 6:00 with tip slightly above the surface.

 1. Squeeze hard, letting icing fan out generously as it forces the tip up.

2. Gradually relax pressure as you lower tip. Pull the bag toward you until tip reaches the surface. Relax pressure and pull tip along the surface to form a point.

 3. To make a shell border, start your next shell so that the fanned end just covers the tail of the preceding shell to form a chain.

REVERSE SHELL

Reverse shells look spectacular as top and bottom borders and as framed areas on your cake. Practice with tip 21 and medium consistency icing. Hold bag at 45° angle at 6:00 with tip slightly above surface.

1. Squeeze bag to form a shell. As you begin to form a shell, squeeze hard, letting the icing fan out. To form

curve, lift tip up and over the shell as you move tip from 9:00 (right- or left-handed) to 12:00 to 6:00. Relax pressure and lower tip. Pull tip straight toward yourself at 6:00 to form tail. Relax pressure and lower tip. Pull tip straight toward yourself at 6:00 to form tail.

2. Repeat with another shell, curving from 3:00 (right- or left-handed) to 12:00 to 6:00. To continue the reverse shell border, pipe a chain of swirling reverse shells, with the fan end of each new shell covering the tail of the previous shell. If you are making the border on a round cake, turn the cake as you go so that the back of the bag is at 6:00 and you are working toward yourself.

SOTAS

An impressive, yet quick and easy technique you can perfect on the first try! The lacy texture of sotas looks magnificent on borders, outlined areas and as a background for flowers. The keys to simply executed sotas are thinned icing and using a small amount of icing in your bag—this puts less pressure on your hands. Practice with tip 1 and thin consistency icing. Hold bag at a 90° angle with tip slightly above surface.

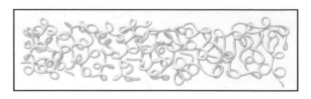

1. Squeeze bag and allow icing to drop randomly in a series of overlapping loops. Cover area edge-to-edge.

STAR

The star tip creates some of the most celebrated decorations! The serrated edges of the star tip makes ridges in the icing as you squeeze it out. After squeezing out a star, be sure to stop pressure completely before you pull your tip away. This will give you a perfectly formed star shape, without peaks. Practice with tip 16 and medium consistency icing. Hold bag at 90° angle straight up with tip about ⅛ in. above the surface.

2. Stop pressure completely. Pull tip straight up and away.

PULL-OUT STAR

1. Squeeze the bag to form a star. Increase or decrease pressure to change star size.

For pull-out stars, while still squeezing, pull tip away from surface until you reach desired length and gradually decrease pressure as you pull away. Stop pressure and pull tip away. Work from the bottom to the top of the area to be covered with pull-out stars.

STAR FILL IN

This technique covers a section on the entire surface of a cake, cupcake or cookie with stars. Because these close together stars require so much piping from the same bag, it's a good idea to keep replenishing the icing. Replenish icing when it gets soft to prevent stars from being poorly defined.

Practice with tip 16 or triple star tip 2010, which covers large areas quickly and easily; use medium consistency icing. Hold bag at 90° angle straight up with tip ¼ in. above surface.

1. Pipe stars uniformly and close together.

2. Pipe a row of stars beneath the first, adjusting tip position so that the points of the stars interlock and cover the area without gaps.

3. Continue to fill in entire area.

SWIRL DROP FLOWER

The swirled look of the petals happens when you twist your wrist the proper way. Practice your wrist movement, keeping your knuckles in the position described below. You can also create a star flower by not moving your wrist and letting icing build up as you squeeze. Practice with tip 2D for petals, round tip 3 for center and use medium consistency buttercream icing. Hold bag at 90° angle straight up with tip lightly touching the surface.

 1. Before piping, turn your hand ¼ turn so the back of your hand is away from you and your knuckles are at 9:00 (3:00). Lightly touch the surface with tip 2D.

 2. As you squeeze out icing, slowly turn your hand until the back of your hand returns to its natural position, with knuckles at 12:00.

3. Stop squeezing and lift tip away.

 4. For flower center, hold the bag straight up and squeeze out a tip 3 dot of icing. Keep the tip buried as you squeeze.

5. Stop squeezing. Pull tip up and off to the side, shaving off the point on the dot.

VINES

In a flower spray, your eye is drawn to the point where vines meet—the focal point. This is where you will place the most flowers. Always use an odd number of main vines.

Practice with tip 3 and thin consistency buttercream icing. Hold bag at a 45° angle at 3:00 (9:00) with tip lightly touching surface.

 **1.** Touch your tip lightly to the surface as you start to squeeze, then lift slightly above the surface as you draw out the stem.

 **2.** Move tip gently up and down to form "hills and valleys." To end the line, stop squeezing and pull the tip along the surface.

3. Add secondary curved stems, starting at main stem, stopping pressure as you pull to a point.

VIOLET

These petite flowers are great for cupcakes. Gather them on an icing mound to create a center bouquet with all the elegance you could want. Practice with tip 59s (right-hand) or tip 101s (left-hand) for petals, tip 1 for center dots and medium consistency royal icing. Use flower nail No. 7 and violet template from flower nail templates set covered with a Pre-Cut Icing Flower Square. Hold bag at a 45° angle with tip lightly touching surface.

1. Squeeze with light pressure, move tip out slightly as you spin the nail to form first bottom petal. Relax pressure as you move tip back to starting point. Stop and lift away.

2. Repeat to make two more bottom petals.

3. Make one shorter rounded top petal. Repeat to make the second top petal.

4. Add two center dots.

- -

WRITING

Personalize a celebration cake with a message written in perfect penmanship! Achieving beautiful results is easier than you might think, following these easy steps. And, practice makes perfect! You'll find you have more control if you let the icing draw out slightly over the surface as you write. Practice with tip 5 and thin consistency icing with ½ teaspoon piping gel added per cup. Hold bag at 45° angle at 3:00 (9:00). Left handers may have to adjust the bag position to fit their writing style.

1. Squeeze with a steady, even pressure. Glide tip along the surface in a smooth, continuous motion.

2. Remember to keep your wrist straight, moving your entire forearm as a single unit. Use your arm, not your fingers, to form each line, letter or word.

3. After you begin to master the curves and swings of the letters, lift the tip up slightly as you write.

ZIGZAG

When piping zigzags, think about two motions simultaneously. The movement of your arm determines the height of the waves and the distance between them. The pressure on your bag determines the thickness of the line. Strive for uniform thickness and even spacing as you go.

Practice with tip 16 and medium consistency icing. Hold bag at 45° angle at 3:00 (9:00) with tip lightly touching surface.

1. Steadily squeeze and glide tip along the surface in an up and down motion.

2. Continue piping up and down with steady pressure.

3. To end, stop pressure and pull tip away. For more elongated zigzags, move your hand to the desired height while maintaining a steady pressure. For a more relaxed look, increase the width as you move the bag along.

THE WILTON ROSE

Create this magnificent rose—the most popular icing flower of them all. With practice, your roses will have the just-picked look of real fresh garden roses! If you are going to be placing your roses on your cake immediately, parchment squares are not needed. Slide flower from nail onto cake using a spatula or Flower Lifter.

You'll need round tip 12 for the base, petal tip 104 for petals, flower nail No. 7 and stiff consistency royal or buttercream icing. Hold bag at 90° angle straight up for base with tip slightly above flower nail; hold bag at 45° angle at 4:30 (7:30) for petals with wide end of tip touching base.

ROSE BASE

1. Using heavy pressure and tip 12, build up a base, remembering to keep your tip buried as you squeeze. Start to lift the tip higher, gradually raise the tip, and decrease the pressure.

2. Stop pressure, pull up and lift away. The rose base should be 1½ times as high as the petal tip opening.

CENTER BUD

3. Make the center bud using tip 104. Hold nail containing base in your left (right) hand and bag in right (left) hand. The wide end of the tip should touch the cone of the base at or slightly below the midpoint. The narrow end of the tip should point up and angled in over top of base.

4. Now you must do three things at the same time: Squeeze the bag, move the tip and rotate the nail. As you squeeze the bag, move the tip up from the base, forming a ribbon of icing. Slowly turn the nail counterclockwise (clockwise for lefties) to bring the ribbon of icing around to overlap at the top of the mound, then back down to starting point. Move your tip straight up and down only; do not loop it around the base.

5. Now you have a finished center bud.

TOP ROW OF THREE PETALS

6. Touch the wide end of tip 104 to the midpoint of bud base, narrow end straight up.

7. Turn nail, keeping wide end of tip on base so that petal will attach. Move tip up and back down to the midpoint of mound, forming the first petal.

8. Start again, slightly behind end of first petal, and squeeze out second petal. Repeat for the third petal, ending by overlapping the starting point of the first petal. Rotate the nail ⅓ turn for each petal.

MIDDLE ROW OF FIVE PETALS

9. Touch the wide end of tip 104 slightly below center of a petal in the top row. Angle the narrow end of tip out slightly more than you did for the top row of petals. Squeeze bag and turn nail moving tip up, then down to form first petal.

10. Repeat for a total of five petals, rotating the nail ⅕ turn for each petal.

11. The last petal end should overlap the first's starting point.

BOTTOM ROW OF SEVEN PETALS

12. Touch the wide end of tip 104 below the center of a middle row petal, again angling the narrow end of tip out a little more. Squeeze bag and turn nail to end of fingers, moving tip up, then down to form first petal.

13. Repeat for a total of seven petals, rotating the nail ½ turn for each petal.

14. The last petal end should overlap the first's starting point.

15. Slip parchment squares and completed rose from nail. This is the completed Wilton Rose.

• •

SMOOTHING ICING WITH FINGER

When piping some facial features or details, such as dot eyes or piped in shaped, you may want to smooth out the area for a clean look. To do this, gently pat the area with your finger dipped in cornstarch.

USING ROLLED FONDANT

The dough-like consistency of fondant makes it the perfect medium for covering cakes and creating ruffles and braids, stately molded accents, distinctive borders, fun trims and beautiful flowers. Decorators agree that fondant is an icing that is truly easy to work with. It's even easier with Wilton Ready-To-Use Rolled Fondant—no mixing, no mess!

FONDANT AMOUNTS

Use this chart to determine how much ready-to-use rolled fondant to buy. Wilton fondant is available in 24 oz. (1 lb., 8 oz.) or 80 oz. (5 lb.) packages. Amounts listed do not include decorations.

Sheet 2 in. high

Cake Size	Fondant
7 in. x 11 in.	30 oz.
9 in. x 13 in.	40 oz.
11 in. x 15 in.	60 oz.
12 in. x 18 in.	80 oz.

Oval 4 in. high

Cake Size	Fondant
7.75 in. x 5.5 in.	24 oz.
10.75 in. x 7.8 in.	36 oz.
13.5 in. x 9.8 in.	48 oz.
16.5 in. x 12.4 in.	72 oz.

Round 4 in. high

Cake Size	Fondant
6 in.	18 oz.
8 in.	24 oz.
10 in.	36 oz.
12 in.	48 oz.
14 in.	72 oz.
16 in.	108 oz.
18 in.	140 oz.

Round 3 in. high

Cake Size	Fondant
6 in.	14 oz.
8 in.	18 oz.
10 in.	24 oz.
12 in.	36 oz.
14 in.	48 oz.
16 in.	72 oz.
18 in.	108 oz.

Heart 4 in. high

Cake Size	Fondant
6 in.	18 oz.
8 in.	26 oz.
9 in.	32 oz.
10 in.	36 oz.
12 in.	48 oz.
14 in.	72 oz.
16 in.	96 oz.

Petal 4 in. high

Cake Size	Fondant
6 in.	18 oz.
9 in.	30 oz.
12 in.	48 oz.
15 in.	72 oz.

Square 4 in. high

Cake Size	Fondant
6 in.	24 oz.
8 in.	36 oz.
10 in.	48 oz.
12 in.	72 oz.
14 in.	96 oz.
16 in.	120 oz.

Hexagon 4 in. high

Cake Size	Fondant
6 in.	18 oz.
9 in.	36 oz.
12 in.	48 oz.
15 in.	84 oz.

Paisley 4 in. high

Cake Size	Fondant
9 in. x 6 in.	20 oz.
12.5 in. x 9.5 in.	48 oz.
16.5 in. x 12.5 in.	72 oz.

Diamond 4 in. high

Cake Size	Fondant
10.25 in. x 7.4 in.	24 oz.
15 in. x 11 in.	36 oz.
19.25 in. x 14.25 in.	60 oz.

Pillow 4 in. high

Cake Size	Fondant
6.75 in. x 6.75 in.	16 oz.
10 in. x 10 in.	28 oz.
13.25 in. x 13.25 in.	48 oz.

HOW TO COLOR FONDANT

COLORING FONDANT

You can easily tint Wilton White Ready-To-Use Rolled Fondant using Wilton Icing Colors. Or, another way to color fondant is by blending portions of pre-tinted fondant from multi packs.

TO TINT WITH WILTON ICING COLORS

1. Cut off the desired amount of white fondant and roll into a ball, kneading until soft and pliable.

2. Using a toothpick, add dots of icing color in several spots.

3. Knead color into your fondant or gum paste ball, stretching and folding until color is evenly blended.

COVERING A BASE BOARD WITH FONDANT

Use Wilton Cake Boards or a Silver Cake Base. If using cake boards, note the faint lines on board top; this shows the direction of the corrugate grain. Stack two or more boards together, crisscrossing the direction the lines run on each; this strengthens the base. Tape boards together to secure. Wrap boards with foil.

1. Lightly coat board with piping gel to help the fondant stick to the foil.

2. Roll out fondant about 2 in. larger than base size, ⅛ in. thick. Position over board using a rolling pin, draping fondant over edge.

3. Trim excess fondant from edges under bottom of board. Smooth top and sides with fondant smoother.

COVERING A CAKE WITH FONDANT

Just follow our instructions for the right ways to knead, roll out and lift the fondant, and you'll find that covering a cake is easy.

 1. Prepare cake by lightly covering with buttercream icing.

 2. Before rolling out fondant, knead it until it is a workable consistency. If fondant is sticky, knead in a little confectioners' sugar. Lightly dust your smooth work surface or the Roll-N-Cut Mat and your rolling pin or fondant roller with confectioners' sugar to prevent sticking. Roll out fondant sized to your cake (see "Fondant Amounts" p. 217). To keep fondant from sticking, lift and move as you roll. Add more confectioners' sugar if needed.

 3. Gently lift fondant over fondant roller and position on cake.

 4. Trim off excess fondant using the fondant cutter, a spatula or sharp knife.

 5. Smooth and shape fondant on top and sides of cake using the Wilton Fondant Smoother. Beginning in the middle of the cake top, move the fondant smoother outward and down the sides to smooth and shape fondant to the cake and remove air bubbles. If an air bubble appears, insert a pin on an angle, release air and smooth the area again. Use the straight edge of the fondant smoother to mark fondant at the base of cake.

COVERING A LARGE CUPCAKE WITH ROLLED FONDANT

1. Bake and cool top and bottom halves in Dimensions Large Cupcake Pan. Turn cupcake bottom narrow end up. Prepare for rolled fondant by lightly icing with buttercream.

 **2.** Roll out fondant ⅛ in. thick using 20 in. Fondant Roller to create a circle about 14 in. dia.

 **3.** Lift fondant onto fondant roller and move onto cupcake bottom.

 4. Use hands to smooth fondant on top and around sides, pressing into indented areas of cake.

 5. Turn cake upright and trim excess from top edge. Follow project directions for positioning cupcake top and completing cake.

COVERING A LARGE CAKE

 In most cases, the smaller your cake, the easier it will be to cover with rolled fondant. However, there is an easy way to position and smooth fondant on cakes that are 12 in. dia. or larger. Follow the steps below to lift fondant onto the cake without tearing.

1. Cover cake with buttercream icing. Roll out fondant sized to fit your cake.

2. Slide a large cake circle that has been dusted with confectioners' sugar under the rolled fondant. Lift the circle and the fondant and position over cake. Gently shake the circle to slide the fondant off and into position on the cake.

3. Smooth and trim as described in Covering a Cake with Fondant (p. 219).

FONDANT AND GUM PASTE DECORATING TECHNIQUES

FONDANT BOW AND LOOPS

Nothing says "celebrate" like a cake topped with a lush fondant bow. While the bow looks intricate, it's really just a grouping of fondant strips, folded, wrapped and arranged to create a full effect.

 1. This bow can be assembled directly on the cake or ahead of time, using a 2 in. to 2½ in. fondant circle as a base. Lightly dust Roll-N-Cut Mat with cornstarch. Roll out fondant ⅛ in. thick. Cut strips for bow loops using dimensions listed in project instructions. Your bow may use more loops than shown here. Fold strips over to form loops. Brush ends lightly with damp brush. Align ends and pinch slightly to secure. Stand loops on side to dry, or stuff loops with crumbled paper napkin and let dry.

 2. Position six or seven bow loops in a circle to form base of the bow. Attach to fondant circle with thinned fondant adhesive or melted candy.

 3. Attach remaining loops, filling in center area of bow. Trim loop ends, if needed, to fit.

SIMPLE BOW

Create a simple bow using one strip of fondant or gum paste to decorate your cakes or treats.

 1. For simple bow, roll out fondant ⅛ in. thick. Cut strip, ¼ in. x 12 in. Fold to form loops and streamers.

 2. Cut strip, 1½ in. x ¼ in., to wrap around center for knot.

 3. Let dry on cornstarch-dusted board.

FONDANT RIBBON ROSE

This quick and easy flower can be placed on your cake right after you roll it.

 1. Roll out fondant ⅛ in. thick on Roll-N-Cut Mat lightly dusted with cornstarch. Cut strip following dimensions stated in project instructions. Brush bottom edge with damp brush and begin rolling from one end of strip,

 2. Gradually loosen roll as flower gets larger, gathering and pinching bottom edge to shape and secure. Fold cut edge under and attach with damp brush.

 3. Use veining tool from the 10-Pc. Gum Paste/Fondant Tool Set between spirals to open up petals. Trim to desired height with scissors. Let dry on cornstarch-dusted cake board or Wilton Candy Melting Plate.

FONDANT CURLICUES

You know how much flair curling ribbon adds to a package. Here's an easy way to make fondant curls. Curlicues also are great used for hair, tails and confetti streamers. Toothpicks, lollipop sticks or dowel rods may be used for various sizes.

 1. Roll out fondant ¹⁄₁₆ in. thick on Roll-N-Cut Mat lightly dusted with cornstarch. Cut into thin strips.

 2. Loosely wrap strips around a lollipop stick several times to form curls. Let set 5 to 10 minutes.

 3. Slide curl off lollipop stick and let dry. Attach to cake or treat with thinned fondant adhesive or melted Candy Melts candy.

• •

APPLYING FONDANT TO FONDANT

Add fondant details easily to fondant-covered cakes with the Wilton Brush Set and water.

 1. Brush back of fondant decoration with damp brush. Be careful not to use too much water or the fondant decoration can slide around rather than stay in one place. If using colored fondant, this will leave a tinted residue if it slides.

 2. Position decoration on fondant-covered cake. Press lightly with finger to smooth if needed.

FONDANT LEAF

Natural-looking leaves can make your fondant bouquet come alive. Use the veining tool from the 10-Pc. Gum Paste/Fondant Tool Set to mark vein lines and let leaves dry on Wilton Flower Forming Cups or Wave Flower Formers to form a lifelike curved shape.

 1. Roll out fondant ⅛ in. thick on Roll-N-Cut Mat lightly dusted with cornstarch. Cut leaves using leaf Cut-Outs fondant cutters, cookie cutters or cutters from gum paste decorating sets, such as the Wilton Stepsaving Rose Bouquet Flower Cutter Set.

 2. Place leaf on thin foam from Fondant Shaping Foam Set. Using veining tool from tool set, mark vein lines, starting with center line. Add branch veins on both sides of center vein.

 3. Remove leaf from foam and let dry. For curved leaves, dry on Wilton Wave Flower Formers or in Flower Forming Cups dusted with cornstarch.

FONDANT ROPE BORDER

The twisted texture of fondant ropes is outstanding for cake borders. If you've ever piped a rope in buttercream icing, you'll love the flexibility of fondant.

 1. Use palms of hands to roll fondant logs, ¼ in. dia. or following project instructions for exact measurements. Twist two ropes together to make each rope section. Lay pieces side by side and gently press together at one end to join.

 2. Holding the joined end in a stationary position, twist the other end two to three complete turns. Continue twisting as needed.

 3. Attach rope to bottom border using a damp brush. Moisten cake slightly and position rope, pressing ends lightly to secure.

HINT: For multicolored ropes, follow rope instructions for rolling individual logs, using two or three logs in different colors. Follow the same twisting procedure, but twist more loosely to create wider space between colors. After twisting, roll back and forth using palms of hands to create a smooth rope.

GUM PASTE CARNATION

A dazzling multi-layered flower that will create an amazing cake-top bouquet.

1. Use fondant roller with guide rings to roll out gum paste ⅛ in. thick. Cut with medium round Cut-Out coated with a film of shortening. Roll gum paste into a ball. Roll one side of ball between your fingers to form a golf tee shape with a stem about ¾ in. long.

2. Dust work surface with dusting pouch. Flatten the round portion of the tee to form a circle around the stem and place flat side down on work surface. Use thick pointed modeling tool from 10-Pc. Gum Paste/Fondant Tool Set to roll flat portion very thin. Roll from center to edges.

3. Center medium round Cut-Out over tee shape and cut.

4. Move base to thin foam that has been dusted with dusting pouch. Use small end of veining tool 10-Pc. Gum Paste/Fondant Tool Set; hold like a pencil (hold at about a 30° angle). Press heel of tool down on outer edge of circle and pull out. Continue working all the way around edge, virtually overlapping the impressions. (This will thin and possibly tear the edges, and that's okay.)

5. Set aside to dry 3 to 4 hours; flat side down.

6. Use dusting pouch to lightly dust Roll-N-Cut Mat with cornstarch. Roll out a small piece of white gum paste less than ¹⁄₁₆ in. thick. Cut five or six circles for each carnation using the medium round Cut-Out fondant cutter. Place one circle on thin foam from Wilton Fondant Shaping Foam Set dusted with dusting pouch. Place others under Wilton Practice Board flap. Holding small end of veining tool (from the 10-Pc. Gum Paste/Fondant Tool Set) like a pencil, press heel down at edge of circle and pull out to form a ruffle.

7. Continue all the way around circle. Overlap impressions to create a torn ruffled look. Repeat for two more ruffled circles.

8. Brush center of carnation base with gum glue adhesive. Gently press one ruffled circle on top of base to attach. Repeat with other two ruffled circles.

9. Make more ruffled circles following previous steps. Attach each immediately after it is ruffled, until flower is complete. To help place the last petal, fold it around tip of veining tool before inserting petal into center.

FULL BLOOM ROSE

This may be your proudest moment when you can hand shape a rose this realistic!

 1. In advance, make the rose center. Roll a ball of gum paste, ½ in. dia., on Roll-N-Cut Mat and form into a teardrop shape. Use 6 in. lengths of 22- or 24-gauge florist wire or toothpicks. Bend back end of wire into a ¼ in. hook. Dip hook end into gum glue adhesive and insert at bottom of rose center, inserting halfway through base. Press bottom of center to shape and smooth against wire. Let dry at least 48 hours.

 2. Roll out gum paste ¹⁄₁₆ in. thick. Using the large rose cutter from the Stepsaving Rose Bouquet Flower Cutter Set, cut blossom shape. Use a knife to make a ½ in. cut between each petal toward middle of blossom. Place on thin foam from the Wilton Shaping Foam Set and use ball tool from 10-Pc. Gum Paste/Fondant Tool Set to soften edges of petals. Move blossom to thick foam and cup center by pressing in middle with ball tool.

 3. Apply gum glue adhesive to rose center. Insert the wire holding the rose center into the middle of the blossom and thread blossom up to the bottom of the rose center. Visualize the 5-petal blossom as a stick figure, with petals corresponding to "head," "arms" and "legs." Wrap the head petal around rose center.

 4. Brush bottom half of one "arm" and opposite "leg" with adhesive and wrap around the center bud. Repeat for remaining petals. Gently press bottom to shape. Petals should overlap each other. Pinch off any excess gum paste from bottom. Furl back petal edges of the outer layer of petals.

 5. Prepare the next blossom; cut slits and soften edges as in step 2. Transfer to thick foam from the Wilton Shaping Foam Set and use ball tool to cup the two "arm" petals. Turn over blossom and cup two "leg" petals and "head" petal. Turn over blossom again and cup the center. Brush adhesive on bottom of rose center. Thread blossom onto wire. Brush the two "arm" petals with adhesive and attach, centering over the seams of the previous two petals.

 6. Brush bottom half of remaining petals with adhesive and attach, spacing evenly. Press bottom to shape; pinch off excess if needed.

 7. Add a third blossom; cut slits and soften edges as in step 2. Transfer to thick foam from foam set. Using the ball tool from tool set, cup all petals. Turn blossom shape over and cup center. Brush adhesive on bottom of rose center. Thread wire through the center of the blossom shape. Brush adhesive on bottom half of petals as needed.

 8. Turn rose over and let petals fall naturally into place. Gently press petals against the rose center to attach.

 9. Roll out gum paste ¹⁄₁₆ in. thick and cut calyx using calyx cutter from flower cutter set. Brush bottom of rose center with adhesive and thread wire through center of calyx. Brush adhesive on bottom half of sepals and press to attach. Bend top half of wire stem down and let rose hang down to dry on Wilton Gum Paste Flowers Drying Rack. For roses made on toothpicks, place in bottom of inverted foam cup to dry.

GUM PASTE MUM

Let fall's beautiful bloom grace your cakes with the mum technique.

 1. Roll ½ in. ball of gum paste. Dip end of 3 in. spaghetti piece into gum glue adhesive then all the way into the ball (mum base). Place into bottom of inverted foam cups. Let dry for 48 hours.

 2. Use dusting pouch to lightly dust Roll-N-Cut Mat with cornstarch. Roll out a small amount of colored gum paste less than ⅟₁₆ in. thick. Cut six medium daisies using cutter from daisy cutter set. Place under flap of Wilton Practice Board.

 3. Remove one small shape from the practice board. Move to thin foam from Wilton Fondant Shaping Foam Set. Use round end of thick pointed modeling tool (from 10-Pc. Gum Paste/Fondant Tool Set) to cup each petal by pulling it from the point to the base of each petal.

 4. Brush the mum base with gum glue adhesive.

 5. Thread spaghetti with mum base through center of petals. Press petals to base to attach.

 6. Brush gum glue adhesive on mum base around spaghetti, extending to where petals separate from the base. Repeat with remaining five daisy shapes.

 7. Place 2½ in. flower forming cup on top of an inverted foam drinking cup. Thread spaghetti through hole in flower forming cup and press into foam cup to dry.

 8. This is the completed mum.

RUFFLED FANTASY FLOWER

The delicate-looking petals of this fantasy flower can be made with any size round Cut-Outs fondant cutters.

 1. Cut a piece of 26-gauge wire to 4 in. long. Bend one end into ¼ in. hook.

 2. Roll out gum paste ¹⁄₁₆ in. thick on Roll-N-Cut Mat. Cut circle using largest round Cut-Out fondant cutter. Set circles on medium shaping foam from Wilton Fondant

Shaping Foam Set. Use veining tool (from 10-Pc. Gum Paste/Fondant Tool Set) to frill edges by pressing down and pulling out.

 3. Fold circle in half and brush center area with gum glue adhesive. Place hook end of wire in adhesive, place on center of folded circle and fold circle in half again.

 4. Open edges slightly and curl to randomly shape flowers. Insert in craft foam block to dry.

• •

USING A FONDANT IMPRINT MAT

Create textured fondant quickly using Wilton Fondant Imprint Mats.

 1. Roll out fondant ⅛ in. thick on Roll-N-Cut Mat using 20 in. fondant roller.

 2. Lift fondant onto fondant imprint mat using fondant roller, or place fondant imprint mat on top of rolled fondant. If fondant is on top of fondant imprint mat, smooth by pressing firmly with Wilton Fondant Smoother or roll with fondant roller. If fondant is below fondant imprint mat, roll with rolling pin.

 3. Lift fondant imprint mat with fondant attached and center imprinted fondant on cake. Peel back mat. Smooth fondant around cake by gently pressing with heel of hand.

PEARL DUST AND COLOR DUST COLOR EFFECTS

Pearl Dust and Color Dust are used to brush color on gum paste or fondant designs. You can use a brush to paint wet or apply dry. For fine detail, a small round-head brush works best. For larger areas, use a wider, flatter brush.

 Brushing dry onto your flowers or details creates a softer look. Painting with a mixture of Wilton Pearl Dust or Color Dust and Pure Lemon Extract creates a more vivid look.

 To make a "paint": In a small bowl, mix equal parts Pearl Dust or Color Dust and lemon extract. Dissolve the dust completely into extract before painting. Since the extract can evaporate quickly, mix small amounts of paint at a time and use immediately.

Some projects may take more than one coat of "paint" for even coverage. Let each coat dry completely before starting a new one.

TIERED CAKE CONSTRUCTION

There are many methods of constructing tiered cakes. Here are some used in this book. Visit wilton.com for more construction methods.

TO PREPARE CAKE FOR ASSEMBLY

Place base tier on a sturdy base plate or three or more thicknesses of corrugated cardboard. For heavy cakes, use foil-covered Wilton Silver Cake Bases or a foam core or plywood base, ½ in. thick. Base can be covered with Fanci-Foil Wrap and trimmed with Tuk-N-Ruffle or use Ruffle Boards. Each tier of your cake must be on a cake circle or board cut to fit. Place a few strokes of icing on boards to secure cake. Fill and ice layers before assembly.

ADDING DOWEL RODS TO TIERED CAKES

Use the upper tier for size reference when determining dowel rod placement. All the dowel rods must be placed within the area you will mark (see steps below) to provide adequate support.

 1. Center a cake board the same size as the tier above it on base tier and press it gently into icing to imprint an outline. Remove. Use this outline to guide the insertion of the dowel rods.

 2. Insert one dowel rod into cake straight down to the cake board. Make a knife scratch on the rod to mark the exact height. Pull dowel rod out.

 3. Cut the suggested number of rods (see note) the exact same length, using the mark on the first one as a guide.

 4. Insert rods into tier, spacing evenly 1½ in. in from the imprinted outline. Push straight down until each touches the cake board. Repeat this procedure for every stacked or pillared tier on the cake.

NOTE: The larger and more numerous the tiers, the more dowels needed. If the tier above is 10 in. or less, use six ¼ in. bamboo dowels. Use eight dowel rods for 16 in. and 18 in. cakes; on these larger tiers, use ¾ in. plastic dowel rods in the base tier. When using white plastic dowel rods that are wider and provide more support, the number needed may be less.

SEPARATOR PLATE (2-PLATE) AND PILLAR CONSTRUCTION

This most dramatic method features two, three or more single cakes towered together. Use separator plates and pillars. Check pillars and plates for correct fit before constructing your cake.

 1. Set cake tiers on separator plates 2 in. larger in diameter than cakes.

 2. Add dowel rods to cakes and position separator plates on tiers with feet up.* (Note: Connect only same size separator plates with pillars.)

 3. Position pillars over feet on separator plates.

 4. Carefully set cake plate on pillars. Continue adding tiers this way.*

*Finely shredded coconut or confectioners' sugar, placed in area where cake circles or plastic plates will rest helps prevent icing on the cake from sticking.

PUSH-IN PILLAR CONSTRUCTION

Simple assembly—no dowel rods needed! Use any type of Wilton push-in pillars and plates. Check pillars and plates for correct fit before constructing your cake.

 1. Mark tier for push-in pillar placement. Use the separator plate for the next tier above, gently pressing it onto the tier, feet down, making sure it is centered. Lift plate away. The feet will leave marks on the icing to guide the position of pillars when you assemble the tier. Repeat this process for each tier, working from largest to smallest tier. The top tier is left unmarked.

 2. Place each tier on its separator plate, securing with icing.

 3. Position push-in pillars at marks, and insert into tiers. Push straight down until pillars touch the cake plate.

 4. To assemble, start with the tier above the base tier. Place the feet of the separator plate on the pillar openings. Continue adding tiers in the same way until the cake is completely assembled.*

*Assemble cakes when you arrive at the reception or party.

STACKED CONSTRUCTION

Stacking is the most architectural method of tiered cake construction. Tiers are placed directly on top of one another and pillars are not used. Cakes are supported and stabilized by dowel rods and cake boards.

 1. Dowel rod all tiers except top tier.

 2. Position the middle tier on the base tier, centering exactly.

 3. Repeat with the top tier.

 4. To stabilize tiers further, sharpen one end of a long dowel rod and push it through all tiers and cake boards to the base of the bottom tier. To decorate, start at the top and work down.

GLOBE PILLAR SET CONSTRUCTION (TIERED CONSTRUCTION)

These elegant pearl-look globes are available in separate sets of four 2 in., 2½ in. or 3 in. globes. The 3 in. globes are to be used to support the base cake only. They have a reinforced center channel, which eliminates the need for pillars. The 2 in. and 2½ in. sets should be used with 9 in. "Hidden" Pillars (included in set); do not use these sets to support the base cake. Your cake design may use a base board instead of the 3 in. globes to support the base cake as shown on the following page.

 1. Position base cake on a thick base board. Using the separator plate, which will hold the cake above, mark base cake for pillar placement (see Push-In Pillar Construction p. 228). Lift plate away.

 2. Insert pillars through cake centered over marked area to rest on its separator plate or base board. Place the correct size globe (2½ in. for cake shown here) over the pillars. Mark pillars where they extend above globes. The cut pillars should be equal to the height of the base cake plus the height of each globe.

 3. Trim pillars at markings with craft knife or serrated edge knife.

 4. Insert pillars in base cake. Position globes over pillars.

 **5.** Position the tier above on globes.

 6. Add additional sets for more tiers.

TOWERING TIERS CAKE & DESSERT STAND CONSTRUCTION

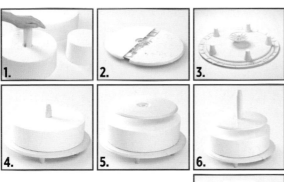

NOTE: Final cake assembly should be done at the cake's final location. Moving the cake once assembled is not recommended. Do not cut cakes directly on the stand and remove first from the stand.

PREPARE CAKE BOARDS

Cake tiers will use the same size cake boards as cake. Each board will need a 1½ in. dia. hole cut in the center to accommodate the center post of the stand. To do that, make a parchment paper pattern for each cake to be used. To find the exact center of the board, fold the pattern in half, and then again in half to make quarters. Snip the point of the paper to make a small center hole. Place a center column piece over the small hole and trace. Cut out the hole and test the size to make sure it fits over the column. Adjust if necessary. Place the pattern on the cake board, trace the hole and cut out. Test the size again to make sure the board fits over the column. Adjust if necessary. Save paper patterns for cake tiers.

PREPARE CAKE TIERS

Ice cake tiers and position on prepared cake boards (with holes). All cake tiers (except for the top tier) will need to have a center hole cut out. Using your parchment paper patterns from the cake boards, mark the center hole on the top of the cake. Using the Cake Corer Tool, gently push the corer into the center of the cake all the way to the bottom and twist a half turn. (See photo 1.) Keep the corer straight, remove it from the cake, leaving a hole in the center of the tier. Repeat for all the cake tiers.

STAND AND CAKE ASSEMBLY

Short center posts are ideal for cupcakes and small individual desserts. Tall center posts should be used for cake tiers up to 5 in. high. First, decide which plates and center columns will be used for the cake setup. The largest plate of the cake setup will be the base tier. For the 16 in. and 18 in. plates, assemble by sliding the half plate sections together and interlocking them on the plate support. (See photo 2.) Use 14 in. plates or smaller as is. Screw the base feet to the bottom of the base plate. Place center post foot on the bottom of the plate or plate assembly (if using a 16 in. or 18 in. plate). (See photo 3.) Place a center post section on the top of plate and screw into center post foot to secure. Once the base assembly is complete, add the first cake tier. Slide the base cake with board over the center post. (See photo 4.)

Place the next sized plate on the center post currently in place. (See photo 5.) Attach another center post. (See photo 6.)

Slide the next cake over center post onto plate. Continue until all tiers are in position.

For the top tier, add the top tier plate and screw on the top nut to the center post. Position top cake tier on the plate. (See photo 7.)

To display cupcakes, first assemble the entire stand using the short posts and the desired number of plates. Start with the largest plate at the bottom and build up to the smallest plate. Position cupcakes on the stand.

CANDY/POP MAKING TECHNIQUES

USING CANDY MELTS CANDY

TO MELT

CHOCOLATE PRO MELTING POT: The most convenient way to melt—no microwave or double boiler needed! Melts large amounts of Candy Melts candy in minutes.

DOUBLE BOILER METHOD: Fill lower pan with water to below level of top pan. Bring water to simmer, then remove from heat. Put Candy Melts candy in top pan and set in position on lower pan. Stir constantly, without beating, until smooth and completely melted.

MICROWAVE METHOD: In microwavable bowl, microwave 1 package Candy Melts candy at 50% power or defrost setting for 1 minute. Stir thoroughly. Continue to microwave and stir at 30-second intervals until smooth and completely melted. Candy Melts candy may also be melted in candy decorating bags. Melt as described above, squeezing bag between heating intervals to blend Candy Melts candy together. When completely melted, snip off end of bag and squeeze melted Candy Melts candy into molds. Throw away bag when empty.

NOTE: Candy Melts candy will lose its pouring and dipping consistency if overheated, or if water or other liquid is added. If coating is overheated, add 1 teaspoon vegetable shortening per 12 oz. Candy Melts candy.

TO COLOR

Add candy colors to melted Candy Melts candy a little at a time. Mix thoroughly before adding more color. Colors tend to deepen as they're mixed.

TO MOLD (1 COLOR CANDY)

Pour melted candy into clean, dry mold. Tap lightly to remove air bubbles. Place mold on level surface in refrigerator until bottom of mold appears frosty or until candy is firm. Pop out candy. For lollipops, fill molds, tap to remove air bubbles, then position sticks in mold. Rotate sticks to thoroughly cover with candy so they remain securely in place. Chill until firm, then unmold.

MULTI-COLORED CANDY

"PAINTING" METHOD: Before filling mold cavity, use a Wilton Decorator Brush dipped in melted Candy Melts candy to paint features or desired details. Let set 3 to 5 minutes after each additional detail. Fill mold and chill until firm.

PIPING METHOD: Use a parchment bag or candy decorating bag filled halfway with melted candy. Cut small hole in tip of bag and gently squeeze to add candy detail to mold. Let set 3 to 5 minutes after each additional detail. Fill mold and chill until firm.

SPECIALTY TECHNIQUES

MAKING A CANDY SHELL

Mold a sweet holder for candies, ice cream or a cereal treat cupcake top! Use Wilton Candy Melts candy and any Wilton standard baking cup in a standard muffin pan or non-stick pan to create the perfect shape.

IN A PAN

 1. Fill pan cavity to the top edge with melted candy. Tap on counter to remove air bubbles. Let chill for 8 to 10 minutes or until a ⅛ in. to¼ in. shell has formed.

 2. Pour out excess candy, then return shell to refrigerator to chill completely. Carefully unmold shells. If you have difficulty removing shells, place pan in freezer for 2 to 3 minutes, then unmold.

 3. Smooth edges by sliding across warmed cookie sheet or warming plate. Excess candy can be reheated and reused. Fill shell following recipe instructions.

IN A BAKING CUP

1. Spoon or pipe 1 to 2 tablespoons of melted candy into the bottom of a standard baking cup. Brush candy up sides to desired height, forming an even edge.

2. Chill 5 to 8 minutes. Repeat process for a thicker shell. Chill until firm.

3. Carefully peel baking cup off candy shell. Fill shell following project instructions.

MAKING A CANDY PLAQUE

You can use Wilton shaped pans as candy molds and any Wilton Candy Melts candy to make solid decorative plaques.

If your pan has detail, it may be painted or filled in with desired colors using a cut parchment bag as you would for any candy mold, letting each color set before adding colors that touch.

1. Pour melted candy into center of pan cavity. Tap pan gently on counter to eliminate air bubbles. Chill to set.

2. Fill pan with additional melted candy. Chill to set before adding colors that touch.

3. Once completely filled for candy plaque, candy should be ¼ in. to ¾ in. thick, depending on project. Chill about 30 to 40 minutes until firm. Check occasionally. If candy becomes too chilled, it may crack.

4. Unmold onto hand or soft towel (tap gently if necessary).

MAKING COOKIE POPS

The convenience of baking your treat on a stick makes Wilton Cookie Pops Pans the perfect choice. Be sure to use the Vanilla Sugar Cookies on a Stick recipe (p. 185), which yields the ideal texture of dough that will be secure on the stick.

 1. Spray pan cavities with Bake Easy! non-stick spray or vegetable pan spray. Fill cavities with cookie dough to ⅛ in. below top edge. Insert Wilton Cookie Sticks into dough, covering 2 in. of end.

 2. Bake according to recipe and cool 5 minutes. Gently loosen with spatula; remove from pan. Turn over to release cookies. Cool completely before decorating.

 3. Decorate with melted Candy Melts candy or icing following project instructions.

COVERING A CUPCAKE USING GANACHE, POURED ICINGS OR CANDY MELTS CANDY

Each of these coatings will give cupcakes, mini cakes and other baked treats a beautiful and delicious finish. Ganache adds a creamy texture and satiny finish to treats. Poured icings, like quick-pour fondant, give you the most color versatility and a smooth finish. Candy Melts candy helps treats set up firmer than icing or ganache.

With Candy Melts candy you can completely cover your cupcakes. First, use a spatula and melted candy to ice the bottoms of the cupcakes. Chill until set. Follow the steps below to cover.

1. Place cooled cupcakes or mini cakes on cooling grid positioned over cookie sheet or pan. Prepare ganache, poured icing or Candy Melts candy following recipe or package directions.

2. Use a pan or measuring cup to pour ganache, melted candy or icing on center of cupcake. Or, use a cut disposable decorating bag or parchment bag to pipe candy or icing.

3. Let dry.

DIPPING POPS

Give your cake pops a dunk in Wilton Candy Melts candy! Dipping is a great way to seal in the flavor and moistness of the cake, and it creates a great surface for toppings and decorations. Melt them in the Wilton Chocolate Pro Melting Pot. For small and medium-sized cake ball pops, try convenient, microwavable Wilton Candy Dips.

1. Holding the lollipop stick securely, dip pop into melted candy.

2. Tap pop lightly to smooth surface.

3. Place pops in Wilton Pops Decorating Stand. Chill for 10 to 15 minutes.

COVERING A POP WITH SPRINKLES

For quick party pops, after you dip in candy, do a second dip in Wilton Sprinkles! Whether you use nonpareils, jimmies or colored sugars, you'll have an instant, colorful treat everyone will love.

1. Dip pop in melted Wilton Candy Melts candy, then dip in favorite sprinkles or sugars.

2. Roll pop until completely covered.

3. Place in Wilton Pops Decorating Stand. Chill until firm.

COLOR FLOW DECORATING TECHNIQUES

MAKING PUDDLE DOTS

Versatile disks of Color Flow icing or thinned royal icing are made in advance, dried and used as accents, buttons and faces.

 1. Thin Color Flow icing or royal icing by adding ½ teaspoon water per ¼ cup of icing. Icing is ready for flowing when a small amount dripped back into mixture takes a count of 10 to disappear.

 2. On parchment paper-covered cake boards, pipe a ball, ¼ in. to 1¼ in. dia., depending on project instructions, using thinned icing in cut parchment bag or disposable decorating bag with tip. Let dry 48 hours.

3. Decorate following project instructions.

COVERING A COOKIE WITH COLOR FLOW

Smooth and shiny decorations are the hallmark of Color Flow icing. To make a Color Flow shape, use full-strength Color Flow icing to outline then pipe in the area with thinned Color Flow in cut parchment bag (if you are using the same tinted icing). Note that Color Flow will need to dry 24 to 48 hours, so plan on decorating your cookies at least 48 to 72 hours before your celebration for ample drying time. If using a different color to outline, let dry for 1 to 2 hours and then fill in with thinned Color Flow in cut parchment bag.

Creating a Color Flow cookie is a fun way to top a cupcake! Find the Color Flow icing recipe on p. 182.

1. Outline shape with tip 3 in cut parchment bag half-filled with full-strength Color Flow. Squeeze, pull and drop icing string following shape. Stop, touch tip to surface and pull away.

2. Thin Color Flow mixture with water following recipe directions (p. 182). Cut opening in parchment bag to the size of tip 2. Fill in design with thinned Color Flow.

3. Let cookies air dry thoroughly at least 24 hours.

WORKING WITH COLOR FLOW

1. Trace your design pattern onto parchment paper, then tape paper onto a cake circle or the back of a cookie pan. Cover with parchment paper, smooth and tape. Use tip 2 and a cut parchment bag half-filled with full-strength Color Flow to squeeze, pull and drop icing string following pattern outline. Stop, touch tip to surface and pull away.

2. If you're using a different color to fill in, let outline dry 1 to 2 hours.

3. Thin Color Flow mixture with water following recipe directions. Cut opening in parchment bag to the size of tip 2. Fill in design with thinned Color Flow.

4. Let decorations air dry thoroughly, at least 24 hours for cookies and 48 for plaques. To remove, cut away parchment paper from board, then turn over and peel parchment paper off the Color Flow piece.

HINT: To easily remove dried Color Flow, pull parchment paper backing over the edge of a table with one hand, while holding decoration with other hand. Parchment paper will pull off naturally. Or, with dried Color Flow resting on cookie sheet, place cardboard sheet over Color Flow, lift and turn over so that top of decoration rests on cardboard. Lift off parchment paper.

Since any moist icing will break down Color Flow, either position Color Flow decorations on cake shortly before serving or place on sugar cubes, attaching with full-strength Color Flow.

STORING A DECORATED CAKE

Take some final precautions and store your cake the best way possible. After all, your time, effort and creativity have made it very special! Beware of the following factors, which can affect the look of your decorated cake.

Sunlight and fluorescent lighting will alter icing colors. Keep your cake stored in a covered box and out of direct sunlight and fluorescent lighting.

Humidity can soften royal icing, fondant and gum paste decorations. If you live in a climate with high humidity, prepare your royal icing using only pure cane confectioners' sugar (not beet sugar or dextrose), add less liquid and add 1 more teaspoon meringue powder to the recipe.

Heat can melt icing and cause decorations to droop. Keep your decorated cake as cool as possible and stabilize buttercream icing by adding 2 teaspoons meringue powder per recipe. Protect your cake by placing it in a clean, covered cake box. Avoid using foil or plastic wrap to cover a decorated cake—these materials can stick to icing and crush delicate decorations. The icing that covers your cake determines how it should be stored—in the refrigerator, at cool room temperature or frozen, if storing for longer than three days. If you want to store your iced cake in a different way than noted, make a small test cake.

Icing type determines care. See Icing Index for individual types and each one's recommendation (p. 196).

NOTE: Cakes with thoroughly dried royal icing decorations should be stored according to the type of icing that covers the cake. However, if royal icing decorations are to be put on a cake that will be frozen, it is recommended that these decorations be placed on the cake after thawing so that they don't bleed from condensation or become soft.

• •

TINTING SHREDDED COCONUT

Place desired amount of coconut in a plastic food storage bag, add a little Wilton Icing Color with a toothpick and knead until color is evenly blended. Dry on parchment paper.

Patterns

Patterns may be copied to reproduce desired designs.

Congratulate the Grad Cake

Copy pattern at 133%

Graduate

A New Spin on Aging Cake

Copy patterns at 200%

Game Wedge (left), **Spinner** (right)

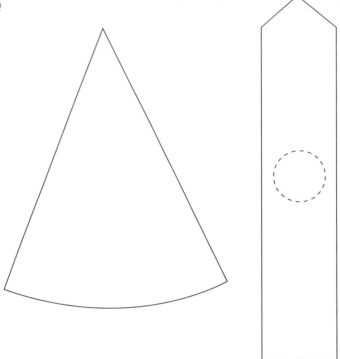

Anniversary Flair Cake

Pattern is at 100%

Numeric Pattern

As Your Journey Begins Cake

Copy pattern at 200%

Large Triangle

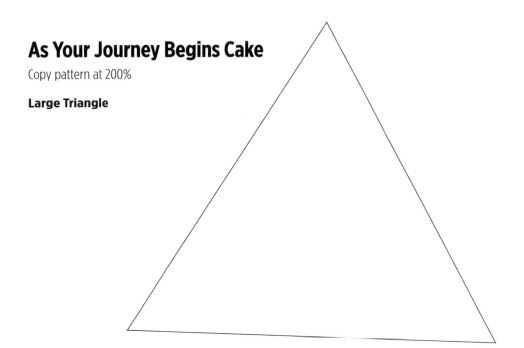

As Your Journey Begins Cake

Copy patterns at 200%

Small Triangle (top),
Medium Triangle (bottom)

As Your Journey Begins Cake

Copy patterns at 133%

Initials

$$A \; B \; C \; D \; E \; F$$

$$G \; H \; I \; J \; K \; L$$

$$M \; N \; O \; P \; Q \; R$$

$$S \; T \; U \; V \; W \; X \; Y$$

$$Z$$

Garden Terraces Cake

Copy pattern at 133%

Garden Greenery

North Pole Penguin Cake

Copy patterns at 133%

Top to bottom: **Penguin Body,
Wing, Feet, Beak**

Formal Fare Tuxedo Cupcakes

Patterns are at 100%

Bow Tie (top), **Shirt/Lapels** (bottom)

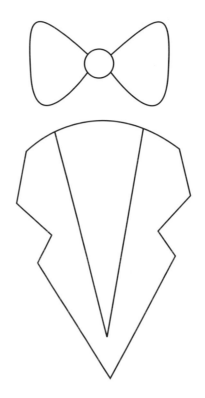

Top Graduate Cookies

Pattern is at 100%

Mortarboard

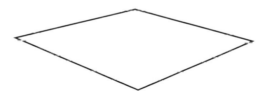

First Birthday Teddy Bear Cake

Copy pattern at 200%

Number 1

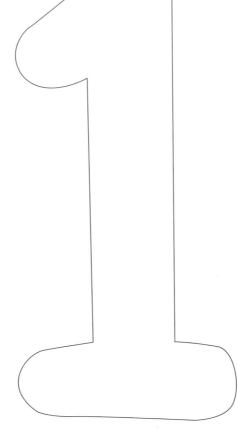

Santa's Surprise! Cake

Copy patterns at 133%

Fireplace (left), **Staircase Riser** (right)

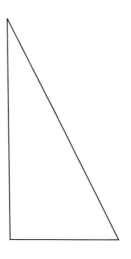

Queen Mom Cake Pops

Copy patterns at 133%

Crown

 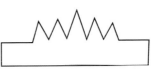

Wise Guy Pie

Copy pattern at 133%

Owl

Witch Cake

Copy patterns at 200%

Witch Hat (left),
Witch Face (right)

Mom-To-Be Baby Shower Cake

Copy pattern at 200%

Half Scalloped Circle

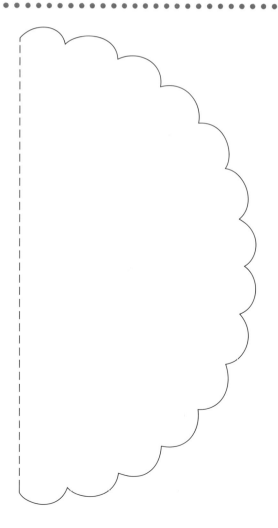

Products

On the following pages, you will see just a sampling of our expansive product line. Visit your local retailer or wilton.com to view the complete selection of Wilton products. Our online store makes it easy for you to purchase what you need for any project in this book.

DECORATING ACCESSORIES

TIPS

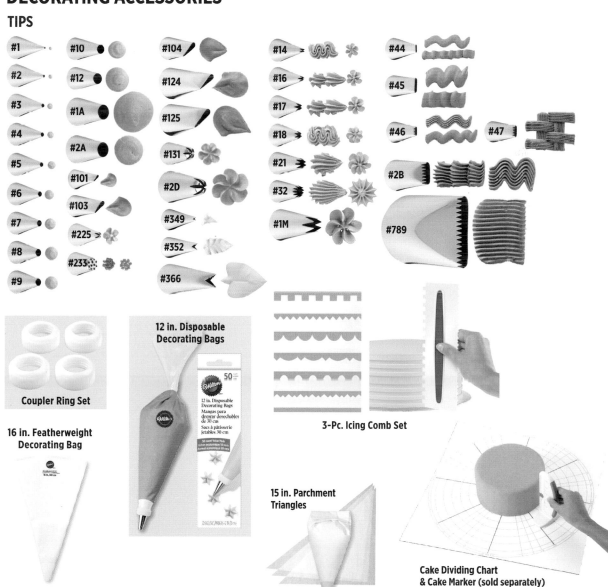

12 in. Disposable Decorating Bags

Coupler Ring Set

16 in. Featherweight Decorating Bag

3-Pc. Icing Comb Set

15 in. Parchment Triangles

Cake Dividing Chart & Cake Marker (sold separately)

BAKING TOOLS

ULTIMATE Cake Leveler

Small Cake Leveler

Bake-Even Strips

SPRINKLES, SUGARS & EDIBLE DECORATIONS

PEARL DUST

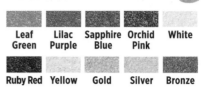

Leaf Green	Lilac Purple	Sapphire Blue	Orchid Pink	White

Ruby Red	Yellow	Gold	Silver	Bronze

COLOR DUST

Purple	White	Periwinkle Blue

Red	Deep Pink	Orange

Brown	Goldenrod	Spruce Green	Lime Green

ICING COLORS

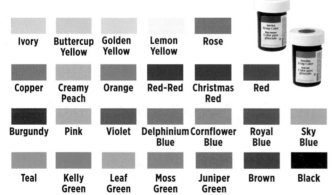

Ivory	Buttercup Yellow	Golden Yellow	Lemon Yellow	Rose

Copper	Creamy Peach	Orange	Red-Red	Christmas Red	Red

Burgundy	Pink	Violet	Delphinium Blue	Cornflower Blue	Royal Blue	Sky Blue

Teal	Kelly Green	Leaf Green	Moss Green	Juniper Green	Brown	Black

FOODWRITER EDIBLE COLOR MARKERS

Primary Color Sets

Yellow	Green	Red	Blue	Brown

FINE TIP   **BOLD TIP**

COLOR MIST FOOD COLOR SPRAY

Red	Orange	Black
Yellow	Violet	
Gold	Silver	Pearl

Blue

Green

Pink

TUBE ICINGS & GELS

DECORATING ICINGS

Colors match Wilton Icing Colors (p. 246).

Red
Violet
Yellow
Orange
Pink
Royal Blue
Leaf Green
Kelly Green
Chocolate
White
Black

DECORATING GELS

Colors match Wilton Icing Colors (p. 246).

Red
Pink
Violet
Yellow
Orange
Royal Blue
Kelly Green
Brown
White
Black

COOKIE ICING (ALL COLORS)

Yellow   Pink

Green   Blue

Red   White

Orange   Black

SPARKLE GEL (ALL COLORS)

Orange   Black   White

Gold   Red   Light Green

Blue   Yellow   Green

Pink

Piping Gel

PRESENTATION

23-Ct. Standard Cupcakes-N-More Dessert Stand

13-Ct. Standard Cupcakes-N-More Dessert Stand

Pops Display Stand

Pops Decorating Stand

FLOWER MAKING TOOLS

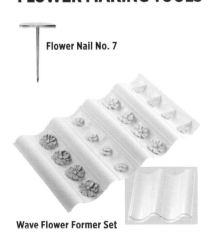

Flower Nail No. 7

Wave Flower Former Set

SUGAR SHEETS! EDIBLE DECORATING PAPER

SOLID COLORS

Orange   Brown   Purple   Red   Black

Bright Pink   Bright Blue   Bright Green   Bright Yellow   White

PATTERNS

Scrolls   Zebra

Damask

READY-TO-USE ROLLED FONDANT

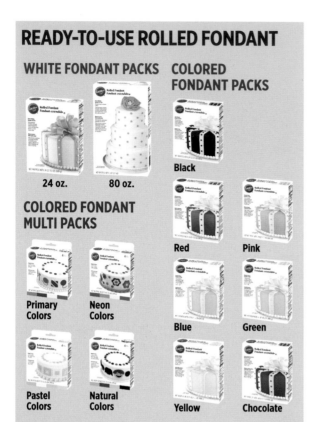

WHITE FONDANT PACKS

24 oz. 80 oz.

COLORED FONDANT PACKS

Black

Red Pink

Blue Green

Yellow Chocolate

COLORED FONDANT MULTI PACKS

Primary Colors Neon Colors

Pastel Colors Natural Colors

GUM PASTE

Gum-Tex

Ready-To-Use Gum Paste

GUM PASTE/FONDANT TOOLS & ACCESSORIES

20 in. Fondant Roller

8 in. Fondant Roller

20 in. Fondant Roller Guide Rings

Fondant Smoother

Dusting Pouch

10-Pc. Gum Paste/ Fondant Tool Set

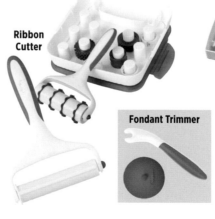

Ribbon Cutter

Fondant Trimmer

Fondant Shaping Foam

Flower Forming Cups

GUM PASTE/FONDANT TOOLS & ACCESSORIES

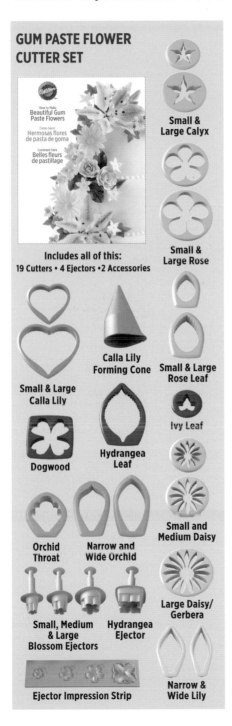

GUM PASTE FLOWER CUTTER SET

Includes all of this:
19 Cutters • 4 Ejectors • 2 Accessories

Small & Large Calyx

Small & Large Rose

Small & Large Calla Lily

Calla Lily Forming Cone

Small & Large Rose Leaf

Dogwood

Hydrangea Leaf

Ivy Leaf

Orchid Throat

Narrow and Wide Orchid

Small and Medium Daisy

Small, Medium & Large Blossom Ejectors

Hydrangea Ejector

Large Daisy/Gerbera

Ejector Impression Strip

Narrow & Wide Lily

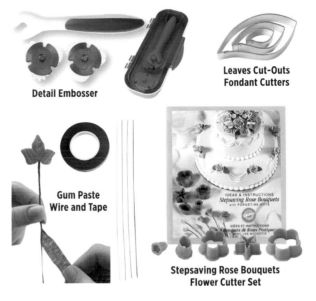

Detail Embosser

Leaves Cut-Outs Fondant Cutters

Gum Paste Wire and Tape

Stepsaving Rose Bouquets Flower Cutter Set

BAKEWARE

Mini Wonder Mold Pan

Classic Wonder Mold Pan

Round Pops

Checkerboard Cake Pan Set

Romantic Castle Cake Set

CAKE STANDS, ASSEMBLY SETS, PLATES AND PILLARS

Cakes-N-More 3-Tier Party Stand

Carousel Cake Display Set

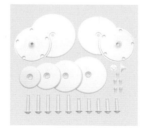

Towering Tiers Cake Stand

Fresh Flower Cake Spikes

"Hidden" Pillars

Baker's Best Disposable Pillars with Rings

Globe Pillar and Base Sets
2 in. globe tier set • 2½ in. globe tier set • 3 in. globe tier set

Crystal Clear Cake Divider Set with 9 in. Twist Legs

CANDY MAKING

Chocolate Pro Electric Melting Pot

CANDY COLOR SETS

Primary

Garden

CANDY MELTS CANDY

| Vibrant Green | Black | Dark Cocoa | Peanut Butter | Dark Cocoa Mint |

| Blue | Yellow | Orange | Red | Dark Green |

| Pink | Lavender | White | Light Cocoa |

COLORBURST CANDY MELTS

Pastels   Brights

Candy Cane

COOKIE MAKING

Comfort Grip Cookie Press

Index

METRIC CONVERSION CHART

VOLUME MEASUREMENTS (dry)

$^1/_8$ teaspoon = 0.5 mL
$^1/_4$ teaspoon = 1 mL
$^1/_2$ teaspoon = 2 mL
$^3/_4$ teaspoon = 4 mL
1 teaspoon = 5 mL
1 tablespoon = 15 mL
2 tablespoons = 30 mL
$^1/_4$ cup = 60 mL
$^1/_3$ cup = 75 mL
$^1/_2$ cup = 125 mL
$^2/_3$ cup = 150 mL
$^3/_4$ cup = 175 mL
1 cup = 250 mL
2 cups = 1 pint = 500 mL
3 cups = 750 mL
4 cups = 1 quart = 1 L

VOLUME MEASUREMENTS (fluid)

1 fluid ounce (2 tablespoons) = 30 mL
4 fluid ounces ($^1/_2$ cup) = 125 mL
8 fluid ounces (1 cup) = 250 mL
12 fluid ounces (1$^1/_2$ cups) = 375 mL
16 fluid ounces (2 cups) = 500 mL

WEIGHTS (mass)

$^1/_2$ ounce = 15 g
1 ounce = 30 g
3 ounces = 90 g
4 ounces = 120 g
8 ounces = 225 g
10 ounces = 285 g
12 ounces = 360 g
16 ounces = 1 pound = 450 g

DIMENSIONS

$^1/_{16}$ inch = 2 mm
$^1/_8$ inch = 3 mm
$^1/_4$ inch = 6 mm
$^1/_2$ inch = 1.5 cm
$^3/_4$ inch = 2 cm
1 inch = 2.5 cm

OVEN TEMPERATURES

250°F = 120°C
275°F = 140°C
300°F = 150°C
325°F = 160°C
350°F = 180°C
375°F = 190°C
400°F = 200°C
425°F = 220°C
450°F = 230°C

BAKING PAN SIZES

Utensil	Size in Inches/Quarts	Metric Volume	Size in Centimeters
Baking or Cake Pan (square or rectangular)	8×8×2	2 L	20×20×5
	9×9×2	2.5 L	23×23×5
	12×8×2	3 L	30×20×5
	13×9×2	3.5 L	33×23×5
Loaf Pan	8×4×3	1.5 L	20×10×7
	9×5×3	2 L	23×13×7
Round Layer Cake Pan	8×1½	1.2 L	20×4
	9×1½	1.5 L	23×4
Pie Plate	8×1¼	750 mL	20×3
	9×1¼	1 L	23×3
Baking Dish or Casserole	1 quart	1 L	—
	1½ quarts	1.5 L	—
	2 quarts	2 L	—